DIRECTOR'S CUT

Lining up a shot.

DIRECTOR'S CUT

MY LIFE IN FILM

TED KOTCHEFF

with **JOSH YOUNG**

Published by ECW Press
665 Gerrard Street East
Toronto, Ontario, Canada, M4M 1Y2
416-694-3348 • info@ecwpress.com

LIBRARY AND ARCHIVES CANADA
CATALOGUING IN PUBLICATION

Kotcheff, Ted, author
Director's cut : my life in film / Ted Kotcheff with
Josh Young ; foreword by Mariska Hargitay.

ISSUED IN PRINT AND ELECTRONIC FORMATS.
ISBN 978-1-77041-361-0 (paperback)
ALSO ISSUED AS: 978-1-77090-991-5 (PDF)
978-1-77090-990-8 (EPUB)

1. Kotcheff, Ted. 2. Motion picture producers
and directors—Canada—Biography. 3. Television
producers and directors—Canada—Biography.
4. Motion picture industry—United States. 5.
Television broadcasting—United States. I. Young,
Josh (Joshua D), author II. Hargitay, Mariska,
1964-, writer of foreword III. Title.

PN1998.3.K6765A3 2017   791.4302'33092
C2016-906347-X C2016-906348-8

Cover design: David A. Gee
Cover images: © vanderveldon/iStockPhoto
Interior images: Courtesy of the author

The publication of *Director's Cut* has been generously supported by the Government of Canada through
the Canada Book Fund. *Ce livre est financé en partie par le gouvernement du Canada.* We also acknowledge
the Government of Ontario through the Ontario Book Publishing Tax Credit and the Ontario Media
Development Corporation.

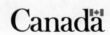

PRINTED AND BOUND IN CANADA   PRINTING: FRIESENS 5 4 3 2 1

I would like to dedicate
these memoirs to
Laifun
whose loving urgings
caused their genesis,
and
to three soul mates,
Mordecai and Florence Richler
and
Francis Chapman,
who bestowed upon me a
lifetime of closeness and devotion

Me, dreaming of the next shot.

by Mariska Hargitay

September 12, 2011. Ted Kotcheff had just completed 12 beautiful, inspiring, envelope-pushing years at *Law & Order: SVU*, and we had all gathered — cast, producers, and crew — to say thank-you, to say goodbye. That night, I wanted to express my gratitude for the gift of collaborating with Ted — I wanted to tell him how much I'd miss him, what working with him had meant to me, how he'd changed my life. But each time I got ready to speak, my emotions got the better of me. So at the end of the dinner, I simply hugged him and said, "Goodbye for now."

As I was leaving, I thought back to when I was first cast as Detective Olivia Benson. (Thank you, Ted.) He had graciously invited me to lunch so we could get better acquainted. Sitting across from him, I knew right away that I was in the presence of someone unique — a man whose charisma came from an unfettered appetite for life.

*Mariska Hargitay and me at her wedding to Peter Hermann, laughing when
I told her I played Cupid by introducing them on the set of* Law & Order: SVU.

With an old-school elegance and the skill of a quintessential storyteller, Ted not only regaled me with the depth of
his experience, he also made some of the most insightful
observations about acting I'd ever heard. Even back then, I
thought, "This guy really needs to write a book." But what
delighted me most was his honesty: he couldn't help but tell
the truth. Now, after a 12-year working relationship and a
lifelong friendship cemented in place, I am deeply grateful
for what I can only call the "Ted Experience" — that rare
time in one's life where you meet someone who will be
both your teacher and friend. Ted speaks the truth, directs
the truth, pulls the truth out of all the actors he works with.
You can see that in the performances he directed on our
show and in all his films. Perhaps most important is that

his passion for the truth beckons us to think more deeply about our own lives.

When Ted directs, he brings that passion to every frame. He engages his entire being in the act of creating. Ted often looks like he's performing an opera, with his keen eyes, full of vitality, glued to the monitor, his entire body acting out the emotions of the scene, almost as if he's an instrument being played by the actors. When he calls "action," he doesn't just say it, he challenges the actors with a forcefulness I rarely hear from other directors: "Ac-TION! Do your best and I will be there with you along the way, so give it everything you've got." We were shooting a television show, but with Ted we always felt like we were shooting a feature.

Most directors shoot scenes with a master shot, then cover the scene from various angles. But this classic approach doesn't apply to Ted; he demands more freedom, more artistic space for the boldness of his vision. Ted's uniqueness was never more evident than when he directed the 2005 *SVU* episode "911" in which Benson is on the phone with a kidnapped girl being held in a basement waiting for help to arrive — for the *entire* episode. I'd faced challenging scripts before, but this one raised the bar, and it was an opportunity to create something with an artist who I had come to see was unlike anyone else. And so Ted and I went to work.

I had the sense that Ted already shot the episode in his head, yet his creativity on the set felt like a flurry of improvisation. Frenetically — even frantically — he would shout, "Give me the fifth line now! Great! Now I need the twelfth line! After you deliver it, I'm going to whirl the camera around and be on top of your head!" He was editing with the camera as he worked, one dramatic shot following on the heels of the next, demanding that I be emotionally prepared at every juncture. It was exhilarating.

One of the most remarkable aspects of that shoot was that although Ted gave me an abundance of ideas, he cherished and respected each one of mine. While he insisted on realizing the vision he had in his head, he remained a true collaborator. I've always thought that the Emmy I was honored to win for the episode belonged as much on Ted's mantle as it did on mine.

I want to reiterate just how extraordinary — and delightful — Ted's spirit of collaboration is. A fierce, bold, lion of a man, uncommonly articulate, with a wealth of experience and a portfolio of cinematic knowledge few can claim, can be more than a bit intimidating. Yet, in a room full of good ideas, if you offered Ted something that was, in his judgment, the *best* idea, his whole being would catch fire. His eyes would light up and he would say, in his inimitable rat-tat-tat, "Yes . . . yes . . . yes! Let's do it that way!" There was no possessiveness in his creativity, no tight-fistedness about where the magic came from, as long as that's what everybody was committed to mining from themselves and each other.

This was a huge lesson for me when I was given the chance to direct my first episode of *SVU* in March 2014. I was more than nervous; I was plain scared. When I called Ted and confided my fears, he told me something that not only got me through the episode, but went in my file of best pieces of advice I ever received: "Mariska, you know more than you think you know." And his support didn't stop there. Like a true mentor, he made my success a priority in his life. He discussed the script with me for hours, a deep, creative exchange of ideas in which he shared his perceptions about the material, delving into psychology and drawing from his own experiences to illuminate his points. His generosity was absolute. He had already given me so much over the years, and now was giving even more. In that moment, I felt not only deep gratitude, but deep joy for his children that they had this magnificent teacher for a father. And I must say, there is probably no greater testament to Ted, and his wife, my dear Laifun, than Alexandra and Thomas. Beyond being enormously accomplished in their respective fields, documentary filmmaking for Alexandra, classical music composition for Thomas, I am struck each time I see them how wonderfully and thoroughly alive they are, how deeply they are engaged in their craft and the world. And to see Ted talk about them is to see joy itself.

A few weeks after hugging Ted at the end of his farewell dinner and telling him "goodbye for now," I wrote him this letter:

Dear Ted,

I was going to give you a toast at your dinner and I'm sorry that I didn't. But as the moment approached, I realized it would have been a situation involving way too much Kleenex, so I thought I should write to you instead. What I want to say is simple: thank you. Thank you for being the artist that you are. I think one of the most difficult things as an artist, and as a person in general, is to listen to your own voice, to march to your own drum, to insist on your own vision. You are an inspiration and a leader in that regard. I think that the most beautiful thing about your insistence on your voice and your vision is that you help other people find theirs. You open up a space for them to be the unique artists they are. You teach them how to claim that room for themselves. You make them stronger, better, braver. Most of the time I don't even think you knew you were doing it. You were just being you. And I certainly don't think that you know how much of that you have done for me in my life. So more than anything, I think that is a gift you have given me, an understanding of the beauty of being a true original, bold and defiant, and true to your vision. I'm sure you're not surprised to hear that it is not the same without you here on the show, but your singular, beautiful imprint is everywhere and on everything we do every day. I miss you immensely, and I am forever grateful.

xoxo

Mariska

I have encountered few artistic flames that have burned as brightly and for so long as Ted Kotcheff's. As you read these pages, my hope is that you will allow Ted not only to illuminate the story of his life, his experience, and the craft he has practiced for so long, but to encourage, foster — perhaps kindle for the first time — the artistic fire in you. Nothing will delight Ted more, or make his eyes shine brighter, than knowing that he has passed the flame forward.

And Ted, I can only end with the words that I've heard you say so often, with your distinct panache and gallantry: "Big kiss, darling!"

Picture This . . .

Want to hear my idea of the greatest life? I wake up in the morning, put on my clothing, have breakfast, and then I go to a film set. I find a receptive film crew and a devoted cast of actors who can make what I'm envisioning even better. I say, "Okay everybody, here we go. Let's put the camera over there. Darling, you stand over here. Sir, you stand over there. At the moment when she looks at you, you rush over to her . . ." And then we all devote ourselves to working together to create a new kind of reality and put it on film.

Not being pigeonholed as the guy who makes one style of film has allowed me to traverse every genre. But it also often landed me in the wilderness when it came to studio executives and producers drawing up their wish lists of directors for projects. More importantly for me, it has hurt me in the search for financing for my own ideas, as moneymen always feel more comfortable when they can say, "Oh, he's done that before, so he'll do it again."

My filmography is a gumbo. I have directed action films like *First Blood*, the first in the Rambo series, and *Uncommon Valor*; dramas of varying levels of intensity from *North Dallas Forty* to *Joshua Then and Now*; and comedies including *Fun with Dick and Jane*, *Switching Channels*, and *Weekend at Bernie's*. Add to this list other titles such as *Wake in Fright*, a noir thriller; *Who's Killing the Great Chefs of Europe*, a caper; and *Billy Two Hats*, a western.

The one thing I have never done is what others expected me to do. I turned down the James Bond film *License to Kill*. I'd like to say the reason was because I felt there was no artistic benefit for me to direct a Bond film because the formula was set in concrete, but the real reason I did not do the Bond film was that they wouldn't pay me as much money as I asked for. It was the only time in my career I allowed money to be the deciding factor.

And I have never directed a sequel, a veritable ATM for a director. Even after *First Blood* became a worldwide blockbuster, I turned down the next Rambo film, which would have yielded a nice beach house in Malibu at the very least. I also said no to the sequel to *Weekend at Bernie's*.

There's no nobility in those decisions, and I don't say this to show that I am an auteur. The Rambo character was being taken in a different direction. In my film, he was a man who abhorred violence, wrestled with the moral dilemma of violence in Vietnam, and did not kill a single person. In the sequel, John Rambo was turned into a gratuitous killing machine. On *Weekend at Bernie's*, I felt that I had run out of dead man jokes, or at least the desire to stage them. I had also lived for a long period of time in those worlds, and so I wanted to move on and see what other new worlds I could explore filmically. For me, making films was always about the production experience and telling a different story each time. Everything else is a distant second.

Commenting on my place in the '70s and '80s, the *Washington Post* recently called me "the under-appreciated Ted Kotcheff."

Hey, I'll take it.

What I believe the *Post* means is that much of my due has come later. Yes, I did have several hits, notably *First Blood*, which grossed $125 million worldwide at a time when that was a huge number. *North Dallas Forty* stirred up controversy over the NFL's treatment of players and notched positive notices for intense realism from critics. *Fun with Dick and Jane* broke out at the box office, and *Weekend at Bernie's* became a cult hit all over the world. One of my first films, *The Apprenticeship of Duddy Kravitz*, won the highest prize, the Golden Bear, at the Berlin Film Festival in 1974. My films have also generated largely positive reviews.

And in recent times, two of my films received the ultimate artistic accolade by being named Cannes Classics by the Cannes Film Festival, long the world's most prestigious film festival. The first was *Wake in Fright*, a dark Australian film that came out in 1971 and was recognized by Cannes in 2009. The second was *The Apprenticeship of Duddy Kravitz*, released in 1974 and honored at Cannes in 2013. What I love most about that is not the recognition, but the acknowledgment that the films have longevity.

My first and best love is the filmmaking process.

"

The Apprenticeship of Duddy Kravitz is the axis on which my career and, in many ways, my life has rotated.

The film was based on the novel by my dearest friend in the world, the late Mordecai Richler. I met Mordecai in 1958, and we shared a grungy flat together in London where he wrote the novel. When I read it, I told him that not only was it the finest Canadian novel ever written, but that one day I was going back to Canada to make a film of it. We both laughed at the absurdity of such an idea. At that time, there was no film industry in Canada, which is why I had moved to London.

As I established myself as a director of live television and theater in London, I struggled for 14 years to get *Duddy Kravitz* made. Eventually, the film was co-financed by the Canadian Film Development Corporation, formed to jump-start national film production. It was one of the most popular Canadian films of the 1970s, and critical support of the film from the likes of Pauline Kael helped boost its profile.

The film raised the prospect that Canadian stories might just have a place on the big screen. It has always been my belief that a flourishing film industry defines a nation and that together with homegrown literature, theater and music reflect its essential character. These art forms are part of any nation's very heart and soul. Despite the fact that my family and I had a very checkered relationship with Canada, I am glad that I played a small part in boosting my country's film industry.

I grew up in the slums of Toronto, poorer than poor. My parents each arrived separately from Bulgaria thinking the streets would be paved with gold. Unfortunately, soon after, they found themselves squarely in the middle of the Great Depression, at a time when immigrants were regarded as the lowest of the low. The houses in our neighborhood were overcrowded with immigrants like my family who had no heat in the winter and a lack of social services. Our house was so cold that I nearly froze to death when I was two; my life was saved by a doctor who defrosted me in a pot of boiling water.

I never went to film school, or took a filmmaking class. My film school was the strange jobs I held. I worked in my dad's diner that was frequented by Damon Runyonesque characters — bookies, bootleggers, small-time crooks, pimps, prostitutes, professional wrestlers. After graduating with an English degree and not being able to find work as a poet, I worked in Swift's slaughterhouse, then at Goodyear Tire in the foam rubber department, which is the closest I've ever come to Dante's *Inferno*.

My break came when the Canadian Broadcasting Corporation (CBC) moved from radio into television. I managed to land a job as a stagehand before the CBC was even on the air. Working as a stagehand and watching live TV plays being done every day slowly shaped my interest in becoming a director. Television expanded at such a ferocious pace that within three years, at age 24, I was given a chance to direct.

Directing captivated me. My primary focus in directing has always been on characters. There's a story about the brilliant writer Anton Chekhov that illustrates this point better than I can explain it.

Chekhov, who is my hero, sent all of his short stories to a literary critic in Moscow for review. On one particular story entitled "The Horse Thief," the critic wrote back that the story was terrific, except for one thing. Chekhov had not taken a moral stance on the stealing of horses.

Chekhov replied that he was not interested in judging a horse thief. "First off, if you need me to tell you that stealing horses is wrong, are you ever in moral trouble. I don't care what the character does, I want to know what he's thinking when he does what he does," he told the critic. Then Chekhov wrote a sentence that still sends a shiver down my backbone when I read it: "I'm not the judge of my characters. I'm their best witness."

Wow! That was what I wanted to bring to filmmaking.

Chekhov also used to say that the most important thing is that no character should be humiliated. When I first read that statement, my heart skipped a beat.

More than any advice I've ever received, those two observations were heaven sent. They became the cornerstone of my directing philosophy. Any time I felt lost or overwhelmed, I would say to myself, "Kotcheff, be their best witness and don't humiliate them."

When I was directing *Duddy Kravitz*, I wanted to get inside Duddy's head. He is a likable, if indefensible, 18-year-old hustler, who betrays friends and his lover in his desire to make something of himself. I wanted the audience to know where he was coming from. The basic question of the film is posed by a gangster, who asks, "Kravitz, why do you always run around like you've got a red hot poker up your ass?"

I hope the film — aided in large part by Richard Dreyfuss's complex portrayal of Duddy, which he has called the best of his storied career — provides the answer to that question.

Duddy Kravitz was my entrée into Hollywood. After it was released, I was offered my first Hollywood studio film, *Fun with Dick and Jane*, starring George Segal and Jane Fonda. Some 25 years later, Dick Wolf, creator of the *Law & Order* series, hired me to put together and executive produce *Special Victims Unit* because he thought *North Dallas Forty* was the greatest sports movie ever made in America.

What is the connection between doing a network TV show set inside the world of the officers who handle the most horrendous crimes perpetrated largely on children and women and professional football? I haven't the slightest idea, but such are the strange links that make up my career.

One of the things that my eclectic career shows is that I love films with dynamic actors. My favorite part of the filmmaking process is working with actors to pull out the best performances. How lucky am I that I've directed a veritable who's who: William Shatner, Gene Hackman, Richard Dreyfuss, Jane Fonda, Gregory Peck, George Segal, Sylvester Stallone, Nick Nolte, Ingrid Bergman, Tom Selleck, Don Ameche, Kathleen Turner, Burt Reynolds, Christopher Reeve, Jacqueline Bisset, James Woods, Alan Arkin, James Mason, Micheline Lanctôt, Brian Dennehy, Kurt Russell, Jean Simmons, Laurence Harvey, Donald Pleasence, Jack Thompson, Chris Meloni, and Mariska Hargitay, among many others. Yes, I'm a movie fan at heart.

"

Directing is a strange process. The director is not only creating what will be on the screen, but in the process he or she is also playing chief psychiatrist with the actors, air traffic controller for the crew, and conductor of many different segments of the art forms involved, from camera work to music to production design. You need a lot of other qualities besides knowing how to make films. You need to able to control the people working together and get the best out of everyone or you will not be able to achieve the film you envision. All of this needs to be done while kowtowing to the moneymen.

Put more crassly, a director must be a policeman, a

I'm totally involved with George Segal while filming The Desperate Hours *in 1967.*

---

midwife, a psychoanalyst, a sycophant, and a bastard, as the great Billy Wilder once said.

I've concluded that "director" is not a clear word for what my peers and I aspire to do. A "director" sounds like someone sitting in a boardroom dictating corporate actions. The best word for my job on a film is the French term — *réalisateur*, or realizer. A director has a vision of a film in their head that he or she must turn into reality — realizing it.

When I work on a film I become possessed, a possession I have never quite understood. I am totally consumed by the process. It's all I think about. When I'm sitting on the toilet or shaving in the morning, I'm envisioning how the scenes will play out. On the set, I become so involved that I practically act out each scene as I conduct the actors.

My directing style is noisy, but not loud. I gyrate, wince, laugh, cringe, or tear up, depending on what the actors are doing. I demand the full attention of everyone on the set. My catchphrase when I see people veering off into chitchat is "What is this cocktail party conversation going on while we are trying to film!"

I'm not the only one who demands the full attention of the crew. When I met the great Swedish director Ingmar Bergman many years ago, he told me that when he says "Action," he needs the attention of everyone on his crew to be focused on the action, pouring their psychic energy into the actors to the nth degree. One day, feeling negativity, he turned around during a take and saw an electrician on top of a tall ladder reading a newspaper. He yelled out, "You! Get out of my studio!"

The one constant in my work is that I have always been attracted to characters who don't know themselves, who aren't sure what's motivating them, and who are on a voyage of self-discovery. And so, after directing 17 feature films, some 13 TV movies, more than 40 episodes of live television, and one short film that my daughter produced and my son scored, and executive producing 289 (and directing several) episodes of the hit TV series *Law & Order: SVU*, I decided it was time to examine my own trek, to search for answers about creativity.

Commercially, there were times when I could hit the zeitgeist (*First Blood*, *Weekend at Bernie's*) and other times when I couldn't find it with a map (*Winter People*, *Folks!*). I learned that I cannot tell what audiences will want to see, so I focused on what moved me, what made me laugh, and what thrilled me and hoped that my audiences felt the same.

I have wrestled with what to make of my career on and off for years, and with how my own life and history has affected the films I have made. No answer has yet been found, but this dilemma came into full view over the course of two months in 2011, though not entirely by my choosing.

That September, I ended my 12-year run as executive producer of *Law & Order: SVU* just a few days before a retrospective of my work was being shown at the Oldenburg Film Festival in Germany. A month later, the Directors Guild of Canada presented me with its Lifetime Achievement Award. Aside from underscoring the fact that I am indeed old, these events forced me to look back over my 50-plus years behind the camera and the years prior that deposited me there.

My ancestors, the Bulgars, have a saying: "There are many roads to the top of the mountain." I feel like I've tried them all but not yet reached the summit. This book is another one.

CHAPTER ONE

How I Was Branded a Communist

Before my career could even get started, I was branded a Communist and banned from America. This disbarment was a huge stigmatic obstacle, as it marooned me professionally in Canada, which had no film industry whatsoever at that time.

It was 1953. I was 22 and had been working one year as a stagehand at the Canadian Broadcasting Corporation in Toronto on dramatic plays that were shown live on television. Another stagehand, Phil Hersh, and I decided to go to New York for a short holiday. I was incredibly excited. My father had always said that New York was the most interesting place in the world to live. Certainly, it was the mecca of theater and drama. I could not wait to see the lights of Broadway and lap up the spirit of the Great White Way. Phil and I were looking forward to having the full-on New York experience. We would go out for a feast in Little

Italy and eat the famous cheesecake at Lindy's in Times Square. We had heard that the most beautiful women in the world were in New York, so we also planned to sample the bars and nightclubs.

Quite possibly, I thought, this could be a life-changing trip. Well, it certainly proved to be life changing, but not in the way I imagined.

Traveling by railroad was the most economical. We took a train from Toronto to Montreal, where we switched for a train to New York. The closer we got, the more our anticipation grew.

As the train approached the U.S. border crossing from Canada into Vermont, U.S. immigration officials came through for a passport check. Phil and I presented our documents. Phil's was stamped without ceremony. Mine was not.

An overweight, toady immigration official studied my passport as though it were in hieroglyphics. He harrumphed and walked away, taking my passport with him.

When he returned several minutes later, the immigration official informed me that I would have to disembark at the next stop in St. Albans, Vermont. There, I would be examined for admissibility. "If you pass the examination, you can go on to New York this evening," he said.

I didn't take this hiccup very seriously. I figured it was some kind of formality, as I had never entered the U.S. before. I assumed that they were going to ask me the kind of standard questions that customs officials ask, things like where are you going to stay, is this trip business or pleasure, are you carrying any fruit, et cetera. I told Phil to go ahead to New York, check into our hotel, and scope out a local bar. I would see him later that night.

The train pulled in to a dingy railway station in St. Albans, an ugly little one-horse burg. It was raining heavily.

The immigration official and I disembarked. With my two pieces of luggage banging on my legs, I accompanied Mr. Bullfrog up a hill to a charmless, three-story stone building.

The official checked me in and escorted me to the second floor. He directed me into a room. I took a few steps inside and heard a loud clang behind me. I quickly turned around to see that the door had metal bars on it.

Holy shit, I thought, *I'm in jail! Jail?!*

Mr. Bullfrog scowled at me. "We have decided to detain you for a variety of reasons," he said. "You will go before a board, and they will decide your admissibility to the U.S."

I was stunned. I didn't know what to do. I lay down on the bottom of a bunk bed. The walls were covered in graffiti, some in English, mostly in French. "*Baise mon cul, Oncle Sam*" being typical. A two-way radio could be heard from next door: "Those baby smugglers are expected to try crossing the border tonight."

I sat and stewed for several hours. Thoughts of seeing the lights of Broadway and carousing with beautiful women were long gone. Now I was only concerned with why I was here, and how I would get out. I was a 22-year-old who was incarcerated but had no idea why. Only one person knew where I was. But what if they moved me? Then no one would know.

At one point, an orderly brought me a ham sandwich for lunch, but made me pay for it. Periodically, some official type would come to the cell door and ask me a personal question, then go away. One guy with a military attitude and spit-shined shoes to match his demeanor told me that "if I played ball with them, I would be in New York that night."

I didn't find him particularly convincing, and I began to grow increasingly worried as time passed. What had I done? Surely, this was a case of mistaken identity. Wasn't it?

19

Eventually, two immigration officials appeared and began peppering me with questions. They asked me my mother's maiden name, which I told them was Diana Christoff. This was followed by a series of benign questions about where I lived and what I did for a living.

Every six or seventh question, they would again ask my mother's maiden name. Finally, I had had enough.

"I already gave it to you, several times!" I said curtly.

"Give it to me again," one of them growled.

"Christoff," I said curtly.

"How do you spell Christoff?" he asked.

"C-H-R-I-S-T as in Jesus Christ, and O-F-F as in fuck off," I answered.

"Don't get so smart with me, young guy," he said.

"You keep asking me as if I'm lying to you," I replied.

Finally, around 4 p.m., I was granted the promised hearing. I went before three strict and humorless Justice Department officers in a gloomy boardroom. After a few perfunctory questions, one of the officers looked down at a piece of paper and then solemnly asked, "Were you ever a member of the Left Wing Book Club?"

In fact, I had been.

When I was a teenager, in the school's summer holidays, I worked at my dad's diner, Norm's, at the corner of Dundas and Pembroke in Toronto. The place was full of lowlifes and colorful characters. One of them was an aging leftie who wore a beret and a cape. From the looks of him, he was very hard up. He sold copies of *The Daily Worker* for a meager living, and I sometimes bought the paper, more out of charity than political interest.

One day the leftie spotted me sitting at the cash register reading a book. He pressed me to join the Left Wing Book Club, which he promised me would provide good books at low prices. Though I demurred, he kept nagging at me. Finally, feeling sorry for his indigence, I allowed myself to be persuaded by him. I filled out the coupon in *The Daily Worker* and gave it to him.

It was a kind of Socialist Book of the Month Club. Over the next seven months, I passively received three club selections. The first was volume one of the writings of Lenin. The second was *Wind in the Olive Trees*, a critical and damning account of Generalissimo Franco, Spain's fascist dictator for 30 years. Lastly, I received a biography of the Scottish poet Robert Burns, who was admired in Socialist circles, presumably because of his proletarian roots.

The books seemed random and unrelated. I found Lenin's writings unreadable and gave up on them early. The book on Franco was too much of a polemic to be engaging, but I did enjoy the Robert Burns biography and all of his poems that were included, and still do.

During one of the book deliveries, the postman spoke to my mother and reproached her for allowing her son to belong to a "Commie front" book club. The postman! I suppose this should have alerted me to the fact that I was being snooped on by the Royal Canadian Mounted (i.e., Stuffed) Police. But in any case, bored with their books, I resigned from the Left Wing Book Club after seven months. I never heard from them again.

How did the U.S. Immigration Service know any of this? I had thoughts of conspiracy.

Answering the Justice Department officer's question about my membership in the Left Wing Book Club, I protested my innocence. "Sir, that was when I was 16 years old," I said. "Six years ago . . . and I was only a member for seven months. And I was so bored with their offerings that I quit!"

"Be that as it may, you belonged to a book club that

disseminated literature that advocated the forceful over-throw of democratic government," one hearing officer said.

The officials didn't seem to care what my explanation was. They issued their verdict: "I'm afraid we have to reject your application for entry into the United States."

"Your banishment comes under the provisions of sections 212(a)(28)(H) of the Immigration and Nationality Act in that you are an alien who has been a member of an organization that circulated and distributed printed matter advocating the economic, international, and governmental doctrines of World Communism."

"Communism?! What do you mean? I'm not a Communist! I'm the opposite! I'm violently opposed to Communism!"

Their three countenances were studies in stony disbelief. I could read their eyes: diehard Commie. I realized I could protest and argue from now till doomsday, but it would be to no avail.

I was refused entry and informed that I would be escorted back to Canada that evening. The hearing was over.

I was handcuffed to Mr. Bullfrog, handcuffed! And together we walked back down the muddy hill to the railway station. Passing people looked at me strangely, some even fearfully. As the train arrived in the station, in an unexpected act of thoughtfulness, Mr. Bullfrog said that if I promised to behave myself he would remove the cuffs, saving me embarrassment when we boarded the train. However, as I was escorted to my seat by a uniformed man, who clearly had some sort of official capacity, people eyed me curiously. Mr. Bullfrog took a seat two rows behind me.

When the train crossed the border, he left the train without a look or a word at the first Canadian station. I proceeded to Montreal in the gathering darkness. My mind swirled with confusion, as I began to ruminate on the events of the day.

I had been imprisoned for hours, harassed with endless questionings on the deceptive pretext that if I played ball, I would be allowed to go to New York. This was followed by that sham hearing as to my admissibility with its predetermined outcome, and then the final humiliation: handcuffed like some dangerous criminal, all done to me by a country I liked and admired.

I became livid, to put it mildly. I was boiling with rancor. A wave of contempt rose within me for the hypocrisies of the Yanks. The freest country in the world! Freedom of thought! Freedom of belief! What bullshit! I was condemned for something I had read. I concurred with the sentiments of that anonymous French Canadian, *"Baise mon cul, Oncle Sam!"* Kiss my royal Canadian asshole, Uncle Sam!

As for our Royal Canadian Mounted Police betraying me, one of their own people, to the Yanks, it was disgraceful. They not only dropped their trousers and bent over, they put Vaseline on their posteriors to make it easier for the Yanks to bone them. I've never forgiven them, even to this day.

"

I sat fists clenched and ransacked my mind: was there something else besides the book club? Was I perhaps paying for the misinterpreted beliefs of my parents? My entire family was extremely left wing, a product of what had happened during the 1930s Great Depression, when the unacceptable, ugly face of capitalism truly showed itself: when people were allowed to starve to death and freeze to death, even me — almost! My parents' political and social beliefs had somewhat become my own.

Both my parents had participated in a left-wing theater club, which put on weekly plays in a Bulgarian-Macedonian hall, which had its share of Communist members. The auditorium held about 200 people, and it was always full for performances.

Most of the plays were about the plight of the Bulgarian and Macedonian people, who lived under the oppressive rule of the Turkish Ottoman Empire for some 500 years. The desire of the people to be free and to overthrow their savage rulers was an underlying theme in many of the plays. More than once, my dad played a rebel soldier who was killed by the Turkish army.

While the left-wing philosophy was ingrained in me from their theater group, the experience also led to my love of theater. It taught me what Bulgarians and Macedonians had endured for centuries, and it showed me how story-telling could be a critical outlet in the desire for freedom and dignity. The fact that it was left wing was secondary to the emotional content.

Because my parents could not afford a babysitter, and I was an only child at the time, they took me to all the rehearsals and performances. My parents, then in their twenties, were the leading actors in the troupe. They rehearsed every Saturday night, leaving me to roam the auditorium and gaze up at them under the stage lights. I would stand at the rear of the auditorium peering over the back of a chair, watching my parents transform into other people and become two strangers. I'm sure it was here that the seeds of my directing career were planted.

All my aunts and uncles were also actors in the plays. I actually made my stage debut at five, playing a village child in *The Macedonian Blood Wedding*.

My father, who knew French, also translated classic

Организацията „Вардар" При Македонския Народен Съюз

ПОКАНА

ДРАМАТИЧЕСКИЯ КРЪЖОК ПРИ НАШИТЕ ОРГАНИЗАЦИИ, КОЯТО Е ПОД ВОДИТЕЛСТВОТО НА АНДРО ПАЛМЕРОВ

ЩЕ ПРЕДСТАВИ

НА 28 ЯНУАРИЙ, НЕДЕЛЯ ВЕЧЕРТА

В Залата на Народния Дом, 386 Онтарио Ст.

«ХИМН НА НИЩЕТАТА»

(ДРАМАТА Е В ПЕТ ДЕЙСТВИЯ ИЗ ЖИВОТА НА МИЗЕРИЯТА)

УЧАСТВАЩИ В ПРЕДСТАВЯНЕТО НА „ХИМН НА НИЩЕТАТА"

1. МЕТОДИ ИВАНОВ	Нико (сирах)		7. ЛЮБА ПАЛМЕРОВА	Соня (годеница на Давид)	
2. ЮРД. КОЧЕВА	Феня (дещеря на Саря)		8. СПИКА ДАФОВА	Сара (вдовица, майка на Д.)	
3. ЖЕЧКА ДУЛОВА	Лева (ехевдка)		9. ?? ??	Лакей	
4. ТОМА НАСКАЛЕВА	Берта (дещеря на Кан)		10. АНТОН ДУЛОВ	Мински (търгов.)	
5. НАУМ ГЕОРГИЕВ	Г-н Кан (еврени)		11. ИВАН КОЗАРЕВ	Един Човек (еврени)	
6. ТОДОР КОЧЕВ	Д-р Давид (син на Саря)		12. НЕДЕЛЧО КОЖУХАРОВ	Лазар (студент)	

ДР. РАБОТНИЦИ И РАБОТНИЧКИ,

„Химн на нищетата", изнасяш мизерията и нейната действителност, трогва и най-коравите сърдца. На нашата сцен се изнася за трети пжт и ще требва да се види от всеки честен човек. Трудовата емиграция ще требва широко да пропагитир тая вечеринка, за да бъде най-масово посетена.

Всички добре дошли! ОТ НАСТОЯТЕЛСТВОТО.

*Theatre program from the Bulgarian-Macedonian Theatre Group for a
play in which my parents starred. Mom sits on the floor, Dad sits behind her.*

plays like Molière's *The Doctor in Spite of Himself* into
Bulgarian for the troupe. For these plays, he would serve
as the line prompter. He would stand just offstage and feed

the lines to the actors if need be. I remember standing in the wings next to my father being totally captivated by this process. All the performers had exhausting jobs filling their week, leaving them little time to learn their lines properly. So sometimes every line had to be prompted. My father would whisper the line, and then the actor would utter it.

My father's whispering of each line was loud enough that the audience could hear it. My father would say, "Tell him you love him." A second later, the actor would earnestly declare, "I love you."

But when I looked out at the audience, I could see people weeping, oblivious to the process, not letting it disturb their experience. The audience members were completely riveted. I marveled at their desire not to let anything interfere with their involvement with the play. It was a real lesson for me. Drama entails a suspension of disbelief. Their disbelief was so suspended that they never once flinched — despite the fact that every line was being audibly prompted. They were so emotionally engaged in the story that they were able to filter out my father's voice.

My father had one defect as a prompter: he loved humor and would laugh enormously, even at his own jokes, to the extent that he couldn't get out the punch line. Sometimes, like in the Molière play, my father would laugh so hard at its funny bits, tears would pour from his eyes, rendering him unable to see the lines and prompt the performers. The poor actors were stuck frozen, waiting, only able to throw daggers at him.

The one thing I noticed was that all the performers in the play were working-class people, not professional actors. They used the plays as an outlet for their creativity, and for their deeply held political beliefs and frustrations.

The plays were followed by music, a Bulgarian choir

and solo performances of tap dancing and even the violin. I did both. At age five, I began playing the violin and became accomplished very quickly, so I often performed for the crowd. The performances were followed by a political speech and a collection of money to support the theater group, as all performances were free and funded through contributions.

The guiding spirit of that theater group was my mother's elder brother, my uncle, Andrew Palmeroff. At the end of the evening's entertainment, Andrew would take the stage and deliver a political speech. He was a fiery orator. He passionately railed about how important the plays were to the psyche and soul of each and every member of the community, which caused them to give more than they intended. I became a champion debater at high school, having picked up many rhetorical tricks from my uncle.

Uncle Andrew worked days as a chef in his restaurant, but the theater group was his true love. He would tape his lines that he had to learn above his culinary workstation. At breakfast once, he was studying his lines and making pancakes at the same time. He reached up on the shelf for the baking powder but someone had put rat poison next to it on that shelf, but he didn't notice that because he was so absorbed in preparing for his role. He dumped a nice shaking of rat poison in the batter, making a patron violently ill.

Politically, he was an extreme left-winger. Aside from running the theater, he also wrote for a Bulgarian-Macedonian newspaper published in Canada called *New Times*. He had a big influence on me.

Ironically though, I was totally turned off Communism because of Uncle Andrew. His son, Julian, was very gifted athletically, an outstanding player on the Pape Public School hockey team. He was also a champion pole-vaulter.

I was very fond of Julian — he was a very lovely and amusing man — but my uncle thought sports were for knuckleheads and oafs, and he wanted a son who was an intellectual, like me, with whom he could talk about Freud and Marx and their ilk. He even told me he wished I were his son.

He gave me a copy of the *Communist Manifesto* and Sigmund Freud's *The Psychopathology of Everyday Life* at age 11! Freud was interesting. I remember once Julian, an ardent hockey fan, came in excitedly and said to me, "Hey, Boston's playing tonight." His father looked up from his tome and inquired acidly, "Who's conducting?" He demoralized his son until he lost all belief in himself, giving him a deep sense of worthlessness. He could have been a professional hockey player, but instead ended up nowhere.

When I saw how he belittled his son, I decided that his beloved Communism and all his high-minded talk about its humanism and justice and compassion for the "masses" was a pile of crap, sanctioning his mistreatment of children who were not up to his high-minded standards. I've always disliked and mistrusted thinkers who put ideas ahead of people, something that characterized many Communists all the way up to their god, the monstrous Joseph Stalin.

It was a mixture of adolescent rebellion and events in my life like the one I just related (and other dramatic ones that I shall reveal) that rendered both my brother Tim and me deeply antipathetic intellectually and emotionally to political philosophies of the Left. It was not empty hyperbole when I said to the Justice Department officers that I was violently opposed to Communism — I meant it.

"

All these thoughts and memories swirled round in my head as I rode the train back to Montreal. The rhythmic sound of its wheels calmed me down. Instead of fruitless venting, I turned my mind onto the important question of what I was going to do. Life ahead seemed riddled with doubts and obstacles.

First off, was there any way I could submit an appeal to have my disbarment overturned? If there was, I knew it would be a lengthy and tortuous process. And I had to face the fact that my ban might be irrevocable. My thoughts turned to how all this impinged upon my career. Now I was only a stagehand, but I dreamed of ultimately becoming a filmmaker. With no film industry in Canada, and the door to Hollywood now slammed in my face, I felt confounded and doomed.

What irony that three small books capsized the whole of my future life as I had envisaged it. How appropriate! As my life had started upside down, perhaps this was right side up.

CHAPTER TWO

Cabbagetown Kid

When I was two, I was involved in a serious accident rendering me comatose — which I will regale you with later in this chapter. What I want to say now is that when I regained consciousness, when I opened my eyes, the whole world appeared overturned: our yellow home, our blossoming pear tree, my keening family on its veranda — everything was downside up.

This was my very first vision of this terrestrial sphere of woe, an image that has stayed vividly in my memory ever since.

Later in my life, I thought this was a perfect metaphor for where I found myself, as I was born square in the middle of Canada's dire Great Depression, made even harsher and more lunatic by our country's two prime ministers in turn. They were the Liberal Party leader, William Lyon Mackenzie King, and the Conservative Party leader,

R.B. Bennett, known as Iron Heel Bennett, you can guess why. They were two of the most demented, idiotic political leaders ever allowed to run a country.

Half of Canada was unemployed and had been for some time. During the '30s there were 30,000 people out of work in my hometown, Toronto, alone. Mackenzie King would not take this seriously, refusing to believe there was a crisis. He thought the problem was seasonal, and any form of relief would unbalance his beloved budget. This gullible man met Hitler in Germany in 1937 and thought he was a nice man, "an affectionate, sympathetic man who truly loves his fellow man, and has a sincere desire for peace." All this at the very moment Hitler was inaugurating Buchenwald.

My father exploded at this news: "Hasn't this horse's ass read Hitler's *Mein Kampf,* where that maniac details the horrors he's about to unleash on the world?" But, as a Royal Canadian Mounted Police colonel once pointed out to me, "Your parents were premature antifascists," meaning, they were Communists because only Communists were against Hitler before World War II. Can you believe this?

R.B. Bennett not only looked like a bloated capitalist, he *was* a bloated capitalist. One of the richest men in Canada, his wealth was not earned but inherited. Bennett thought the Depression was psychological and not real, and that it wouldn't last very long. Being a diehard conservative, he was against any form of government relief to the unemployed and destitute for, as he once said, "It would sap people's initiative, making them soft, and produce a generation of sloths, feeding from the public trough," and other such Calvinist rubbish.

This is just a sampling of the endless flow of inanities from these two men, and their firm belief that any healthy

Me, at five years old, with my parents, Diana and Ted Kotcheff.

man could always find a job, and that if he was unemployed, it was deliberate, and not society's fault, and to ask for handouts from the government was shameful. Boy, did this country ever need a Roosevelt.

Canada at that time was a racist country. The vast majority of Canadians, from the prime minister down, were anti-Semitic and anti-foreign. Toronto especially was the citadel of WASP privilege. Banks, department stores, financial and insurance firms, and corporations from the likes of Procter and Gamble to Maclean Hunter barred Jews from employment. Jewish doctors were refused hospital affiliations. Universities refused to hire Jewish faculty and had quotas for Jewish students, and high offices in the federal government, from the Senate to the Supreme Court, were barred to Jews. In Montreal, there was a march through the streets with participants yelling, "*A bas les Juifs!*" (Down with the Jews), followed by front windows of Jewish shops smashed, exactly like Hitler's *Kristallnacht*. Some crazies even accused the Jews of having created the Depression.

I remember when I was five and learning to read, my father took me to one of Toronto's eastern beaches and there was a sign at its entrance, "No dogs or Jews allowed." I read it haltingly and said, "Dad, what should I do with my apple juice?"

"No, Billy, it's people they don't want."

"Are we Juice, Dad?"

"Almost."

Us "Bohunks" and "Polacks" (Bennett's terms) were equally in trouble. Foreigners who applied for relief or became radicalized or committed any illegality, no matter how minor, were taken into custody and, without any trial, herded aboard trains and, without any right of appeal, put on freighters and deported back to their home countries. In the worst years of the Depression, from 1930 to 1935, Canada deported more than 28,000 foreign men, women, and children. I always thought this was Bennett's way of trying to solve the unemployment problem.

The threat of deportation always hung over my parents like a sword of Damocles. My mother worried constantly: because they were involved in protests, demonstrations, and becoming radicalized, and also because my father, trying to help his family survive, was making illegal whiskey for a local bootlegger in the basement of our home. If caught for either of these offenses, we would all be repatriated to Bulgaria.

You can imagine how tenuous my identity as a Canadian felt, when at any moment the government could tell me to get out and go back to Bulgaria. Hey, I was born in

Canada, thus a first-generation Canadian, yet I was still a "foreigner." My whole family and I were treated as second-class citizens. My father was Bulgarian, the lowest of the low, and my mother was Macedonian, lower still. Slavs were especially vilified. We weren't outsiders; we were lepers who smelled like garlic, and often told to go back to where we came from.

Unlike most of the working-class people who came to Canada from England and Scotland, my father, Theodore Kotcheff, came from an upper-middle-class family. His father, my grandfather, was the court-appointed architect for all of the public buildings in Bulgaria. My father graduated from *Gymnasia*, the term for secondary school in Bulgaria, which was unusual at the time.

Though I never knew the reason, my father immigrated to Canada in 1927 when he was 17. His real surname was Tsotcheff, but upon his arrival in Canada, the Canadian immigration official couldn't read Cyrillic, and didn't know how to spell it, and my father, knowing no English, kept repeating "Ts," "Ts," "Ts," but the official couldn't get it and, becoming impatient, baptized my father on the spot: "Kotcheff! Next!"

My mother, Diana Christoff, came to Canada at 18 from Bulgaria with her younger sister, Sophie, and elder brother, Andrew. She had lived in Varna for 15 years with her family after they had fled Macedonia for Bulgaria to escape the brutal Turkish Empire that was terrorizing her country.

My parents' marriage in 1929 was something of an anomaly. My father was 19, my mother 20. Most Bulgarian marriages in my parents' time were arranged, but they met independently of their families and had a romantic courtship. My father then took a job as a waiter in a restaurant, where my mother worked as a waitress. The restaurant was owned

My parents in front of my dad's restaurant, Norm's, in 1946.

by my Uncle Andrew. My father and mother began dating. One day at work, my father put his hand on my mother's rear. This was witnessed by Uncle Andrew, who promptly fired both of them.

The reason my mother fell in love with my father is that she felt safe and protected with him. After her tumultuous childhood, this was of the utmost importance to her. They first met at a demonstration: she was protesting the government's total indifference to those in desperate need. My mother became cornered, trapped in a shop doorway by a policeman on a horse. The policeman began slashing at her with his whip. My father was nearby. He ran over and covered my mother with his body and took the beating for her. This was how they met.

When I first heard this story later in life, it stuck with me as one of moving sacrifice. When I was directing the film *Joshua Then and Now*, I inserted a similar scene to show how the female lead, played by Gabrielle Lazure, would quickly and completely fall for the male lead, played by James Woods. That one scene — in real life and on film — depicted the creation of a bond of true, selfless love. And filmically, it happened to be a wonderfully romantic way of meeting.

My parents got married on October 27, 1929. They planned their wedding and reception for a Sunday, the only day that my parents and practically all of their guests were not working. It was held at the Bulgarian-Macedonian People's Hall on Ontario Street in Toronto. They had a live Macedonian band that played all the classic horos.

The large gathering went round and round, dancing and leaping, having the greatest time, when suddenly the police arrived and shut the reception down. There were complaints from neighboring religious, joy-killing Brits that a bunch of apostates were violating the Sabbath with our loud, foreign music and noisy dancing. We should be at home, reading the Bible and praying. "Toronto the Good," as it was called then, had strict blue laws. And so that was the anti-climactic end to my parents' joyful and romantic wedding.

Bad as this was, my parents didn't know that their wedding would be followed two days later by Black Tuesday, the catastrophic stock market crash that led to the Great Depression. My parents always had an impeccable sense of timing.

"

My early childhood was made all the worse by the fact that I was born on April 7, 1931, in the hardest part of the Depression. Because there was no money to go to a hospital, my birth occurred unceremoniously on our rickety, Formica-topped kitchen table, and I'm sure you don't know anyone else who has this particular distinction. My given name was William Theodore Constantine Kotcheff. William was my dad's elder brother, Theodore was my father, and Constantine was my grandfather, who had immigrated with my grandmother and my father but died very soon afterward in the worldwide flu epidemic that killed an estimated 50 million people.

For the first 22 years of my life, I was Bill Kotcheff. It was only when I went to work for CBC Television that I had to use my second name and became Ted Kotcheff. (Why that came about, I'll deal with later.)

The area we lived in was called Cabbagetown. It was so named because the Irish immigrants who settled there in the 1840s were so poor, they grew cabbages for food in their front yards. It was considered the slums of Toronto.

The Depression magnified the area's destitution. Poor families moved to Cabbagetown to live crammed in the row houses with their relatives, because they could not afford their own residences. Many houses were not safe for occupancy. Our house did not have a proper working furnace and, as I mentioned, in the winter of 1933, at two years of age, I came within a hair's breadth of freezing to death.

That night, the temperature in Toronto dropped to -40 degrees Fahrenheit. The snow had piled up so high against the first-floor windows in our house that we literally could not see out. We had so little money, my father couldn't afford any wood or coal to keep the furnace burning, or even fuel the pot-bellied stove in the kitchen.

On that bone-chilling night, no amount of blankets could keep out that kind of cold. My labored breathing awoke my mother. She took one look at my ice-blue carcass, stiff as a plank like a frozen slab of meat, and she screamed. Because we had no phone or car, my father sprinted ten blocks through the arctic midnight to fetch the doctor. Fortunately for me, my dad was an amateur marathon runner. He got to the doctor very quickly, but what I was desperately in need of was heat.

My Uncle Gyorgi, my father's brother who lived with us, was rattled by the sight of his frozen nephew. He lamented the conditions with his trademark refrain, "son of bitch," which he pronounced "beetch." "Sons of beetch Canadians turning our house into igloo!" he ranted. "Son of beetch rotten government not helping us to get fuel!"

Gyorgi then took up arms to save me. He grabbed an axe and dashed to a nearby snow-covered park. He chopped down two good-sized blue spruce trees and dragged them back to the house, taking a surreptitious route to avoid the authorities who surely would have arrested him for his illegal tree hack, and deported him back to Bulgaria post-haste. He risked this for love of me. Back at the house, he threw the wood into our pot-bellied stove to warm up the kitchen where I lay and to heat water in a baby-sized washbasin.

Dr. Malin, a saintly Bulgarian, finally arrived with my dad. He stuck a thermometer in my ear and then up my posterior. My body temperature was 84, two degrees away from death. "Hypothermia!" he cried out, and he snatched me from the couch and plunged me up to my neck in the almost boiling water.

I felt like I had been transported from the North Pole at midnight to the Sahara Desert at high noon. Shocked and scalded, I glared at the doctor who was still holding me and howled my very first words: "Beetch! Beetch!" Not "Mama" or "Dada," but "Beetch!"

Dr. Malin said, "That's right, Billy, when the summer comes, you'll be able to go to the beach." But my mother and dad knew what I was trying to say and looked accusingly at Uncle Gyorgi, who was smiling with satisfaction because he had provided his nephew with his very first word: "Bitch!"

How precociously discerning of me to come out with *le mot juste* that encapsulated my life in Cabbagetown hitherto. It certainly was a "beetch."

"

My mother, father, me, and Uncle Gyorgi all lived on the ground floor of a yellow wooden house with a chocolate-colored front door. My Aunt Sophie (with whom my mother had emigrated from Bulgaria) and her husband, my Uncle Stavro (an arranged marriage), lived upstairs with my baby cousin Rudolf, who had been named after his mother's big-screen love, Rudolph Valentino. We all lived happily together. However, Uncle Gyorgi's stay with us was suddenly cut short.

I loved my Uncle Gyorgi. No matter how bad things got in our life, he was never down. There was always a twinkle in his eye, he was perpetually in good spirits, a tonic we all so desperately needed. He would come out with amusing quips in his broken English: once when we were absolutely penniless, he said to me, "No money, no funny." And, of course, I never forgot that he had saved my life.

My uncle participated in demonstrations, because he was deeply angry at how mean and parsimonious the politicians were to the impoverished and unemployed, allowing people to literally starve and freeze to death. At one demonstration at Queen's Park (beside the provincial legislature), Gyorgi was peacefully protesting when, totally unprovoked, he was attacked by a policeman on a horse.

Of course, this was not unusual, as the cops hated protesters, especially foreign protesters. The policeman began to furiously whip him all over his head and body. Gyorgi knew the story of how my parents had met, so he always came prepared. To stop the onslaught, he pulled some marbles from his pocket and hurled them under the horse's hooves.

The horse lost his footing, and he and his rider came crashing down on the pavement. Gyorgi almost escaped, but another cop galloped over, knocked him down with his horse, and arrested him. Gyorgi told us that a bystander, some dried-out WASPy woman, said to him, "Serves you right for being so cruel to that horse."

Gyorgi was tried, found guilty, and deported back to Bulgaria. His final words on Canada, as he was taken away, "The weather is cold, so are the pipple." Oh, how I missed him! What an insane time it was!

"

Getting back to *my* tribulations, what follows is the serious accident I promised you, which happened right outside our Cabbagetown house, on Sydenham Street. I wrote a poem about the experience (later published in one of three volumes of my poetry entitled *First Looks and Beyond*), and here are some of its lines:

> I, a tyke, had toddled
> Onto the horse-appled road,
> When round the corner,
> From Tracy Street,
> Came a black Model A,
> It never slowed,
> *Wham!* I went flying!
> Then straight away
> The Ford rode over
> Where I lay

With demoniac wheels,
Front and back,
Howling squeals,
Leg bones crack,
The jeering enthronement
Of Happenstance.

After the assault,
I lay still as debris
On the black asphalt.
A deathly hush.
Uncle Stavro raised
The limp remains,
Its shattered legs, tire stained,
Protruding gristle and bone,
My mother unmoving
Turned to stone.
My lifeless head,
Loosely lolling,
Hung backward
Over Stavro's arm.
The sisters' voices rose to heaven
With Slavic lamentation
Of funereal pain.
Roused from the dead,
Eyelids fluttered in my inverted head;
A strange first sighting:
Straw yellow home,
Pear-blossomed tree,
My barking Scottish collie
My keening family,
Downside up,
Upside down,

And topsy-turvily.
Flowers and grass up in the sky,
While scudding clouds pass knee high.
My very first remembrance
Of being on this earthly manse,
A haunting image, its afterglow
Still luminous as a rainbow.

On our veranda, my upside-down mother was screaming, weeping because she thought I was gone. My Aunt Sophie was holding her with a comforting arm.

I was rushed to Toronto's Hospital for Sick Children by the man who ran over me, where I was accepted as an emergency charity case. The doctors worked furiously to reset my legs in the hope that one day, they would again be usable. The operation was successful. I ended up staying in the hospital for four strange weeks.

The hospital wasn't strange, the support was. There were no visitors allowed in after 7 p.m. — no exceptions. Both my parents worked until 8:30 p.m., so my Aunt Sophie would spend the afternoons with me. My aunt showed my parents which window was my room's, and occasionally, late at night, my parents would yell up to my window from outside, four stories below, that they loved me.

I vividly remember that accident and the ensuing weeks in the hospital. I understood the Depression through the oddity that my parents could not visit their three-year-old son in the hospital because they had to work. Not that I fully grasped the situation then, but I understood that I was living in this upside-down world.

Why Lord Death had it in for me, I don't know. After He tried to rub me out by Glaciation, then by Auto, we were almost pals. I've never been afraid of Him since.

99

Life was indeed a "beetch" in Cabbagetown. Kids don't take in, or understand the economic status of their parents, as long as they have food on the table. Until I was five years old, I lived in what I now realize was abject poverty. We were two families jammed into a two-story house in the poorest section of town.

The Cabbagetown where I spent the first five years of my life no longer exists. Our house has long since been torn down. Now it is a gentrified area of pleasant apartment complexes and row houses, with nary a cabbage to be seen.

We were so poor that we could not afford to go to a hospital — for anything. My mother had her tonsils taken out in our house by the same doctor who dunked me into the boiling water and saved me from hypothermia, Dr. Malin. I remember seeing her passed out after the operation and thinking that she was dead. Literally, she was a patient etherized upon a table — that Formica-topped kitchen table which was my birthplace.

Decent-wage jobs were hard to come by in what became known as the Hungry Thirties. Any jobs were hard to come by no matter how badly underpaid, and were they ever. Thousands of Canadians were paid unbelievably low wages, working such long hours their lives were close to slavery. A 50-hour week for 10 cents an hour, and more often less, was common. We always lived on the edge of disaster, my father working on one itinerant job after another, interspersed with long periods of unemployment.

Every morning, my father and two chums went to the corner of Queen and Yonge, smack in the center of Toronto, because that was where the *Toronto Daily Star* was first delivered hot off the presses around 11 a.m. The three men were literally penniless. But what my dad did was absolutely brilliant: he arranged that each one of them would approach different affluent-looking business types, prevalent in that area, and ask if they would give one cent. The amount, being so small, they were rarely turned down.

So between them, the three men collected the three cents needed to buy one copy of the *Toronto Daily Star*. They immediately opened the newspaper to the Want Ads section under Employment Opportunities, but, day after day, there would not be one single job offered. Finally, eureka! Six men were wanted by Swift and Company, the prosperous abattoir.

As I told you earlier, my father was a weekend marathon runner, and he immediately set out on foot. He ran all the way, arriving second to a man with a bike. He was hired. Great excitement in Cabbagetown! Many years later, I measured the distance by car from Queen and Yonge to Swift's, located at Keele and St. Clair. That day, my father ran seven and a half miles.

When I remember my father now, I always see him running, running, running through the streets of Toronto as fast as he could, running to provide food for my mother and me. This image of him running always brings tears to my eyes.

The job that my father got at the Swift abattoir consisted of piling up the skins of the slaughtered cows to be sent to shoe companies. The skins were stiff and heavily salted to protect them. But my father had no gloves, couldn't afford them, so the salt cut his hands to shreds, and he would arrive home at night with his hands bleeding. Fortunately for his hands, but not for us, it turned out to be a temporary job, and after a few weeks he was laid off.

But it was not all Sturm und Drang in old Cabbagetown. First off, my dad had some very amusing idiosyncrasies:

he thought bathing was very bad for you, as scrubbing the skin removed the body's protective oils, making you vulnerable to all sorts of infections, illnesses, and afflictions.

My mother put up with it until his ankles got rusty, then she would force him to bathe. But there was never a scintilla of B.O. emanating from my dad. My father also never brushed his teeth because he believed that brushing wore off the enamel. As proof of his hypothesis, he would point to the kitchen sink, where frequent cleaning with Dutch Cleanser had removed the white enamel in places, revealing the dark metal beneath. He said, "You see, that's what happens with tooth brushing." He never went to the dentist (who could afford that anyway?), and amazingly, when he died at 87, he had all of his teeth. He did make virtuoso use of the toothpick, carefully removing all food.

Aside from these peccadilloes, he was a neat man, trousers always pressed, shoes always shined.

My mother never stopped: it was always a time of "busy hands." She made her own feta cheese, so there was always cheesecloth dripping whey, hanging from the kitchen faucets. She made sauerkraut, soaking the cabbage leaves in salt water in a small barrel lying on its side by the front door that my father would kick when he passed it to stir up the salt. She pickled peppers in two styles, in brine and in olive oil. She canned tomato sauce, buying all her produce at the end of summer when it was cheap. For example, a three-pound basket of field tomatoes would cost 10 cents, and she made enough of everything to last all winter. She preserved peaches and pears for our dessert.

And she always made yoghurt. She kept the same yoghurt culture for 12 years! One day, I came home and ate her precious, active cultures. She was beside herself, but fortunately, she had given some to her sister Sophie, which allowed her to continue yoghurt making with the same 12-year-old Lactobacillus Bulgaricus to the end of her days.

She was always repairing holes in our socks, stretched over a used light bulb; always crocheting and knitting lop-sided sweaters; knitting overlong scarves; making dresses using *Vogue* patterns for herself and her sister Sophie. She even made scatter rugs. She embroidered, doing petit point of idyllic pastoral scenes on cushion covers, always singing old country songs in a beguiling voice. She and my dad even gave me haircuts, placing a bowl over my head and cutting around it.

"Busy hands" indeed. All this, with her continued search for a paying job.

My parents had an eating habit that I thought was true of all married couples, but I later discovered that it only characterized my mother and father's relationship. They always had dinner from the same plate, which my mother placed between them.

Years later, this was reduced to eating the salad that we always had with our evening meal from the same plate. They did this for the whole of their married life. This sharing seemed to me to be emblematic of their conjugality, the oneness that love creates. I sang of this in one of my poems:

Now there is no separateness,
There is no you,
There is no me,
Oh, miraculous love!
You transmute mine
And my beloved's soul,
Two become one,
A perfect whole.

No matter how bad things were, my father made sure that there was always Slavic culture in our lives. The rooms were decorated like a typical Bulgarian home, with vibrant tapestries my mother made hanging on the walls. We always spoke Bulgarian at home, and I didn't learn English until I went to school at five! My mother always cooked Bulgarian dishes, bop (bean soup), lentil soup, kebabcheta, stuffed peppers, stuffed cabbage, tarator, banitsa, baklava, and other Bulgarian classics.

Every Sunday, the whole family would gather together, usually at our house, for a Sunday dinner: my Aunt Sophie and Chiche Stavro (Uncle Stavro) from upstairs; Chiche Andro and his wife, my Aunt Luba; and my mother's first cousins whom I called "uncle," Chiche Dono and his wife, and another Stavro we called Dubel Stavro (Fat Steve), to differentiate him from Sophie's husband, and his wife. These two Stavros played an important part in my life later on, as did all of my close relatives. They all brought their kids, my cousins, to play with me.

They would all drink wine, usually made by my uncle Fat Steve. Then, after dinner, they would sing Bulgarian and Macedonian folk songs with tears in their eyes as memories of the old country haunted them. They would get out of their chairs and start dancing to their own songs; "*Haide!*" They would hold hands, *horo* style, and dance out of the dining room, through the living room, into the hallway, then through the kitchen, and back into the dining room. Round and round they would go, singing and dancing their hearts out, full of the joy of life.

These bacchanalian Sunday afternoons were an object lesson for me. No matter how difficult life may be, how depressing, never surrender to it, enjoy every second of your existence on this strange planet. Let loose, and make merry whenever you can.

Many years later, I saw Ingmar Bergman's film *Fanny and Alexander*. I was astonished to see this Swedish family behaving exactly like my family, dancing round and round through the house. When I met Ingmar Bergman, I asked him about this scene, and he told me his family used to behave in the same way as mine, every Sunday.

This whole way of life during my childhood left indelible memories that had a deep effect on me. In my heart and soul, I have always felt Bulgarian.

My father loved films. When he originally immigrated to Canada, he first went to live in Edmonton, Alberta, where an elder sister lived. His first job, in 1927, was as an usher in a posh movie theater. He became enraptured with films. He always took me to the cinema, at first sporadically of course, even though movies were only 25 cents for an adult and 10 cents for a kid, and no popcorn — we couldn't afford it. Later, when he got a steady job, we would all go, including my younger brother, Tim, two or three times a week for a double feature, and it was then that my love of movies was born. Remember, there was no TV to watch, so this was our primary form of entertainment.

I was mesmerized by what I saw on the big screen. These movies versed me in cinema. I loved *The Thin Man* with William Powell and Myrna Loy. Humphrey Bogart became my idealized version of a leading man. When I began smoking, I held my cigarette exactly like Bogie did, not between two fingers but cupped in my hand.

Oh, and those women! Greta Garbo in *Ninotchka* took my breath away. I fell in love with Ingrid Bergman (whom I came to work with later), the talent of Judy Garland bowled me over (when I met her, the story of her life devastated

Family portrait: Grandma, Mom, Dad, a distant relative, my younger brother Tim, and me.

me), and when I saw Bette Davis, that spunky free spirit, outspoken and independent, I thought, "That's the woman for me."

One of the biggest treats of my life, when I first went to Hollywood, was to have an intimate dinner with Bette Davis, just her and me and a mutual friend who had arranged it. She was, thrillingly, exactly like her screen image — peppery, high-spirited, full of sharply observed experiences told with a soupçon of acidity.

49

And I remember watching the great Hitchcock's films and starting to sweat, they were so suspenseful and incredibly well crafted.

I saw practically every film made between 1936 and 1950, some multiple times. Even today, when an obscure film from that period comes on the TV late at night, I will recognize it and spoil the plot for my wife.

"

Besides deportation, the other thing that stressed my parents was the constant threat of eviction hanging over them. It was hard not to think of being evicted, for, in Cabbagetown, it was practically a daily event. I remember seeing this happen to our neighbors: bailiffs storming in with the landlord, forcing them out of their dilapidated home because they were unable to pay the $1.50 monthly rent. The father, the mother, their children whom I played with sat on the sidewalk as their pathetic, decrepit furniture was piled up around them. Any decent piece of furniture was commandeered by the bailiffs as payments toward the outstanding delinquent rent. Tossed from his home with nowhere to turn, sitting in a sagging chair on the sidewalk, the look in the father's eyes, of defeat and desperation, was unbearable to see.

Evicted families, sitting on the sidewalk, were the capitalist icon of the Great Depression. As I sit here writing, some 80 years later, I still vividly remember this last image of my neighbors.

My father was frequently unemployed and often could not make our monthly rent, which was $2. I remember him telling the landlord he didn't have that month's $2. The landlord said, "How about $1?" My father shook his head and repeated that he had absolutely no money. The landlord then said, "Okay, how about 50 cents?" At that point, I saw my humiliated father demonstrate his final reply by pulling out the insides of his two empty pockets. My mother held her breath: would he evict us? After a long pause, the landlord said, "Okay, I'll see you next month," and left.

His hesitation was entirely due to what happened to our neighbor's house after their eviction. That night, the emptied house was broken into and dismantled by all the men in our neighborhood. Everything was taken, all the doors, storm windows, railings, plumbing, toilets, washbasins, wiring, light fixtures, and any furniture left behind, like some antiquated gas stove or icebox. Even floorboards were ripped up, to be used, as we did, in stoves for heat.

After several houses were gutted in this fashion all over Cabbagetown, with some abodes stripped to their joists, landlords were reluctant to evict; they didn't want their houses turned into useless skeletons. So, my mom and dad relaxed; we were all safe for the time being.

Before you start moralizing about these blatant thefts, remember, as Bertolt Brecht pointed out: "Even saintly folk may act like sinners, unless they've had their customary dinners."

My father tried everything to keep food on the table. At times, his impotence at being unable to do so would rob him of his normal good humor, and get him down. It was at one of these moments that an angel of sorts appeared. How this man knew my father, I don't know, for my dad was not a drinker, even when he had the money to do so. Our malignant angel was the owner of a very successful blind pig — a wonderful metaphor of unknown provenance. (I never *metaphor* I didn't like.) The man suggested my father

51

make moonshine (another metaphor!) in the basement of our house. He would pay for a still to be installed. After that, he would pay 25 cents for every bottle of hooch Dad made.

My father disliked the idea of doing something illegal; he had a deep fear of being arrested. But desperate times need desperate measures; with us almost starving, he had little choice.

Every morning, my dad went down to the farmers' market on Front Street and waited until it was closing time so he could buy the necessary ingredients at rock-bottom prices. Sometimes, when the fruit had become overripe and commercially useless, but still perfect for fermentation, being a handsome and charming man, my father would obtain it without cost from generous farmers. Any unsold produce — be it potatoes, parsnips, pears, corn, apples, peaches, beets — all went into the still's hopper to be distilled. It turns out that you can ferment practically any fruit or vegetable that has sugar. After all, classic Russian vodka is made from potatoes!

When fermentation was in progress, which was almost every day, our house reeked of moonshine. It was like residing in a bottle of Seagram's rye. On one fermentation day, there was a knock on our front door, which had a frosted glass panel in its top half. We could see a silhouette of a policeman! Panic! Imminent deportation!

I was sent to answer the door, but admonished to only open it a crack so that the incriminating reek could not sneak out. I opened the door just enough to get my nose through and yelled, "No grown-ups home!" and quickly slammed it shut. My parents breathed a sigh of relief and congratulated me as the policeman departed — until I told them it was the gas man.

No question, life then was adventurous and hazardous, and you needed to be really gutsy to survive it.

One memorable moment from this time was a visit from my favorite uncle, Chiche Dono. He was continually amusing, not unlike my sorely missed Uncle Gyorgi. With my dad's love of jokes, and having a good laugh, the two of them together were an endless, humorous jamboree. I've never cared for humorless people, or humorless art, for life is such a curious mixture of the excruciatingly painful, the breathtakingly beautiful, and the utterly ridiculous — a tragic farce. We desperately need humor.

I wrote a poem about one of Chiche Dono's visits. Here is an excerpt. The long speech he makes was uttered in Bulgarian, of course:

One day, my Uncle Don
Gave a hand to my father,
Raucous laughter arose from the cellar.
I peeped over the shaky railing
And there below, drunk as lords and skunks,
They were both collecting yet another glass
Of the early drops, dripping from the still,
Which as every good moonshiner knows
Are potent, one hundred proof alcohol.

My uncle raised his glass to heaven,
"God! You know that in my soul,
I have always doubted your existence.
Why, of course you know, you know everything.
I thought you were a fairy tale,
But here I am, no job for six months,
Not one red cent in my pocket,

About to be evicted and no food on the table
For my beloved wife and daughter.
But am I unhappy? No!
Because in the kindness of your enormous heart,
A heart as big as this house,
You have made this delicious potion
Of sweet forgetfulness
That magically makes my fear,
My cares, my worries and pains, all disappear.
Now I know that you exist!
Now I know! — that you exist!
I toast your health!"
My dad joined the toast
To God's thoughtfulness,
They gulped the throat-burning hooch
And reached with their glasses
For more forgetfulness.

The still saved our ass for a while, but the illegality was too much for my dad's nerves, and he decided to give it up. What finally saved us financially was that, in 1936, when I was five, for the first time my father got a steady job delivering bread to homes in a paneled truck for the Co-operative Bakery. Eight dollars pay, every week! A fortune! We were rich! Goodbye, Cabbagetown.

CHAPTER THREE
Escape from Cabbagetown

The bakery where my father worked was in York Township. It was too far for my dad to commute each day from Cabbagetown, so we moved to a nice, two-story brick house on Silverthorne Avenue. It was a semi-rural area on the edge of Toronto. The house was on a dirt road with empty lots on either side of it, one of which was covered in bushes. All the houses there were scattered hither and thither across the pastoral landscape like flung dice. There were vast, empty fields and large wooded areas. After the claustrophobic slums of Cabbagetown, I felt like a bird let out of a cage.

The woods were filled with chokecherries from which my dad made a tasty wine. We picked the leaves from wild grapevines growing in the woods that my mother stuffed with paprika'd rice, exactly like a Greek dolma. My mother would pick the leaves from sweet, young dandelions for her salads. There were lumps of wild rhubarb, which my mother collected, which together with the wild strawberries I picked from the endless beds of them along the railway embankment, my mother would blend into a delicious compote. I described it as "eating wild."

Three important things happened at our new residence. First, I started school. You had to be six to start grade one at Silverthorn Public, but I was so insistent on going, my mother lied about my age, and I started at the age of five and a half.

Second, my parents now having the money purchased a quarter-sized violin and paid for my lessons. The family were all great believers in the importance of a musical education, and in playing an instrument. This has been the quintessential pleasure of my life, and I'm still playing the violin 80 years later. My brother, Tim, studied the clarinet and became very proficient.

Third, backing up a bit, Tim was born! We still were not affluent enough for Tim to enter this world via a hospital, so he was born at home but, at least, he was not born like me on a decrepit Formica-topped kitchen table. Tim was born on a newly purchased, splendid oak dining room table. Obviously, we were moving up in the world.

One of the advantages of home birthing was that I was awakened by the sounds of my mother's labor pains. I stood at the top of the stairs, unseen, and watched Tim miraculously come into this world, emerging slowly from my mother's vagina. After this shocking, yet intriguing education in childbirth, I went downstairs.

My Aunt Sophie, who was the assistant midwife, brought the slimy baby over to me. She cooed and told me that this was my new brother. I took one look at the crinkly faced blob and declared, in an initial burst of sibling rivalry, "That's the ugliest baby I've ever seen." Tim later inherited my father's handsomeness and became a beautiful boy, and a very good-looking man.

Tim was part of my dad's bi-weekly movie visits. While I was interested in the characters and storytelling of the films, Tim was fascinated by the events covered in the 15-minute "Movie Tone News" that always accompanied every screening. This was a harbinger of things to come: Tim later began a professional career in broadcast journalism. He rose to become a major figure in television news, as the vice president in charge of news, documentaries, and current affairs for both CTV, a commercial network, and later the CBC, Canada's public broadcaster. And in 2014, the Governor General of Canada presented him with the Michener-Baxter Special Award for his distinguished contribution to the Michener Awards Foundation and for encouraging public service journalism in Canada.

When World War II struck in 1939, it brought the flush of health to the pallid cheeks of capitalism. So, after delivering bread, my dad landed a more lucrative deal delivering milk via horse and wagon for Roselawn Dairy. He was paid so well that he was able to put some money away. Soon, my father saved enough to buy into a partnership in a restaurant.

This was something all of my uncles wanted to do. Practically all of them ended up in the restaurant business. They were good cooks and it was a relatively small business they could cope with. Uncle Andrew had the Carlaw Grill and many others subsequently; my Aunt Sophie's husband, Chiche Stavro, had the Purity Tea Room on College Street; after a series of eateries, Chiche Dono finished with the Flame Steakhouse in Port Credit. And now my father entered the business: the restaurant was called Queen's Grill on north Yonge Street.

Better still, it was next door to a Famous Players movie house, the Bedford Theatre. The manager saw my love for movies and took a liking to me. Because he knew I could not afford to buy a ticket, he would unlock the back door and let me enter for free.

My dad finally found his niche in life, the work that was perfect for him. He knew how to prepare food, he loved serving food, his customers loved him for his affability.

We moved into an apartment on top of the Queen's Grill. My bed was directly over the jukebox. Because the floor was paper thin, I could hear the music clearly, disturbing my sleep until midnight, when the restaurant closed.

I remember the lyrics of all the *Hit Parade* songs of the time. "Pistol packin' mama, lay that pistol down," echoed in my head for weeks. I loved the totally politically incorrect "Too Fat Polka": "I don't want her you can have her, she's too fat for me." But the one song that really pulled me in was "Paper Doll" by the Mills Brothers. It sat at number one on *Billboard* for 12 consecutive weeks, from November 1943 through January 1944, and I must have heard that song 1,368 times, give or take. It was about a guy whose girlfriend always gets stolen away, so he wants a paper doll he can call his own.

So, as uncertain as things were, I was always able to focus on the escapist possibilities that movies and music, both classical and popular, provided.

"

Becoming a partner in the Queen's Grill turned things around for my father and us. He knew how to run a restaurant successfully, which he did for the next 50 years. His abiding advice to his staff was that old chestnut: the customer is always right. If the customer is unhappy about anything, take the offending plate away and replace it immediately. His menu was always an interesting mixture of Canadian dishes with a sprinkling of Bulgarian cuisine.

He had great success with his next restaurant, Norm's, a diner-style eatery at the corner of Pembroke and Dundas — not far from the old Cabbagetown neighborhood. All the locals came, sometimes for breakfast, lunch, and dinner! This was followed by an even greater success with The Senator on Victoria Street, just below Dundas, which still exists there to this day with the original '40s red leather banquette décor.

When I was 12, my father cobbled together enough money from his Norm's profits to move us to a lovely single-family house in the suburbs on Humbercrest Boulevard, where backyards overlooked the Humber River and valley. It was in close proximity to what was probably the most upper-class area in Toronto, where people like Conn Smythe, the owner of the Toronto Maple Leafs, resided, a place called Baby Point. People there were very snobbish and thought the word "baby" was vulgar; so they called it "Babby Point." So we had now become middle class! We had a telephone! We had a car!

The house we bought had been owned by a man who made coffins for a living, and it looked like it had been styled by a production designer for a Vincent Price horror film. All the woodwork, the doors, and the window frames on the two-story edifice were painted jet black, and the front yard was a patch of mud with a scrubland of crab grass. Before we moved in, the coffin maker's large pick-up truck was always parked on the street directly in front of the house, with his latest models stacked in the back in full view of the whole neighborhood.

The families on either side of his house didn't seem to mind their macabre neighbor, for he was a Brit, but within days of us moving in, they both posted For Sale signs. My parents were horrified and deeply insulted. The coffin maker was fine, but garlic-eating Bulgarians were not. There goes the neighborhood, they felt. What African-Americans have had to endure forever and a day.

My father set out to turn them around. He went about his business, shaping up the house. He painted it stark white and planted a new lawn, complete with a spruce tree in its center, with a flower garden around the base of the house. The house now looked beautiful. In a matter of weeks, the neighbors introduced themselves — the Lindsays on one side, the Wilsons on the other. They apologized for their snap judgment and took down the For Sale signs.

I always admired my parents in as much as they were way ahead of their time, and way ahead of most people in North America in that they partook in protests against the barbarous treatment of African-Americans in the American South. This especially revealed itself in 1931 in the trial of nine black youths accused of raping two white women on a train, a crime punishable by death in Alabama. They were called the Scottsboro Boys.

I won't go into the convoluted details, only to say that the two white women were prostitutes who perjured themselves. The all-white jury found the nine black youths guilty and all but the 12-year-old were sentenced to death.

My parents joined in the huge protests in the North,

which were led by the Communist Party, who took the case to the U.S. Supreme Court and got the convictions overturned because of the jury having no black members. But the vicious Alabaman racists didn't give up! They relentlessly kept trying the Scottsboro Boys over and over.

They totally wrecked the lives of these nine black men and the last member of the Scottsboro Boys was given a full pardon by the Governor of Alabama in 1976 — 45 years after the supposed commission of the crime! If you don't know about this case, investigate it. It has to be one of the most shocking miscarriages of justice ever committed in the United States.

My parents were on the forefront of the protests way back in 1931, my birth year. They both felt very passionately that any form of irrational prejudice and hostility directed against an individual or group because of their race, sex, religion, color, nationality, or characteristics was a vicious societal cancer that had to be pulled up by its roots and extirpated.

And they were bloody well going to make sure that their offspring would never have even a trace of this loathsome, abominable cancer. So, to experience Jewish life firsthand and never be capable of anti-Semitism, when I was twelve and my brother Tim six, we were sent to a Jewish summer camp, Camp Naivelt (Camp New World). They would have sent us to an African-American Camp, but there was no such thing at that time. So for three consecutive years — 1943, 1944, and 1945 — Tim and I spent the whole summer at Camp Naivelt.

It was a great experience, with the usual camp activities, games, and sports. The other boys were congenial, and I became good friends with a boy named Stan Horowitz and with my 18-year-old camp counsellor, Dusty Cole, whom

I adored and who later became an important figure in the Canadian film industry.

Tim and I were the only two boys in 200 who were still in full possession of their foreskins. The only time there was a slight problem was in the showers, when my uncircumcised member was duly noted, and my friend Horowitz and I got into a mild contretemps on the subject of circumcision. I maintained that Nature would not have provided men with a foreskin if it had no purpose, and Horowitz accused me of being a reactionary conservative, that the true socialist position is not to go along with nature but to change it. I accused him of being a victim of a stupid, outdated religious shibboleth, and there was nothing socialist about it at all.

The issue was never resolved.

Every morning, the entire camp would line up and sing our camp song, "Camp Naivelt, *unzer zumer haim* [our summer home]," and then our camp leader would deliver a homily in Yiddish on some moral theme. He was a saintly, idealistic man, a devoted Labor Zionist, working for the creation of Israel.

I was bored listening to him, not understanding a word. After a couple of weeks of this, I said to myself, "Kotcheff, if you are going to be listening to this every morning for the rest of the summer, why don't you listen carefully and learn Yiddish."

Well, I did. Because I went there for three whole summers, I learned to speak it. Later in life, I would taunt Jewish friends asking them if they spoke Yiddish. If they didn't, I'd say, "What kind of Jew are you, anyway? I speak Yiddish!" Using Yiddish expressions in Hollywood increased the number of the denizens there who thought I was Jewish.

A moment of enlightenment I treasure was when the atomic bomb was dropped on Hiroshima, then Nagasaki, killing at least 100,000 in each city. I rushed up to our camp leader, crying out, "Isn't this great? The war is over. That'll teach those slant-eyed, yellow bastards," an expression I had picked up from a comic book.

My camp leader looked at me, "First of all, Billy, you know better than to use racial slurs like that," he lectured. "Haven't you learned anything in our camp? While I share your gladness that this war will finally end soon, I want you to think, Billy, of who was in those cities whose demise you're celebrating. No military there, they were away fighting on some Pacific atoll. No, the cities had only women, children, and old people. One hundred thousand of them were obliterated in each of those cities. People like us."

There were tears in his eyes. Later, I thought, what a morally elevated human being he was to have these feelings when everyone else at that time was in the grip of extreme jingoism and blind patriotism.

But ultimately, of course, it was my parents' feelings and activities that shaped Tim and me. They did their job well. Both of us have not a trace of anti-Semitism or anti-black racism. When I went to live in England, I became an ardent activist in the South African anti-apartheid movement, raising money for it by directing charity shows. And I have my parents to thank.

”

Though I left Cabbagetown far behind when I was almost six, Cabbagetown never left me. I couldn't escape it. I never shook off the image of living in one of the largest

Anglo-Saxon slums in North America. I always identified with the ragged kid growing up in hardscrabble and hearing music or seeing films that transported him out of his daily existence. My parents were indelibly stained and scarred by what transpired in Cabbagetown. They were convinced to the end of their days that a market crash, and ensuing Depression, would devastate us again.

I would later draw on my memories of those years. I filled several notebooks with poems about that time of survival, self-exploration, and character building. And I actually came to embrace those years much later in life.

When I accepted a lifetime achievement award from the Directors Guild of Canada in 2011, I quipped that at heart I was just a Cabbagetown kid. Laughter rose from the audience. They all knew exactly what I was talking about.

CHAPTER FOUR

The Garlic Revenge,
the Principled Principal,
and the Diehard Rebel

My high school, Runnymede Collegiate Institute, was a strange mixture of poor pupils from an area north of the railway tracks, who arrived at school in disintegrating sneakers, and upper class Baby Point, or should I say Babby Point, students who arrived at school driving Buick convertibles. I was somewhere in the middle but, as a foreigner, the lowest of the low socially.

Students had fun with my name. I got "Bill Ketchup," "Bill Katshit," "Bill Kutyacockoff," and "Bill K- K-K-(sneeze)Kawcheff." I didn't mind. I thought it was amusing, but being a foreigner, I carried a permanent chip on my shoulder during my time at Runnymede.

One day when I was 15, a group of popular, snooty WASPs offended me in some way. I thought, "If you think I'm a garlic-eating foreigner, I will really show you."

I doubted they had ever eaten garlic in their lives, so I decided to give them the full olfactory experience.

Early one morning, when even the caretaker hadn't arrived, I brought the biggest head of garlic I could find to school. I snuck down to the basement and unscrewed the plate to the heating and cooling system. I wet the garlic thoroughly, and still dripping, I embedded it deep into one of the main pipes of the system, and I screwed the plate back on. And then I waited.

In three days, the garlic began to rot. By day five, the rotting garlic permeated the heating system and the entire school smelled of garlic. It was all anyone could talk about. Teachers pleaded with the principal and the caretaking staff to eliminate the putrid odor. I thought, "That'll learn ya to cross the old Kotch."

Boy, did I ever enjoy my garlic revenge.

In the midst of this smelly crisis, I was called to the principal's office. The principal, Bruce Clark, was a liberal man. Politically, he was a socialist and, unusual for his time, he believed in the "progressive" education philosophy that he had studied at private schools in England, like Dartington Hall, the essence of which was: he did not believe in any form of punishment, neither corporal nor writing a Shakespearian sonnet ten times on the blackboard. He was permissive of students' behavior and dealt with any offenders in a creative way. Even the most heinous offender in our school, the playground pyromaniac, was given edifying treatment and totally turned around. Mr. Clark radiated a warm benevolence and an easy good humor.

I sat down across from his desk. The assistant principal was also present. Mr. Clark came right to the point. "Kotcheff, we know it's you."

Innocently, I asked what he was talking about.

"The garlic in the heating system . . . we can't find it, but we know it's your handiwork."

I asked whatever made him think that.

"First of all, you're the only one in this school that has the inventiveness to dream up such a prank, and the gumption to execute it," he said. "Moreover, it also fits your Slavic cultural background. So here's the deal. Get it out. There will be no punishment, and we'll tell nobody that you're the culprit, and forget it ever happened."

Even at that age, I almost had to laugh that he partly fingered me because of the cliché of the garlic-eating foreigner, but I also felt complimented by him calling me inventive.

I led him and the assistant principal down the stairs to the HVAC room. I unscrewed the plate, reached deep inside and removed the mushy, rotted head of garlic. The assistant principal opened a trash bag. I dropped the malodorous offender into the bag. He promptly sealed it and rushed out of the building as if he were carrying a ticking bomb.

Principal Clark looked at me admiringly (!) and said, "Kotcheff, you are going to go far."

Two years later, I returned the favor to the principal. He ran for a leadership position in the CCF, a socialist party that later became the New Democratic Party. This was the final straw for the Board of Education, which consisted of a bunch of retrograde Tory fossils who had already harassed him because they thought he was far too soft on discipline. So they fired him now for being a lenient socialist.

I whirled into action. Not only did I respect him for the way he handled my prank and endorsed my future prospects for success, my leftist-leaning upbringing propelled me into action. Two classmates and I organized a student strike. I made a passionate speech, which rallied the whole school, 800 kids strong. We made picket signs that said "HANDS OFF OUR PRINCIPAL" and marched back and forth, picketing in front of the school all day, for three days. All the local newspapers covered the protest and ran pictures of the demonstration. When interviewed, we told them that we were not going back to school without our principal being restored.

The protest worked. We won! We defeated those old WASP farts! The Board of Education was forced to reinstall Mr. Clark as principal of Runnymede Collegiate.

"

All through high school I was always up to some piece of devilry. I remember trading identities with another student in a class with a new gruff teacher. I became Ted Smith, my friend became Bill Kotcheff. We kept up this charade for weeks. When asked by the assistant principal about Bill Kotcheff's behavior, the teacher said, "Bill Kotcheff is perfectly well behaved; it's that Ted Smith who's a problem."

On another occasion, my Latin teacher, Mr. Westlake, asked me to stand up and recite the present indicative of *facere* (the "C" is pronounced as a "K"), which means "to make."

I stood. *"Facio, facis, facit, facimas, facitis, fa-CUNT,"* I said, slightly tweaking what was the final third person plural, *faciunt.*

"Okay, Kotcheff! To the principal's office!" he exclaimed.

"Why?" I asked with outraged innocence. "You asked me for the present indicative of *facere* and I gave it to you."

"You know what you did, Kotcheff! To the principal's office!" he repeated.

Me and my cup: at 15, I was the Regional Debating Competition winner.

Any other principal in Toronto would have expelled me for using that word in class, but here's an example of Principal Clark's special techniques for dealing with offenders. "Billy," he said, "our educational system is geared to the slowest student in the class. You have a very high IQ and learn incredibly quickly, so while you're waiting for the rest to catch up, you get bored and you turn your fecund mind to creating pranks and mischief. So what I'm suggesting is for you to become a proctor to your class, and assist the slower members of it like an assistant teacher."

And that's what I did, in both the Latin and algebra class. I was very impressed with how cleverly he dealt with me. Punishment, justified or especially if it's felt to be unjustified, only invites rebellion and repetition of the offense.

I did, however, distinguish myself as a champion debater. My partner, Donald Blenkarn (who later became an MP for the Conservative Party during the years Prime Minister Brian Mulroney was in office), and I together won the regional debating competition in three consecutive years. I was known for being particularly caustic during rebuttal and totally demolishing my opponent's arguments. I got this knowledge from the fiery speeches my Uncle Andrew delivered while raising money for his theater group.

"

One piece of great luck in my life was that I had close relatives on both sides of my family who had lived lives of unbelievable bravery, possessing indomitable wills, who refused to be subdued and overcame seemingly insurmountable obstacles. They became my life models. My Uncle Stavro Grozdanov (the fat one) was probably the ultimate in this regard.

When I attended Runnymede, he lived close by with his wife, my Aunt Grozdanova. I often went there after school and frequently stayed for dinner. I was the son he never had. He was a tall, imposing man with large, powerful hands. He had been a commander of about 100 Macedonian guerrillas living wild in the Macedonian mountains, only descending to ambush the occupying, vicious Turkish military. I loved his stories of derring-do; he was of that military school that you don't shoot until you see the whites of their eyes.

In 1903, there was a mammoth rebellion against Turkish rule. The Turks came down hard, sent in a battalion of their fiercest soldiers, who successfully wiped out most of the rebels. All the Macedonian commanding officers retreated to the top of Bear Mountain. The Turks surrounded its base. The Macedonian officers did not want to be captured by the Turks, who they knew would torture them to extract the names of all their comrades and their family names so that their whole family could be obliterated.

The Turks were masters in the art of torture. Compared to them, the Nazi SS were amateurs. My uncle felt he would not be able to resist their torture and was terrified that he might not be able to conceal his family name. Had he revealed it, I would not be here writing this sentence, for the whole of my mother's family, including her, would have been massacred.

Consequently, all the Macedonian officers, including Stavro, decided to commit suicide. Which they did. But Stavro just couldn't shoot himself, so he asked one of his remaining comrades to shoot him instead, handing over his loaded gun. Just as he was about to be done away with, a Turkish sniper shot my uncle in the chest, knocking him off the edge of the mountain where he stood, and he fell down the precipitous face of the cliff, ripping his body to shreds. Somehow he survived both bullet and fall and was gleefully captured by the Turks and sent to Istanbul to be grilled there by the Turkish High Command.

He was imprisoned in a semi-conscious state. The Turks waited for him to regain enough consciousness to torture him for the answers they wanted. He exaggerated his injuries to delay the questioning. Then Ramadan serendipitously happened, when (as you may know) many Muslim convicts are released from prison. Through a bureaucratic error, Stavro got out, mingling with the mass of released Muslims, and escaped.

Wounded and still frail, he traveled by night, sleeping by day, eating raw potatoes from farms that he passed, drinking from streams; he made his way to Syria. From there, he reached the Mediterranean coast, where he got a job on a freighter going to Italy. There, he landed a job on an Italian passenger liner, taking immigrants to Montreal.

And now, he was here in Toronto, recounting this story to me.

I was bowled over. What guts! What tenacity! What lion-heartedness! What defiance of danger! I wanted to be him! Though one is always in the midst of a forest of dilemmas, I swore that I would not let anything deter me from following the path of my choice, trodden or untrodden! Nothing was going to intimidate me from achieving what I wanted to achieve.

CHAPTER FIVE
The Rain It Raineth Every Day

Principal Clark's educational philosophies attracted ideal-
istic teachers to Runnymede. Case in point: John Barr, a
short Scotsman with a thick burr, invited me to study ancient
Greek with him. A chance to read Homer in the original?!
I jumped at it! School ordinarily started at 9 a.m.; Johnny
Barr came in every morning at 8 a.m. to teach me ancient
Greek. Being the only student, I made fantastic progress and
got a 96 out of 100 in the final exam. More importantly, I
read Homer and Plato in the original language! This is what
I mean by an idealistic teacher: starting every day an hour
earlier just for one student with no additional pay.

But the teacher who changed my life completely and
irrevocably was Miss Edna Shaw, my English lit teacher.
She introduced me to poetry and opened up a whole new
world to me. At a crucial point in my life, she turned me
around and steered me in the right direction. I immediately

fell in love with poetry — and her — and she became something of a surrogate mother to me, and I a son to her.

She led me to T.S. Eliot, one of the greatest poets of the 20th century. I'll never forget the moment when I first read the opening lines of Eliot's *The Love Song of J. Alfred Prufrock*. The opening image hit me like the light fantastic:

> Let us go then, you and I,
> When the evening is spread out against the sky
> Like a patient etherized upon a table.

With one quintessential metaphor, one searing image, Eliot introduced the whole of the English-speaking world to modern poetry, and hooked a young Canadian student searching for an escape and definition in his life. Poetry became my outlet for all the complexities and conflicting emotions that were bottled up in me. Poems were snapshots of time, fragments of people's lives rendered in elegant prosody. The rhythmic patterns of language conveyed urgency and painted a picture of the poet's thoughts in a way that prose did not. They eventually allowed me to make sense of the extremes of my youth.

Miss Shaw was a proper Victorian dame. She had silvery gray hair, carefully coiffed and powdered, and wore flowery blouses with startling red patterns, a large bow at her neck, and a seashell cameo fixed above her breast. In her sensuous voice, she read the masters to us: Byron, Shelley, Keats, which were intellectual treats. She introduced me to Andrew Marvell, John Donne, William Blake, Robert Frost, and Ezra Pound. I began to devour volume after volume of poetry. I loved her insightful lectures on the dramas and poetry of Shakespeare. As much as I loved films, poems were like hidden treasures to be discovered.

One of my most memorable moments with Miss Shaw happened during a high school production of Shakespeare's *Twelfth Night*, which she directed. She had cast me as Feste, the clown — very appropriately. Feste has a great song which concludes the play that has this refrain:

When that I was and a little tiny boy,
With hey, ho, the wind and the rain,
A foolish thing was but a toy,
For the rain it raineth every day.

But when I came to man's estate,
With hey, ho, the wind and the rain,
'Gainst knaves and thieves,
Men shut their gate
For the rain it raineth every day.

When we were rehearsing, I stopped singing mid-song. "Miss Shaw . . ."

She approached. "What's the matter, Billy?"

"What's Shakespeare going on about here — it doesn't rain every day?"

A strange look of distant pain came into her pale blue eyes. "When you grow up, Billy, you'll find that it does."

In fact, it was already raining then, but I didn't see it.

99

There was a dark side to my childhood that greatly affected my life in ways that I wrestled with well into adulthood, and eventually relied on poetry to ease the pain.

My father was a great believer in spare the rod and spoil the child, the saying that dates to the King James Bible and insists that if a child is not disciplined for wrongdoing, he will always get his way. Biblical significance aside, quite frankly, he beat the shit out of my brother and me, usually with his belt. As a result, my brother and I became very close and joined in a survival alliance.

The beatings stemmed from any number of ordinary transgressions. One time, for example, my brother and I were horsing around in the kitchen. He threw an orange at me; I ducked, and the orange hit a window and broke it. My father was furious and told me that I would be punished. When I protested that I hadn't even thrown the orange, he berated me, saying that I was older and I should know better. He proceeded to beat me with his belt. Unjustified punishment, I felt deeply. Another time, he beat me with the poker from the furnace, leaving thick welts criss-crossing my back. If I raised my arm to deflect a strike, it would enrage him, causing him to redouble his blows.

Because my dad used to beat me, I felt unloved by both parents — by my father because of what he did, and by my mother because she never objected. In fact, my mother was complicit in the beatings.

Whenever my brother or I did something wrong, my mother would slap us in the face. If we somehow eluded the back of her hand, she would say that she was going to tell our father that night, which meant we would be taken down into the basement and whipped. When dad came home from work, and we all sat down for dinner, Tim and I sat anxiously, our stomachs churning. Would she tell Dad or, please God, had she forgotten? But she never forgot; she was always betraying us. I felt angrier toward my mother because she could have protected us and she didn't; in fact, she snitched on us.

The void created by feeling unloved haunted me through

my adolescence. But much worse was the feeling that I was unlovable. I suffered this cruel feeling well into my adulthood. After all, if your parents, who should love you, don't love you, how can anyone else? The situation was exacerbated because I couldn't fill the void with a girlfriend. For whatever reason, girls did not want to go out with me. I was known as a smart kid and a good student, and certainly presentable, but I was not a guy to be considered in romantic terms.

The high school formal dance was a case in point. As the big day approached, I asked a particularly attractive girl to go to the dance with me, but she turned me down. Her reason was that her parents wouldn't let her to go to the dance. It was a lie. She turned up at the dance with a handsome rich guy from Baby Point who drove a Buick convertible.

The beatings ended when I was 16. I finally realized that I was bigger than my father. One night at dinner, I spilled my milk. My dad ordered me to the basement, and as he was loosening his belt, he came out with his standard line, "I'm going to give you a licking!"

I had reached my boiling point. Instead of complying, I stood up and turned the entire dinner table over. The dishes crashed to the floor and food splattered everywhere. I glared at my father and said, "Listen, you asshole, you'll never touch me again or I'll smash your face and you will have no teeth, no eyes, and no nose!"

I was tremendously angry with my parents during my teenage years. At age 18, at the beginning of my second year at the University of Toronto, I left home and shared an apartment with a classmate. When I left the house, I slammed the kitchen door so hard it went through the doorframe, and I yelled at my mother, "You are a Judas and you allowed him to beat us! No more!"

My parents knew the beatings upset me horribly, but it didn't stop them, nor did they ever seem to feel like they were doing anything wrong. My guess is that they were brought up that way. Later when I went into psychotherapy, my therapist, a Freudian, said, "Ted, your father beat you, he was beaten by his father, and your grandfather was beaten by his father, and so on back into time. It is an endless chain of child abuse and you are breaking that chain."

Indeed, I did. In my entire life, I only hit one of my children once. I slapped my youngest son. Afterward, I nearly had a nervous breakdown. It affected me so much that I went to bed for three days. I literally wanted my hand to fall off. I swore I would never hurt any child again.

Interestingly, in the end I actually loved my father but not my mother. I was with my father once when we witnessed a dog being run over by a car, breaking its legs. It was whimpering; I looked at my father — the dog's pain brought tears to his eyes. *How could he beat me?* I thought. He must have suffered doing it. When my father was beating me, I loved him at the same time because I felt in my bones what the psychiatrist pointed out: that he was a victim of his father, and a pussy-whipped victim of his relentless wife egging him on. But I could not forgive my mother for not standing up for her children. I never loved her — and I never liked her, and she knew it. I felt for her because in later years she grieved sorely because of it.

My deep anger with my parents lasted until my early 30s. When I went to work in England at the age of 27, I never wrote to them, or phoned them, or contacted them in any way for years. Finally I forgave them, but only in my mind — not to their faces. I wouldn't give them that satisfaction.

"

The desire to be loved led me to love. Literally. Around the age of six, I started what can only be considered a wild sex life in my childhood.

Sigmund Freud wrote in *An Autobiographical Study*, "It is so easy to convince oneself of the regular sexual activities of children, that one cannot help asking in astonishment how the human race can have succeeded in overlooking the facts and in maintaining for so long, the agreeable legend of the asexuality of childhood."

Well, I can attest to Freud's contention that childhood was a highly sexualized stage of life. Where I derived my sexual knowledge from I haven't the slightest idea, whether it was street scuttlebutt or watching the local canines go at it. But at the age of six, I was an expert.

Seriously, as comical as it may sound.

One of my early adventures was with Thelma B. She allowed me to lower her panties. I attempted to enter her from the back, which was not the correct aperture. I'm not sure where I came up with this idea, whether it was from my Bulgarian genes or watching Mac Cannon's German Shepherd in action. But I did try to Bulgar her — totally unsuccessfully.

The next step in my sexual awakening at this tender age happened when Mary G. and Bill J. asked me if I would join them in the bushes on Kane Avenue to play family. They were slightly older so we were cast accordingly: Mary played Mom, Bill was Dad, and I was their kid. Bill would enter a small clearing, as if coming home from work. Mary would greet him by unbuttoning his fly, then putting her hand inside his trousers and pulling out his member. They would then lie together on a bed of branches. I would watch and learn how it was done correctly.

Armed with this knowledge, I approached Maureen J.

in a garage. I asked her if I could pull down her panties and gaze at her biscuit. She said that surely I had seen one before. The silver-tongued Lothario replied, "Of course I have. But yours is probably much prettier."

It worked. So she shyly allowed me to take down her panties and have a long appreciative look, but she refused anything further.

Using similar seductive talk, I persuaded Norma B., a quiet girl who lived close by, to go all the way with me. She removed her delicate panties and sat on my lap. Recalling the visual Mary G. and Bill J. had treated me to, I entered her at the correct aperture and we rocked back and forth. It was unbelievably delectable.

Afterward, we sat in the high grass in back of her house, surrounded by the soft sounds of a summer afternoon. Norma gazed at me with her pale blue eyes, quietly full of erotic pleasure. She smelled of violets.

Each day, we couldn't wait to see each other and repeat this deliciousness in a corner of her backyard. It was paradise. We had no sense of doing anything wrong.

Inevitably, one day, her mother came out to hang the washing, saw what we were doing, and rushed over. Brandishing a broom, she chased me and cried out, "Get out of here, you filthy little foreigner!"

That night, Norma's father came to our house to have a talk with my parents. He told them what had occurred and informed them that I was notorious throughout the neighborhood for pulling little girls' panties down. He wanted to make sure my parents knew I was a pervert. My parents listened but seemed to pass no judgment.

After his departure, my father asked his young Don Juan to re-enact how I had entered Norma. I sat on the living room floor, pretended to sit Norma on top of my legs, and rocked back and forth.

In the glances my mom and dad exchanged, I saw a mixture of astonishment and a touch of admiration — especially from my father. *How had I learned this?* he was thinking. Later, in retrospect, I felt I had taught Dad a new position.

In any case, I was severely reprimanded. The snake of guilt entered the Garden of Eden I had created with Norma. My parents let me know, in no uncertain terms, that what I had done was dirty, horribly wrong, and that I should never to do it again.

I wondered how anything so delicious and so beautiful could be wrong. But for the time being, I became celibate. If you want to know what happened to poor Norma, I don't know, but she was kept away from me, far away from me.

A year later, I went into the bathroom in our home and saw a "safe" or "sheik" (condom to American kids) floating in the water in the toilet bowl. I knew what these things were, because we kids often saw them left behind in small clearings in the woods in our neighborhood. But I had no idea what they were for. I thought they simply made entry easier.

I rushed over to talk to Dickenson, a 14-year-old who lived in an abandoned bakery up the street from me. I told him about what I had seen. He said, "So?"

"Well, where did it come from?" I asked naïvely.

"What do you mean, where did it come from?" he shot back.

"How did it get there?"

"Your dad dumped it there, and it didn't flush down."

"What?!"

Dickenson smiled. "Your dad fucked your mother and then got rid of the sheik in the toilet, but it didn't go down," he said.

"My mom and dad don't fuck, you bastard! They don't do dirty things like that!" I protested.

"Of course they do, you stupid kid," he said. "How do you think you came into the world?"

I insisted that my parents didn't do such nasty deeds. Then I took a pathetic swing at him. Dickenson shoved me away good-naturedly and went inside his bakery house, chortling.

I rushed home in a panic of uncertainty. Was he right — that fucking led to me? I had seen my brother emerge from my mother's privates on our dining room table. I was going to have to become a sleuth and discover the truth.

One day, when my parents were out, I searched through the drawers in their bedroom. Under a pile of underwear, I discovered a tin of sheiks. Sheiks were sold in a small tin, like a contemporary aspirin tin, which contained three rubbers. On the tin's cover was a colorful depiction of an Arabian sheik; I suppose he was a symbol of potency and licentiousness.

I opened it and saw two unused sheiks.

My parents did fuck, as Dickenson had told me! I was angry. What a pair of hypocrites! They reprimand me. They deny me the delicious pleasure and accuse me of doing dirty things.

I also had them to blame. My father was sexually besotted with my mother. Every time she passed him, he would put his hand on her rear, like a grocer feeling a melon for its ripeness.

Sexual innuendo was rampant in our house. At the end of many meals, my father would say, "Darling, do you know what I want for dessert? Peaches and cream . . ." He thought he was being coy: the Bulgarian word for vagina is *peachka*, which my brother and I well knew.

So much for the hypocrites. Freed of moral constraints, I immediately went to Mary G. I invited her to come to my fort. In the overgrown lot next to our house, hidden away among thick bushes, I had dug a hole about six feet across and three feet deep, and then covered it with some discarded sheets of corrugated metal.

Mary was always up for this kind of thing. I admired her ready sensuality. We entered the hidden fort and took off all our clothes. I lay on her, and we went to it.

My pleasure was enhanced enormously one summer day. As Mary and I were enjoying each other, I looked through a small opening and saw my father sunbathing in our backyard. This made the moment perfect. I was enjoying what he had strictly and hypocritically forbidden. Mary was my first prolonged affair. I remember her with fondness and affection.

"

My high school career ended with a slap in the face. Though I had the best academic record, because of my shenanigans the teachers bumped me down to the number-two spot and gave the valedictorian scholarship to Lorne Wrigglesworth. I seethed at the injustice, but such was life for a misbehaving, dirty foreigner.

One thing happened at my high-school graduation — it was attended by my parents, obviously, and my Aunt Grozdanova. As we all approached the school, they were speaking loudly and volubly in Bulgarian, turning WASP heads and embarrassing me. I tried to separate myself from these Polacks in the school hallway. *I don't know who these people are, nothing to do with me.* My dad and mom noticed that I was trying to disassociate myself from them. My dad asked me (in Bulgarian, of course), "Are you ashamed of us?" As I lay in bed that night, a vortex of unpleasant feelings overcame me: I was ashamed that I had been ashamed of my parents, and I was angry at the world that made me feel ashamed. I was upset and full of self-reproach that my shame was so glaring and unconcealed that I had upset and hurt my aunt, my mother, and my father. All in all, my high school graduation celebration was not a happy experience.

Though I wanted to be a poet — and felt that I had ample material with my family's background, my abuse as a child, my sexual appetite, and my being blackballed as a stinky foreigner — when it came time to enroll at the University of Toronto, I followed a more practical route. I set aside my affection for Shakespeare, Eliot, poetry, and Miss Shaw. In high school, I had been merely okay in English and French, but brilliant in math and physics. In fact, I had some of the highest science marks and test scores in the province.

My relationship with Miss Shaw came to a head in my graduating year at Runnymede, when I told her that I was going to the University of Toronto to study MP&C: mathematics, physics, and chemistry. She tried so ardently to dissuade me, "Billy, there's not a single scientific bone in your body. You're a born artist; you'll be unhappy, desperately so." But I thought to myself, *Shouldn't one pursue something that one is brilliant at, and not study something that one is only okay at?* The die was cast, MP&C.

I entered the university and spent my first year working all day long on integral calculus and differential calculus problems, puzzling over complex logarithms, unsolvable equations, conducting endless lab experiments with strange chemicals — nothing for the soul, only for the brain. Miss Shaw was right: I was miserable in MP&C. In the spring semester, I dropped out, sat all day long moping and agonizing in the junior common room, totally panicked, feeling depressed and lost. I had blown a whole year; I had wrecked my life. What was I going to do?

In desperation, I went to see my surrogate mother. Miss Shaw forbade saying "I told you so." She said, "Billy, this time do what's right for you," and she advised me to switch to English language and literature. I committed a rude gaucherie: "What can I do with an English degree? Become a high school teacher? Oh, sorry Miss Shaw."

There followed from her a great, impassioned speech that I remember almost word for word: "Billy, I know you. You're so artistic. Why are you being so pragmatic and so utilitarian? Why are you worrying about what you will do when you go out into the world? You love drama, you love poetry! You love reading novels! You love art! Study what you love, follow your passions, then something extraordinary, something gloriously unforeseen will come of it, something you've never conceived of, something that you will love to do for the whole of your life! That will happen, I promise you. You may be brilliant at MP&C, but you don't love it, and without love, it might as well be dust! Follow your loves, Billy!"

These inspired words were the fulcrum of my life.

She shaped me,
She made me,
She was my surrogate mother.
I loved her then, and I love her now.

When I became a director, I often thought of her prophetic words — that something unforeseen but glorious would happen to me. How right she was! Oh, by the way Miss Shaw, as always, you and Shakespeare were totally right: it does rain every day.

"

I met with the University College warden. I informed him that I wanted to switch from majoring in mathematics, physics, and chemistry to English language and literature. He thought about my request for a minute and then remarked that it was a very big change. "Mind you, however, one of our students once switched from botany and zoology to Oriental languages," he remarked. "I think that was an even bigger switch than you, so you should be fine."

And with that, I switched my major to English language and literature, known by its students as "eng, slang, and shit."

The rewards were immediate. My mood shifted: I no longer felt like I was wasting my life on pragmatism but pursuing something that was romantic. Not surprisingly, rather than feeling stuck in a morass of 1s and 0s, I excelled.

My French professor, Robert Finch, was a distinguished Canadian poet. Considered a modernist poet, his poems about the Depression were landmark works, and he twice won the Governor General's Award, Canada's top literary honor. One day in class he singled me out. He told the class that we had a budding poet among us who had written four well-crafted, memorable poems for the college's literary magazine: Bill Kotcheff.

CHAPTER SIX
Disturbingly Human

I graduated in May 1952 with a B.A. in English language and literature and aspirations to become a poet. Unfortunately, I had no money and there were no want ads in the newspaper declaring "WANTED: A Poet." I was determined that I wouldn't move back home to the purgatory I had escaped, but I still needed a place to live. Reluctantly, I went back to living at home until I could save enough money to get my own place.

I entered the work force. My first job was at Swift's Canadian Packing, an abattoir. My job was to load boxes of Spam into freight cars. But to take my wheel cart of Spam to the freight cars, I had to go through the slaughterhouse. I would literally pass within yards of the pigs that were being butchered. The odor was asphyxiating. I would cover my nose and mouth with my baseball cap.

My graduation from the University of Toronto, with a B.A. in English literature, in 1952. With my proud mom.

But my work station was immediately adjoining the cow slaughtering section.

The phantasmagorical happenings that were being played out next to me were beyond anything I had experienced, or even imagined.

The haunting sight became a permanent image in my memory. Some 60 years later, I detailed it in my eight-part poem, "Abattoir, The Eyes," perhaps the first poem ever written about a slaughterhouse. In part 2, I captured the grisly sight:

Blades in hand,
The packers spring forward,
Skinning, decapitating.
Butchering, amputating,
Cleave, sever, slice, rive,
A fountain of blood.

The carcass's belly is slashed,
Split open, wide,
Disclosing the viscera.
Purple, yellow, green,
Like exotic flora.
Slit free,

They slither, gelatinously
From the loin's gaping cavity.
Primal cuts:
Liver, kidneys, heart
Are bagged apart.
Nothing wasted,
No leavings left,
Each and every hair and bone,
Hoof and horn,
Ears and lips,
Eyes, nose and cheeks,
Every last sliver of flesh,
Every shred and scrap
From head to tail,
Collected.

But for me, what I could never overcome was seeing the animal's eyes, which I wrote about in part 3 of the poem.

But it was the eyes,
The eyes—,
The aqueous, bovine eyes,
So large, so dark
So deep, so intense,
So disturbingly human.
Gouged and scooped
From the skull's bony sockets,
They are hurled onto a heap
On the rough, cement floor
With a sickening, viscous splatter,
Eyes and more eyes,
Higher and higher,
Intact and entire.

By the time the day's slaughter was over, the pile of eye-balls on the cement floor looked like a surrealistic Man Ray sculpture. But even worse was watching a steak dinner being prepared. I would watch with repulsion as my mother removed the sirloins from the refrigerator and unwrapped the brown butcher's paper, unleashing the reek of raw meat that I endured all day. Thankfully, I left the job after a few months.

Six decades have passed, and I've had trouble with red meat ever since. The reek of obliteration still assails me.

I took a less gruesome job at Goodyear Tire and Rubber. I worked in the foam rubber department making car seats. At the time, all the American cars had foam rubber cushions. It was a tedious job. The molds were filled with liquid rubber, dipped into hot water, and pulled out. While still soaking wet, they were placed on large trays and baked in the oven.

Every Monday, the workers would all meet. Unbeknownst to management, we would vote on how productive we were going to be that week: A, B, or C piece rate, A being the highest. One guy might say that he needed a super productive week to make the instalment payment on his car, while another would moan that he was exhausted and couldn't work that hard. I became a pivotal figure in this debate.

Here was how it worked. If the assembly line were shut down due to technical issues, every worker was sent home with full pay and the highest rating for the day (A). Because I was the only one who moved about the factory floor and everyone else was pinned at his station, as I moved past the large molds on the conveyor belt I had the ability to nudge them and jam up the works, shutting down the assembly. The workers were always pleading with me to sabotage the assembly line, but I could never bring myself to do it.

At Goodyear, we also made "falsies," the foam rubber cups that women wore over their breasts to make them appear firmer and larger. One night, on a date, I was dancing with an attractive girl and all I could think of was the acrid smell coming off the rubber falsies under her blouse. Unforgivably, I asked her to go in the ladies room and remove her falsies because I could not stand the smell — which marked the end of that date. I never forgave myself for being so gauche and insensitive. To this day I still cringe at my behavior. How could I?

The two jobs were unfulfilling, but extremely well paid. I wasn't sure exactly where I was headed career-wise. I continued to write poetry but didn't hold out much hope that I would become a full-time, working poet.

My father tried to dissuade me from my ambition. "Bill, there is no money in poetry," he said.

"You're right, Dad," I retorted. "And there is no poetry in money."

Then one day, four months after I graduated from U of T, my father off-handedly mentioned to me that he had read that the Canadian Broadcasting Company was opening a television network, headquartered in Toronto. "You want to be a writer," he said. "Why don't you see if you can get a job there?"

I felt that, because of these two jobs, I had experience of life that I could bring to the table and help tell stories about the human condition on television. I had grown up poorer than poor in Cabbagetown, as an abused but somewhat clever outcast. Besides, working in television sounded far more engaging than making car seats and much easier to stomach than working at an abattoir.

CHAPTER SEVEN

Adventures in Live Television

Television was in its infancy, and people thought I was making a bad career choice in going to work in it. "It's destined to fail," said a knowledgeable friend of mine. "Ted, people don't want to stay home to be entertained; they want to get away from their homes, get away from their squabbling children and the household bills. They want to go out to a movie or a live theater musical or a hockey game, not sit in their living room staring at a fuzzy square box. It's a novelty that will never last."

This was the opinion, by and large, held by most people. But the ones who knew how big television was going to be were the people who worked for the advertising agencies. They were downright giddy at the prospect. As one guy from a major advertising agency told me, "Television is going to be the biggest thing to hit the advertising business. The man of the house comes home from work, sips his martini, and feels safe and protected in his home. So he lets his guard down. That's when we smack him with our message and ram it down his throat!"

Boy, did he turn out to be right.

In the United States, NBC and CBS, which were both originally radio companies, had gone on the air in 1941. ABC followed in 1945. It took 11 more years for the Canadian Broadcasting Company, also a radio network, to come on the air in 1952. CBC Radio had started in the 1920s to preserve Canadian culture and to provide an alternative to American radio. CBC went into television for much the same reason.

When the U.S. networks started broadcasting, people like my dad were in awe — largely a response to the technology itself. Imagine, pictures flying through thin air.

Personally, in 1952, I had no opinion on the future of television. I just wanted a job in storytelling. Following my father's advice, I somehow managed to wrangle an appointment with the CBC head of programing, Mavor Moore. Bald with owlish glasses, Mavor was a very good actor by trade who had starred in several theater plays and was also an experienced producer. He asked me about my writing and directing experience. I told him about my love of writing poetry and also that I had directed a Tennessee Williams play, *Auto-da-Fé*, for a college drama society while attending the University of Toronto — though I left out one critical detail, that the production was canceled and never actually performed in front of an audience.

He digested my admittedly thin credentials. "Well, have you had any experience in television?" he asked.

I was prepared for this. "Mr. Moore, who in Canada has any TV experience? You're not even on the air yet," I replied.

He smiled appreciatively. In fact, they wouldn't flick the switch for another two weeks. He said, "Okay, do you want to learn about TV production?"

I said, "Of course!"

He didn't hire me as a writer, but he offered me a job as a stagehand. I looked a bit dubious, so he launched into how he felt that television was going to expand exponentially, despite what its critics were saying. Moore believed that those who were in on the ground floor, even as a stagehand, were going to rise to the top.

I accepted the position, but I told Mavor that I had no interest in news, entertainment, or song and dance; I only wanted to work in drama. He obliged and gave me a job as a stagehand in the drama department.

I reported to work in the studio the following day. The excitement of broadcasting live television was everywhere. The scene was frenetic. They were busy doing practice runs, hoping to learn the craft of live television production. Workers were laying cables and shuffling props around the studio, and people were shouting out orders left and right. The head stagehand was named Peter Garstang. He had come out of British theater, as had several other stagehands. I told him that Mavor Moore had hired me. He asked my name.

"Bill Kotcheff," I replied.

"Not in this studio it isn't," he said.

"What?" I muttered.

"Watch this," he said. "Hey Bill!"

On cue, two cameraman, four electricians, and two prop men all responded.

"We have twelve Bills in this studio; I don't need a thirteenth," Peter said. "What's your second name?

"Theodore," I told him.

"Great, from now on you're Ted," he informed me, writing it on his clipboard.

That was my baptism into the entertainment business. From then on, I shed William and Bill and was known as Ted Kotcheff. It took me a long time to turn around when people called to me as Ted. Over time, even friends I had known in college or high school began calling me Ted. Only my mother persisted in calling me "Beelee" to the end of her days.

"

After working as a stagehand for two years, I heard that a documentary filmmaker named Sydney Newman was making ten shows about the new currents of thought of famous people at the University of Toronto, my alma mater. Sydney was one of the best-known documentarians in Canada. To help build Canadian morale during the war he made a series of films entitled *Canada Carries On.* Sydney had been hired by the CBC to supervise the network's documentary and outside broadcast division. I sought out Sydney, told him I was a recent graduate of the University of Toronto, and volunteered to write all ten shows.

To say the least, he was amused by my impertinence. I was a 23-year-old, wet-behind-the-ears kid with two years' experience as a stagehand. But he agreed to give me a shot at writing the first show in the series, which was about Dr. Frederick Banting and Dr. Charles Best, two of the university's scientists who discovered insulin. Banting was deceased. The plan was to do a live broadcast with Dr. Best. We wanted to show their work in detail, using close-ups of Dr. Best in the lab with test rats and all.

On the show, he was going to inject the rats with sugar

1956 was my first year of directing live dramas; I'm pictured here with Sydney Newman, who gave me my first directing job.

---

just before we went live, and then Dr. Best was going to inject them with insulin on the air to show its immediate effect. Problem was, after the rats were injected, we lost the live signal and all the rats died.

Something of a panic set in as the rats began dying. Dr. Best was blasé. "I've got plenty of rats," he said.

Indeed he did. He kept injecting rats until the signal came back.

It was my first lesson in coping with what can go wrong in live television and formulating a back-up plan to deal with it.

I worked diligently on the scripts, writing all ten episodes. When I say I wrote them, I mean I put down the information in what could barely be called a first draft, and Sydney rewrote every word. But he did it in a teaching fashion without any belligerence or belittlement. He also taught me an invaluable lesson.

Sydney showed me the relationship between the words and the pictures in a well-executed documentary: "Ted, in your documentary script, you have the text saying the same thing that the picture is saying. What you want is the picture to give you one piece of information and the words to say something else totally, to add to it. Sometimes the pictures counter the words, sometimes they emphasize them. You essentially get two ideas for the price of one."

For whatever reason, Sydney took a shine to me.

In those days, shows had single sponsors rather than multiple commercials. In America, Goodyear and Kraft sponsored hour-long anthology drama shows. The CBC had followed suit and formed a drama department. Unfortunately, the man running it died three months after it started. The CBC approached Sydney and asked him to be the new head of the drama department.

Sydney came to me with the news. He laughed. "There's only one thing, Ted," he said. "I know fuck-all about drama. I'm a documentary filmmaker. My whole life. But you are a graduate of English language and literature. You know all about drama, so you have to come with me."

"Why not?"

Sydney knew what he wanted and gave all our writers

At an awards ceremony with Sydney Newman and head of ABC-TV Howard Thomas; I was a nominee that night.

and me our marching orders. "I want plays about Canada that deal with what's going on around us *right now*. This is one of the powers of television, immediacy. I want intensely real plays about people like us: their hopes, their needs, their ambitions, their failures." He ended surprisingly by paraphrasing Hamlet's advice to his actors, "The purpose of playing is to hold the mirror up to nature . . . and the very age and body of the time."

So much for his professed ignorance of drama.

We had two anthology series on the air: *General Motors Theatre*, sponsored by all their cars, and a half-hour drama series entitled *On Camera*. All of a sudden, I was a

23-year-old novice working as a story editor for Canada's two highest-profile drama series.

The studio ran on controlled chaos. Directors would rush up to me and frantically say, "Ted, I just had my first run-through, I'm six minutes short, and it's Friday and I'm on the air on Sunday night. I need a six-minute scene, pronto!" and I would stay up all night writing it.

The greatest part about working for the shows was that I wrote in all genres — comedy, drama, mystery, and historical pieces. There was no sameness to the shows or their topics.

However, after two years of watching people make television, I was turning into an arrogant little prick. I would watch a director at work and mutter under my breath, "This guy doesn't know what the fuck he's doing. I could direct better than that any day." Some of those feelings came from the fact that I had written the shows and felt they weren't executing them properly.

One day after about a year of this, Sydney came into my office to talk to me. "You know, Ted, you are a pretty good writer — not a *great* writer, but a pretty good one," he began. "But you know what you would really be good at?"

"What's that, Sydney?"

"You have all the qualities to be a terrific director."

One of the most nagging regrets in my life is that I did not ask Sydney what qualities he saw in me to make him think that I would be a good director. Storytelling? Empathy? Humanity? Arrogance?

It turns out that you need all of those qualities to be a director.

Sydney laid out a proposition for me. He said that he would let me direct one play for the *On Camera* half-hour series. If he liked the result, Sydney promised me a one-year contract as a director. But if he didn't, I'd be out on the street. I could not return to writing for him. "If you don't want to risk it, you can keep your job as a story editor because you are doing good work," he concluded.

It took me less than a minute to decide that I would take the risk. This was my golden ticket to directing — provided I didn't blow it.

I ended up directing a half-hour show about a man in a concentration camp. I sweated over every single detail, probably too much. But Sydney was pleased with the show, and he rewarded me with a contract.

I was now a bona fide director.

The learning experience was without parallel. The great thing about directing live TV — difficult as the logistics were — was that I was able to try my hand at different genres every three weeks. These days, no novice director would have that chance. Indeed, few experienced ones are allowed to move so quickly and effortlessly from comedy to drama to mystery.

Shifting genres was exhilarating at the time, but later in my career, this was a gift that gave back. It allowed me to have a foundation in every genre. People would often ask me how I could do a drama like *North Dallas Forty*, then an action picture like *First Blood* or *Uncommon Valor*, then a broad comedy like *Fun with Dick and Jane* or *Weekend at Bernie's*. I would always answer that it harkened back to my days of directing so many diverse TV shows.

Because the shows were live, with the actors performing almost as if in a play with four cameras and two sound giraffes covering the action, I was constantly worried that something would go wrong. There were no retakes. It was pressure-packed and proved to be tremendous training.

The show, with commercial breaks, had to be exactly one hour. If the show was running long halfway through it, my floor manager would squat under one of the cameras, where the cast could see him and circle his finger rapidly, meaning "*Pick it up!*" If we were short, he would pull his hands away from each other as if he were stretching dough, meaning "*Slow it down!*"

I had to write out every shot, a habit that has stayed with me the whole of my filmic life. Each of the four cameramen would hang his numbered shot list next to the lens. Because there were cables attached to the cameras, we had to be careful that the order of shots did not tangle the cables, immobilizing the cameras in the middle of the live broadcast.

Before the broadcast, a mixture of nerves and adrenaline would kick in. I would think, *My god, this show is going out across the whole country.* Then I'd hear, "Thirty seconds to air!" Butterflies the size of Pegasus would flutter around my stomach. I would tell the guy who was like our DJ to key the music, and then I'd bark out the shots, "Ready with the music! Ready camera 2. Three . . . two . . . one . . . Hit the music! Fade up on 2. Cue him! Cue him for god's sake! Take 3!" waving my finger in front of the face of the camera switcher sitting next to me, indicating that he should cut from one camera to another. And so it went on in similar hectic fashion for the rest of the hour. The theme music that opened the *On Camera* shows was Charlie Chaplin's "Smile."

Dissolve to ten years later. I'm having dinner with a beautiful girl. We're sipping wine, gazing into each other's eyes, looking forward to a romantic evening. All of a sudden, my stomach begins to churn violently. I look down at my gut, "Not now, you bastard!" And then I realize what I hear coming through the restaurant's sound system! "Smile though your heart is aching . . ."

To this day, when I hear "Smile," my stomach knots up.

"

These days, the first question people often ask me, particularly when I'm lecturing at film schools, is "How do you become a film director?" The main thing, I always say, is that you must find someone to mentor you. For me, that person was Sydney Newman.

Sydney taught me how to use pictures to communicate what you are trying to say. He would say things like, "The woman is talking about becoming old, get a close-up of her hands clutching the arms of her mother's rocking chair; they show age." Above all, he taught me that directors need to have a strong point of view artistically.

Once, when Sydney fired a director, I asked him why. Sydney replied, "He was always agreeing with me."

Sydney liked the sparks to fly. He felt that was the only way that interesting, innovative, creative work could be achieved. On one occasion, Sydney and I had a strong disagreement. He barked at me, "Don't talk to me like that, Kotcheff. I pulled you out of the gutter!" I replied, "From the gutter to you is up?" Sydney laughed uproariously, he loved that kind of talk.

Much later in my career, I always let young people watch me work. It's not that I believe that I'm a great model. It's more that when an aspiring director is observing, they see the actuality of what it's like to make a film. They see that you are not only creating the film, but playing chief

Rehearsal with Canadian star John Drainie and my assistant. I was ill, but the show must go on.

psychiatrist with the actors, traffic cop for the crew, story-teller, and much else all at once.

So while it is all very well going to film school because they teach you how to use a camera and tell a story pictorially, there is much else to be mastered. As I say, the best way is to have a mentor. No matter which director you watch, be it Steven Spielberg or a Hollywood hack, the process is the same for everybody, and you have to learn that process.

CHAPTER EIGHT

A Pivotal Moment

When I look back, examining all that befell me, pivotal moments stand out, when the crucial decision taken totally altered the course and tenor of my life and career. Without a doubt, what follows is one of those moments.

I've always felt very grateful to Canada. Where else would I have gotten a chance to direct a major TV anthology drama series at 24? But, at the same time, I've always had a very checkered relationship with my country of birth. It came to a parting of the ways in 1957, when I was 26. I had been directing for the CBC in live television drama for two years. I had directed a number of plays for *On Camera* and for *General Motors Theatre*. I felt ready to expand my talents into theatre and film, which I was determined to do. But, as I mentioned earlier, there was no film industry in Canada whatsoever and precious little theater. What little theater there was, like the Stratford Festival, was in the hands of imported British theater directors. No Canadian had a look-in! A Canadian directing Shakespeare?! Unthinkable. As a friend of mine commented ironically, "Oh, to be in England now that England's here."

No films, no theater available, what was I to do? America and Hollywood were still closed to me. The only alternative was to go to Great Britain. But the prospect of that was daunting: to leave behind my family, my close friends, my first love, my secure and comfortable place of work, cross the Atlantic and plunge into the unknown, where I knew almost no one. I was madly in love with a beautiful girl of Bulgarian descent like me, Maryon Kantaroff, who was a wonderful painter and sculptor. I would have to kiss her goodbye too.

At that time, every Canadian director was faced with the same dilemma. Arthur Hiller left Canada for Hollywood first, in early '57. After he directed a series of films including *Promise Her Anything* and *The Americanization of Emily*, Arthur hit it big with *Love Story* winning the Golden Globes for best picture and best director, and the film netted many Oscar nominations.

The second Canadian talent to depart for Hollywood was Norman Jewison. He made a whole panoply of films, successful both artistically and commercially — *The Cincinnati Kid, The Thomas Crown Affair, Fiddler on the Roof, Moonstruck, Jesus Christ Superstar* — and won the Oscar for Best Picture in 1967 for *In the Heat of the Night*.

Those two went to Hollywood, but due to my banishment from the United States, I didn't have that choice. It was the U.K. or nothing. Compared to distant and foreign London, Hollywood seemed next door. So I hesitated. Part of me desperately wanted to go abroad. At the time, I was in the grip of what I call the Hemingway-Fitzgerald romanticism: that to develop one's artistry, a creative person had to leave North America and go to Europe.

There were many others like me in this regard. Mordecai Richler wrote his first four novels abroad. A Canadian poet and writer friend, Richard Outram, was working in London. A college chum of mine, Clayton Derstine, was writing a novel in Paris, where several other Canadian writers and painters were to be found. So, there was a tremendous pull within me to leave Canada — the irrational feeling that only good could come from it.

Finally, by happenstance, I attended an industry party in Toronto. The vice president of the CBC Television service, Bob Graham, was there. He cornered me, and we got into an alcohol-fueled conversation. He knew nothing of my dilemma and what I was considering. Seemingly out of nowhere, he said, "Ted, you're an extraordinarily talented director." (I had to agree.) "If you want to develop, you've got to get the hell out of this culturally provincial backwater. The people here are totally blind when it comes to assessing Canadian talent; they only recognize it when Canadian artists make it abroad. Go pit yourself against the best somewhere else. Stay here, you'll never grow; you'll stagnate."

All this, from the head of one of the most important cultural institutions in Canada. Well, it had a strong effect on me. I took a deep breath, took my courage into my hands, and decided I must test the waters.

CHAPTER NINE

Horses of the Same Color

In 1955, when I was directing live television drama for the
CBC, Nathan Cohen, our story editor, came into my office
one day carrying a slim volume: *The Acrobats*, by a new
young Canadian writer, Mordecai Richler. Nathan urged
me to read it. He said it was a precocious performance, and
he was now corresponding with the author, who was living
in the south of France, to obtain the television rights. He
knew I was going to Europe for a holiday, and he suggested
that I look him up. He felt that Mordecai and I had very
similar sensibilities, and if we met, we would become good
friends. I don't know what he based this prophecy on, but
there was no evidence to predict if he would be right. This
was the curious instigation of what proved to be one of the
most important relationships in my life.

I read the book, which is about a Canadian painter in
exile and a Nazi on the run, and was deeply impressed by its

sophistication and great seriousness. That it was written by a 19-year-old was hard to believe. It was so assured. I decided that if I was in the area to definitely try to look him up.

I set out for Europe that summer of '57, full of nervous uncertainty about how this whole trip was going to play out. I went first to London, where I stayed with my poet friend, Richard Outram. He was writing poetry but concerned and hesitant about his future. He wanted to be a poet, but how was he to survive? It was almost as if he could hear my father's warning about how "there's no money in poetry." I told him he was too gifted to abandon poetry. Persist! He did and became an important Canadian poet.

I sought out a former CBC drama director, a very good one named Silvio Narizzano. He had done what I was thinking of doing, exported himself to London in pursuit of a film career. I had served as his assistant director in my early years at the CBC and learned a tremendous amount about directing from him. He was presently working at Granada TV directing hugely prestigious plays like Arthur Miller's *Death of a Salesman*.

Silvio said to me, "Ted, can I give you a piece of advice? If you're thinking of coming to live and work in England, don't you think it'd be a good idea, before you commit yourself, to direct a show here and see if you like it?"

I had to agree, and he got me a job directing a play at ABC TV, which produced dramatic shows for ITV, the BBC's commercial competitor. It was scheduled for late in the summer, so I had a chance to continue my European trip.

Later Silvio succeeded in his pursuit, directing *Georgy Girl*, starring Lynn Redgrave as Georgy and James Mason and Alan Bates. It was very successful, with a big hit song also called "Georgy Girl."

I continued on to Paris, where I stayed with a fellow classmate in Eng., lang., and lit., and good friend, Clayton Derstine, who was now striving to become a writer. At some point, Henry Kaplan, another TV director whom I had worked for as his assistant in the early days at the CBC, heard that I was in Europe. He contacted me to come stay with him in his villa in the village of Tourrettes-sur-Loup, nestled in the Alpes-Maritime in the south of France. We Canadians have to be the most peripatetic people, wandering nomads all over the world in search of an identity.

When I arrived in Tourrettes, Henry Kaplan told me that the young Canadian novelist Mordecai Richler was also living there. I was a bit taken aback: I had a distinct sense of inevitability. I got in contact with Mordecai and invited him for drinks. We drank in the village's only bar, a café with tables set up in the town's small square. He looked like a rumpled bed. We sat down, I ordered a Pernod, and he ordered a gin and tonic.

I talked and talked, but Mordecai was unnervingly silent and watchful, hardly saying a word. This was the man I was supposed to have so much in common with? I don't like silences, so I started talking again, and he still said nothing. I thought either I must be the most boring man on earth, or he the most taciturn.

At one point in the conversation, he asked me, "Who's your favorite novelist?"

I replied, somewhat ostentatiously, "Henry James."

"Well, you'll certainly like my novels then," he quipped, causing me to break out laughing, given the huge chasm between their sensibilities.

Well, I thought, this guy has a sense of humor after all. Despite being reserved, when he did speak I enjoyed his wry sense of humor that matched my own.

Mordecai was living in London. We were both 26 at the time — he was only three months older than me. He had grown up in Montreal in the same slummy conditions that I did in Toronto, only he was Jewish. This meant that his family was even lower on the societal rung than my family of immigrant Bulgarians. Mordecai was raised on St. Urbain Street in Montreal, the center of the Jewish ghetto there. He used his upbringing to great effect in his second novel, *Son of a Smaller Hero*, published in 1955, which told the story of a working-class Jewish rebel in revolt against his ghetto family. It was set in Mordecai's childhood neighborhood.

I saw Mordecai every day for drinks for a week, and we struck up the beginnings of a friendship. It was often hard going at first, with me doing most of the talking, but slowly, between bouts of taciturnity, we traded stories about ourselves and discovered that our early lives were extraordinarily similar.

We came from the same slummy world, had the same coarse adolescence. We had identical mothers: They both would have preferred to be men. Mordecai's mom wanted to be a Rabbi, and mine, I told him, wanted to be a business tycoon. My mother sure wore the pants in our family, and I regaled him with an Oedipal dream I had when I was a teenager: I had my mother pinned against a wall, I lifted up her skirt — horror, she didn't have a vagina, she had testicles and a penis. We both laughed. "Boy," I said, "my unconscious got that right."

Mordecai and I had the same endearing loser fathers. When I first met Mordecai's father years later, he was looking at the stock market results in the newspaper. "Hey, my stock went up from fifty cents to one dollar!"

"That's great, Mr. Richler," I said.

"Yeah, only one thing, I bought it at ten dollars."

My father wanted to be a primary school teacher, preferably kindergarten. My mother coerced him into being a businessman, opening bigger and bigger restaurants, and put him on a path to become a tycoon running a chain. Once when my father had to file for bankruptcy, he was so fearful of losing everything, he was vomiting. My mother said scornfully to Tim and me, "Your father is weak; don't be like him."

Mordecai and I were talking about favorite poets one day when we discovered that we had both used the same tactic to induce women we were enamored with to come to bed with us.

We would read them Marvell's witty poem *To His Coy Mistress* that has the same intent as us — to persuade his love to sleep with him. Because, with the celerity of time, next thing you know, age and death have caught up with you, and you have not yet enjoyed the sweetness of love-making: "The grave's a fine and private place, / but none, I think, do there embrace." Mordecai and I laughed uproariously that both of us had tried the same amative maneuver. Talk about being cut from the same cloth!

What intrigued both Mordecai and me at that time was something we discussed often later on: from our identical, totally unpropitious backgrounds, where in hell did we get our aspirations, he to be an important novelist, me to be an important filmmaker? We were never able to reach a convincing conclusion.

One day, Mordecai introduced me to another writer living in Tourrettes, Terry Southern. We had a great time together. Mordecai had brought Terry and his wife, Carol, down from Paris to provide himself with a funny companion and a poker player. I agreed with Mordecai

— Terry was a witty man — and we became friends. Terry was then writing with Mason Hoffenberg, who was also in Tourettes, a wonderful piece of porn called *Candy*. The novel became a cult hit in Paris, London, and New York. He worked for me later in London, doing a fine adaptation of Eugene O'Neill's *The Emperor Jones*, something that would only be done on British TV. Mordecai helped Terry get his first very funny novels, *The Magic Christian* and *Flash and Filigree*, published in London with his publisher, André Deutsch. Terry went on to write the brilliantly funny screenplay for Stanley Kubrick's *Dr. Strangelove or: How I Learned to Stop Worrying and Love the Bomb*.

After I returned to London to direct the ABC play that Silvio had arranged for me, I received a letter from Mordecai apologizing for being so introverted and uncommunicative. "I apologize for being so laconic, but I always get like that when I am in the middle of a novel. That's all I can think about and I cannot provide proper social conversation," he wrote.

It was a very, very sweet letter and a letter that was a window into his craft. He was working on *A Choice of Enemies*, which would be published in late 1957. The novel was based on the lives of his group of friends in London, writers and directors who had fled the U.S. and Canada for England to escape McCarthyism and blacklisting.

He concluded the letter by writing, "I feel you and I are horses of the same color." As did I.

"

Late summer, I finished directing that play for ABC TV. Howard Thomas liked it a lot, so he offered me a very generous year's contract. I was beside myself with excitement.

I was all set. So, in the fall of 1957, I returned to Canada for two months to fulfill my CBC contract. I received another letter from Mordecai, asking me to look him up in London.

I packed all my worldly possessions, tucked my violin under my arm, and in November of '57 I boarded the *Sylvania*, a Cunard liner, and bade farewell to Canada and said hello to Old Blighty. It was a decision I never regretted.

At the time, Mordecai was living with his longtime girl-friend, Catherine Boudreau. I had met Cathy in Tourettes, a tall, slim, dark-skinned French-Canadian working-class lady. She was a very spirited, self-assured woman, forthright to the point of being combative. She had a lively, biting wit that Mordecai enjoyed. She was nine years older than him. They had been lovers in Canada. When Mordecai left for England to pursue his literary career with an interested British publisher, he left her behind. He boarded a ship, the *Samaria*, in Montreal and it departed for England. To his surprise, he discovered Cathy was on board, having purchased a ticket in secret! She was one ballsy woman who was not going to be deprived of her man.

In London, she immediately went looking for a job to support her and Mordecai while Mordecai was writing. She assiduously cared for him, the breadwinner as he wrote his first three novels. Mordecai received $250 for his first novel. One of his uncles said, "Mordecai, you could have earned more money cutting my lawn."

Shortly after I arrived in London, Mordecai felt that Cathy was putting too much pressure on him to get married. They had a bad fight and she moved out. Mordecai asked me if I would like to share his apartment. Needing a somewhat permanent base, I accepted.

The apartment was located at 5 Winchester Road in

Swiss Cottage. Though the area was nice, the Victorian building that it was in was condemned. We had the top floor. The interior design was by Charles Dickens, furniture by Sally Ann. The floor was covered in black tar paper, as were parts of the ceiling. Bookshelves were raw planks of wood, separated by red house bricks. Mordecai gave me the bedroom, and he lived in the living room, where he also worked. The scummy bathroom was one floor down.

The place was disgusting, but we considered it to be merely bohemian and reveled in it. One night I came home drunk and dropped my corduroy jacket on the floor. When I picked it up the next morning, a huge rat jumped out of the sleeves. Another time, I opened a book to find fleas embedded in its pages.

Characters populated the building. There were two Tachist painters, one from France and one from Australia. Tachist derives from the French word *tache*, meaning "stain," which gives you some idea what the pictures look like. The hallways of the house were lined with their paintings.

Mordecai teased the artists relentlessly. One day we bumped into the lead Tachist, who later became a very well-known painter. Mordecai proposed a new approach to the artist.

"Instead of flicking the paint with a brush, why don't you chew on a tube of paint and expectorate on the canvas?" he said.

The painter wrinkled his brow. "That's not a bad idea," he replied. "Very interesting. I think I might try that."

Young men that we were, we would go out carousing and drinking at night. We ran around with expatriate friends, playwright Ted Allan and blacklisted television comedy writer Reuben Ship. We also made close local friends. John Mortimer was one of them. He was an extraordinary talent.

He wrote plays and novels and was the author of two television plays that I directed. He had a very successful TV series with *Rumpole of the Bailey*, and was an accomplished barrister. He was our minister of fun.

Mordecai and I were so inseparable that one of our friends asked me if we were a couple. When I told Mordecai, he thought it was hilarious and too good to pass up. Two nights later, we went to a dinner party. The man who had wondered about our sexuality was there. No doubt he had gossiped to his friends. In the middle of the dinner, Mordecai decided to escalate the suspicion.

"You know when Ted first came to live with me, he was so attentive, so considerate. When he came home from rehearsals, he would always bring me something — lovely Havana cigars," Mordecai began, fluttering his hand in the air as he spoke. "He would bring me my favorite tipple, a good cognac, like Rémy Martin, which I love to sip each night with my cigar. Now, nothing! Absolutely nothing! He just takes me for granted." He stared at me. "So painful . . ."

"Do shut up, darling!" I shot back.

Everyone at the table began looking at us with arched brows as we engaged in a bitchy tiff. I must say it was well done and likely confirmed their suspicions that we were lovers. Of course we weren't. We were red-blooded young men. But the truth was we did develop an unusual shorthand.

During our life together, when I came home from work at the end of the day, there would be a tug of war. All day, I'd be talking to actors, producers, directors, set designers, costume designers, props. I'd have had my fill of interacting with people. Mordecai, meanwhile, would have been alone all day writing. His isolation would weigh on him. So when I got home, I would want quiet, and only an intimate tête-à-tête with Mordecai. He, on the other hand, wanted company, to go out, meet up with chums to drink and carouse. So, as I say, every evening, there would be a friendly tug of war to see whose pressing needs would prevail.

The social Mordecai was a complex character. Usually, he would be witty and entertaining. But there were times when he'd become deeply introspective or, sometimes, contentious. You could never know the Mordecai you were going to get. But whatever Mordecai emerged, he was always diverting and stimulating.

Once, we went together to a party of about a dozen people. Mordecai fell into a heavy silence. He sat alone at one end of the room. The other guests felt the whole room slowly tilting toward Mordecai, his deep self-absorption outweighing all their social interactions and exchanges. Some felt that he was being rabbinical, judging them, critical of their superficialities.

Afterward, I asked Mordecai what he was thinking about so silently. He replied,

"I was rewriting *Hamlet*, so that it could have a happy ending."

99

Mordecai and Cathy got back together and decided to get married. A nuptial party was thrown for them the day before their wedding by his good friends Ted and Kate Allan. The whole Canadian contingent in London was there, including Florence and Stanley Mann.

Florence was an extremely beautiful woman. She was a Dior model — still working as such; David Bailey photographed her for *Vogue* — and she appeared on the

Florence Richler, beauty incarnate, here photographed by Anthony Barbley.

cover of the Canadian magazine *Chatelaine*, whose editor declared her to be "the most beautiful woman in Canada." Her face had a fine, delicate bone structure, and her complexion was flawless. But she was not just a beautiful face; she was smart and thoughtful and well read. She had an old-fashioned femininity that concealed a very strong backbone.

At the nuptial party, Mordecai could not keep his eyes off Florence. He was mesmerized by her beauty, her intelligence, and her dignity. Florence took great exception to his brazen manner, and when he came on to her, and inquired whether she had read *The Acrobats* and what she thought of it, Florence replied in a frosty manner, "Yes, yes, I've read it. I liked it, but not enough to want to meet its author," and she swanned away.

Far from deterring Mordecai, this only inflamed him.

On another occasion, he and I left another social gathering where Florence was present, and Mordecai said to me in too loud a voice, "She's mine. I want her."

"Mordecai, she's married, you're married," I lectured him. "Are you crazy?"

"I don't care. I want her and I'm going to take her."

Some time later, when both their marriages broke up, Florence let him take her. Mordecai used the way he and Florence came to be married in his novel *Barney's Version*.

But before Mordecai and Florence could get married, two divorces had to be obtained. Getting a divorce in England at that time was very difficult. Florence's divorce was fairly straightforward as it was done amicably with her husband's cooperation. They both testified as to their incompatibility. There was only one catch. When Florence secured her divorce, it was entitled a *decree nisi*. *Nisi* means "unless" in Latin — unless you behave naughtily. During the six months after the decree is issued, the divorcing wife had to be totally chaste — no physical intimacies whatsoever.

To ensure this, a squad of "sex police" called the Queen's Proctors could visit you at any time, day or night, and if a man was discovered in your bed, the divorce was canceled. But there was no way Mordecai wasn't going to enjoy this great love of his life for six months. He couldn't bear to be apart from Florence for an hour.

The three of us would have dinner together, often times at Chez Luba, a Russian restaurant that was one of our favorites. Afterward, I would drive the three of us in my Austin-Healey 3000 sports car up to Florence's apartment in Highgate. It would be near midnight. The two of them would go in while I sat outside in my car, engaged by Mordecai to be his cockatoo, his lookout bird.

One night, at about 1 a.m., I saw a stranger approach the entrance of Florence's apartment building, look at a piece of paper, check the address, and then enter. I immediately honked my car horn three times, the agreed-upon signal. Fortunately, Florence had a ground floor apartment. A disheveled and unclothed Mordecai came flying out of its window like Douglas Fairbanks Jr., madly hoiking up his trousers in mid-air. He jumped in my car, and we zoomed away. Those were certainly madcap, Feydeau farce days.

Mordecai's divorce from Cathy was also a farcical sex

comedy. His divorce was much more difficult as he did not receive Cathy's consent. She was very angry at being tossed aside and declined to part amicably. This meant seven years had to pass before desertion could be used to dissolve the marriage. The only other way for Mordecai to obtain a divorce was to commit adultery and be caught in the act. So it had to be simulated.

Fortunately, he had a good director at hand to convincingly stage the necessary scene.

It was set in our flat at 5 Winchester Road. I cast Verity Lambert, my girlfriend, as Mordecai's sex partner. Verity was my wonderful assistant in my *Armchair Theatre* productions. After working closely together, we began to date and fell into a torrid love affair. Later, Verity had phenomenal success as the producer of the endlessly running classic science fiction series, *Doctor Who*.

Verity and Mordecai took off all their clothes which I scattered on the floor around the bed. Verity was hesitant about being totally naked, so she wore a beautiful Dior negligee that Florence contributed. For additional props, I had the remains of an elaborate meal on a side table and an ice bucket with a half-consumed bottle of Dom Pérignon in it. The mise-en-scène completed, the director hid himself in our new john. On cue, a police detective accompanied by a photographer broke down the door and rapidly took flash pictures of the two adulterers in bed together.

Mordecai scripted the scene in a letter to a friend:

Private eye arrives to discover me in bed with a dame.

"I say," says he, "have you been cohabiting regularly?"

"You bet!"

"Will you sign this voluntary statement, please?"

"Damn right."

I flushed the toilet to cover my laughter.

This charade was presented in court and Mordecai was granted his divorce. And very soon, Mordecai and Florence would be able to marry.

There was one dramatic scene that took place at our 5 Winchester Road apartment right after the divorces. One day, Cathy turned up at our flat, shortly after the American edition of *The Apprenticeship of Duddy Kravitz* arrived. Mordecai wasn't home, so I was left to deal with Cathy's rage when she opened one of the copies and saw "For Florence" on its dedication page. She went bananas and began ripping the books — tearing out pages by the handful. I pleaded with her to stop. Cathy grabbed Mordecai's precious ancient Olivetti typewriter that he wrote all of his novels on and hurled it out of the window. *Oh my god*, I thought, *his typewriter falling three stories will be smashed to smithereens.* She returned to the books with intent to destroy every copy. I again begged her to stop, but she wouldn't. Finally, I slapped her hard on the face, knocking her down. She lay on the floor sobbing. "All those years I busted my ass doing awful odd jobs to support him so that he could write his first three novels, and this is the thanks I get," she wailed. I felt horrible. Guilty. As guilty as Mordecai felt later. He knew what she had so selflessly done for him.

But Florence did something very important for Mordecai. She became his literary editor; with her keen creative intelligence, she always made great suggestions to enhance his novels. In the copies that Cathy ripped up, there was a more elaborate dedication, that I'm glad she didn't see then, as it would have really enraged her: "From Mordecai with all my love, all the descriptive passages in this book, the march, the bar-mitzvah film, commencement, etc., all of these because you asked for them after

Me and Florence Mann, Mordecai Richler's wife-to-be.

you read the part about Mr. MacPherson, and the book is certainly better for it. Mordecai." I know this to be true about Florence, because I was living with Mordecai as he wrote this great book that I later turned into an exceptional Cannes Classic film.

The farcical comedy displayed in the two divorces carried over into their wedding ceremony. It was a bizarre happening to say the least. Mordecai and Florence had left London and were now ensconced in Montreal. Florence became pregnant. But because one or the other of their divorces, I forget which, had not been finalized, they had to delay getting married. They discovered that Quebec did not permit civil marriages. It had to be a religious ceremony.

Florence was adopted and she never found out who her biological parents were. But she always thought she was of Jewish origin. Mordecai, of course, was. So a rabbinical marriage would be perfect. But when Mordecai approached a Montreal rabbi, he would not marry them because Mordecai had not obtained a Jewish divorce! Technically, as far as the rabbi was concerned, Mordecai was still married. So, how were Mordecai and Florence to get married?

While investigating this, Mordecai contacted me in London and told me that both Florence and he wanted me to be their best man. I was shooting a TV film and I told him the moment I said, "Cut! Print!" on my last shot, I'd jump on a plane. He told me not to delay it as Florence was now about eight months pregnant.

Meanwhile, Florence discovered that the only religious official in Quebec who would marry them was a woman Protestant minister of the United Church! Getting married in a Christian church ran against Mordecai's grain but what choice did he have?

I went over-schedule on my film. Mordecai sent me special delivery letters: "What's happening, Ted, Florence is going into her ninth month shortly." I kept shooting as fast as I could. Mordecai phoned me. "Ted, I don't want my kid to be born a bastard! When are you coming? We're not getting married without you!" Even though, I have to admit, I thought it was a helluva lot of money for four days, I couldn't say no. He was my closest, most beloved friend; how often would he get hitched to my now dear friend, Florence, who I loved as well?

I went straight from the location where I shot my last set-up and climbed onto a transatlantic flight. On arriving in Montreal, I was met by Mordecai and an absolutely huge Florence. They explained the church situation and their feelings about it. As best man, I was going to handle it. I went down to the St. James the Apostle United Church on St. Catherine Street for a meeting with the woman who was the Protestant minister. I explained the situation to her: that the groom was Jewish, so please keep the Christian religiosity to an absolute minimum; that the bride was in a very late stage of pregnancy, so please keep the ceremony as short as possible:

"Will you take this woman —"

"Will you take this man —"

"I now pronounce you — etc. and out!"

I handed her the fee. She said little and didn't seem to demur from my request.

I reported to Mordecai what had transpired and he relaxed.

On July 27, with no family or relatives invited, just the three of us and an old friend, Bill Weintraub, went to the church for the marriage. I quickly discovered that my special pleading to the minister had fallen on deaf ears. She proceeded to deliver a 20-minute sermon on the nature of holy love and a puritanical homily on the unbreakable bonds of marriage. She asked for the gold wedding ring, which I handed to her. Thank God, it's over! But no, we received another long preaching on how this gold ring was a symbol of eternal love for it was a circle: a circle has no beginning and no end, and so on, and so on. Did this benighted woman think she was going to convert us? Poor Florence, standing for 30 minutes, her back was aching badly and she kept twisting about. And she was struggling with the further discomfort of the 95-degree heat. Mordecai was staring daggers, but the dogged minister kept on discoursing.

Mordecai wanted to kill her. I definitely was going to kill her. But we couldn't even make a moue of annoyance: we had to control our tempers until she pronounced them man and wife. Just as I was about to grab a chair for Florence, the sadistic piece of baggage finally came out with "Florence, will you take this man," and then came those last seven words: "I now pronounce you man and wife." They kissed and I clapped and cheered.

We went home in an incredibly celebratory mood and drank champagne from my wedding gift, Swedish Orrefors wine glasses. Too late now, but the next night, the three of us would have the wedding banquet at the Desjardins restaurant — a lavish lobster dinner.

But the comedy was not yet over. Our plans were upset when late the next day, Florence phoned her obstetrician to complain of pains in her lower back and he ordered her to the hospital. I was about to cancel our lobster dinner but Florence wouldn't hear of it. After all, it was their marriage banquet. She insisted that Mordecai and I enjoy the dinner. Reluctantly, we left, dropped her off at Montreal General, and proceeded to the Desjardins. Mordecai, married and soon to be a father, was out of his mind with joy. We toasted Florence, we toasted the arriving baby, and as we were toasting each other with our Rémy Martins, we got the news: Florence had just gone into labor!

We rushed down to Montreal General. Mordecai tried to join Florence but he was not allowed to enter her room. We were told that this was the law as Mordecai would bring in germs that might endanger the incoming baby. We were both unwelcome because of these hygiene rules. I appealed to a hospital official to no avail. Mordecai became crazed with frustration, cursing and pacing up and down.

Serendipitously, Sean Moore, the brother of our good friend, the Irish-Canadian novelist Brian Moore, was a pathologist at that hospital. He saw us in the waiting room, was apprised of the situation, and quickly fetched a white coat for a freshly washed Dr. Richler so that the brand new husband could be with his brand new wife in the birthing room. The baby boy emerged as he entered.

I was the godfather of the lad who had been spared bastardy by a day. I named him Noah after the character in Mordecai's second novel, *Son of a Smaller Hero*. I always fancied Old Testament names for boys and Victorian names for girls. I suggested Emma for the lovely girl they had next.

These last two wild days confirmed my description of life as a crazy admixture of intense seriousness and ridiculous farce.

"

By the way, the typewriter was saved. Although it fell three stories, it had landed in a bush that cushioned its fall, and it emerged unscathed! There must be a God. Thank goodness! That small Olivetti portable typewriter was Mordecai's good luck charm, his talisman. If anything had happened to it, he'd have been devastated.

He always resisted his family's pressure to get a new up-to-date, electric typewriter; he kept writing on that Olivetti for the rest of his life. Mordecai always pounded it very hard, so soon you couldn't read the type because the typewriter's metal letters were worn out. It would be sent out for repair, which took a fairly long time. In the meantime, Mordecai needed something to write with. Florence couldn't find that now-antique model, so she bought something as close to it as possible.

When his favorite typewriter came back from its lengthy repairs, he dumped the new one in a cupboard. But after a time, his pounding resulted in repairs again. And

Florence would again replace it with a different new one because Mordecai didn't like working on the previous new one. Florence told me that over the decades there came to be seven newish typewriters in that cupboard.

After he died, they were all given to charities by his children.

And Mordecai's revered typewriter was featured in a museum exhibit.

Cathy really knew how to hurt Mordecai, but in this instance, she failed. After the emotional book ripping scene, she disappeared totally. No one had any idea what had become of her, not even Mordecai.

Late one night, 15 years later, there was a knock at my door. I opened it to reveal a strange woman, shorn of all her hair wearing an austere, full-length gray robe. It was Cathy! She had become a Buddhist nun and was living in Taipei, the capital of Taiwan. She said she just wanted to see me for one last time and say goodbye.

Life can certainly take you to unexpected places. I hugged her, and she forgave me that long ago slap.

"

Mordecai had a regimented writing ritual that amazed me. He would wake up in the morning and make his breakfast. It was always either a Jewish omelet with chopped green onion and salami or leftover *cholent*, a bean dish, from the previous night. I used to joke, "Ah, I see you're having the food of your people for breakfast again."

Precisely at 9 a.m., he sat down at his typewriter. Within a minute, clack . . . clack . . . clack. Three hours would pass without one let-up. Then at noon on the dot, he would get up and go out to the local tabac to buy the *International*

Herald Tribune and check hockey scores in the winter and baseball scores in the summer. Next, he would go to a deli and buy some lunch — an equally Yiddish meal of lox, chicken liver spread, or corned beef. This was followed by a short nap. He would wake up at 2 p.m. on the dot, sit back down at his typewriter, and within 30 seconds he was hammering away at the keys again. At 5 p.m. promptly, he would stop — sometimes in the middle of a sentence — and head straight for the gin bottle.

I marveled at his daily schedule. Once I asked him to explain his creative process. "I've read about Hemingway who would drink all day and wait for inspiration and then become a typhoon of creativity, sometimes long after midnight. But you start writing immediately every time you sit down. What about inspiration? What about waiting for the muse?"

Mordecai laughed. "Ted, if I waited for inspiration, I would never write a single word," he said. "I have to discipline myself to write. When I sit down at nine, inspiration knows that this is her opportunity to come to me and there won't be another." And, amazingly, she would.

"

Mordecai could write. His ease in moving from genuine human suffering to absurdist comedy was rare. Under that corrugated surface of his lay a very, very deep feeling man. Nobody ever loved me the way Mordecai loved me. He was capable of great feeling; that was a side of Mordecai that few people saw. Life for Mordecai was painful. He was deeply affected by the irrational injustices of life. I loved his style: moving statements about the human condition were cheek to jowl with hilarious humor. He was always acknowledged by critics as one of the funniest novelists of his time.

Mordecai adapted a stage play, *The Shining Hour*, which was my very first production at *Armchair Theatre*. He wrote two wonderful, original TV plays for me to direct, the first one was called *Paid in Full* and the second *The Trouble with Benny*, the latter receiving an incredible rave review by the *Times*' tough TV drama critic. Mordecai did an extraordinary adaptation of the play *Sunset* by one of our favorite writers, Isaac Babel. I began using him as either a writer or sounding board on everything I worked on, be it theater, television, or film for the rest of his life.

He worked on the script of my first feature film, *Tiara Tahiti*, starring James Mason and John Mills, two of the most famous British actors working at the time. The problem with the film was that the original writer, Ivan Foxwell, was also the producer. Ivan was a very upper-class Englishman and he wanted to make the film into a kind of pantomime, while I wanted to make it into an urbane social comedy.

The other problem was that I was a neophyte director. As the producer, he was always at me, pushing me toward his vision and away from mine, and because I wasn't experienced enough to politely tell him to go fuck himself, I made his film. In the end, I didn't make a film that I had any feeling for.

The reviews for *Tiara Tahiti* were decidedly mixed. One Canadian critic wrote of my directing: "his inexperience shows in the picture's loose, jerky structure, but his talent for working with actors shows too." Another wrote that I "pressed too hard" and concluded that the picture "moved briskly and confidently to its predictable but nicely ironic conclusion."

Still I had lost my cinematic virginity. The experience with Ivan would never be repeated, I promised myself.

Mordecai wrote my second feature film, adapting John Braine's *Life at the Top*, the sequel to *Room at the Top*. The original cast of Laurence Harvey and Jean Simmons returned, and we added Honor Blackman and Michael Craig. In the first film, Harvey's character, Joe Lampton, escapes his blue-collar life by marrying the daughter of a mill owner, who was played by that great Shakespearian actor Donald Wolfit, and he appeared in my film as well. In the sequel, Joe is now living an affluent, upper-middle-class British life, but having trouble looking in the mirror and recognizing himself as anything other than a con man who has married for money.

Mordecai, of course, wrote the final draft of *The Apprenticeship of Duddy Kravitz*, and he later did a rewrite of *Fun with Dick and Jane*.

Mordecai was always there for me. He would read every script I became involved with and make creative suggestions. People always asked me why I worked with Mordecai on every script. The answer was because I didn't have to use words when I spoke to him. Our communication was somewhat telepathic, both ways. I would say, "Mordecai, this scene needs a bit more . . ." Before I could finish the sentence, he would nod and say, "Yes, Ted, I agree with you."

Through all my travails as a filmmaker seeking to get to the quintessence of a film's artistry, I always had the unconditional support of Mordecai. Personally, we became the closest of friends for life. Mordecai was the best friend anyone could possibly ever have. He was the most moral of men in the sense that he took his life responsibilities — be it as husband, father, friend — with unequivocal

LAIFUN CHUNG

Pals forever, me and Mordecai on safari in Kenya.

seriousness and total commitment. If ever I was in trouble, the first person I would contact was Mordecai. Even if I was half a world away, I know he would be on the next plane rushing to my aid.

The love of true friendship is pure. It's always untainted by self-consideration and self-seeking — it is selfless and altruistic, as romantic love should be but frequently isn't. And it was Mordecai who finally dispelled the curse of my life: my feelings of unlovability.

Florence and I also developed a deep and lasting friendship because we shared one very important thing: we both loved Mordecai, and we were both loved by him, deeply and unshakably. I wrote a poem about this when Mordecai was diagnosed with cancer of the esophagus, the cancer that did him in.

Somehow you knew
That we would never
See each other again,
At least, not in this sphere.
Perhaps you felt the claw,
The iron claw that was
To clutch your throat
And take you off so soon.
But we embraced,
Said our farewells
And you walked away.
Then you turned for a moment,
The briefest moment,
And looked back at me
With such love,
I trembled, I was shaken
By the naked feeling
Which radiated everything:
Memories, pleasures, creations,
Laughter, affection, friendship,
Longing, pain, the ineffable;
All this but inexpressibly more.
You knew the curse of my life
That haunted me from childhood
Until now, a snowy-haired man,
Your look dispelled it forever.
Now, wherever I may be,
However I may feel,
I remember that look of love,
It can never be forgotten.
This was your gift,
Your final gift to me.

One of the hardest things to bear on this terrestrial sphere of woe is the loss of one's close friends to gluttonous Death. Mordecai, Clive Exton, the poet Richard Outram, the Irish novelist Brian Moore. With their departure, life became bland and threadbare. It lost its seasoning. They all went ahead, leaving me grieving and bereft. I weep as I write these words.

CHAPTER TEN
London Calling

London was a vibrant, hotbed of artistic activity when I arrived in 1957. That time was dubbed the Carnaby Street years, named after the new fashion trends emanating from London. A creative movement in all the arts had taken hold. The Beatles were about to become a worldwide phenomenon and shine a light on British music, and the Rolling Stones would also soon catch on. The theater was moving from stodgy to edgy, transforming the nature of English stage drama.

In cinema, *The Bridge on the River Kwai*, the epic directed by David Lean that swept the Academy Awards, was released. Ironically, it was written by two blacklisted writers, Michael Wilson and Carl Foreman, with the novelist who wrote the original book, Pierre Boulle, acting as a "front." I was friends with Carl who lived in London. Another young ex-pat director, Kubrick, disenchanted with Hollywood, immigrated to London like me. His first films in London were *Lolita* and *Dr. Strangelove*.

Tony Richardson came out with *Look Back in Anger*, *A Taste of Honey*, *The Entertainer*, and *Tom Jones*. Lindsay Anderson, Richard Attenborough, and John Schlesinger each created wonderful films. These exciting films made so much money that the big Hollywood studios flocked to London, opening offices and financing many British films. Cinematically, London was definitely the place for me to be in — not that I had any choice in the matter, but boy did I ever luck out. My first five feature films were all British financed.

London had become something of a refuge for Hollywood writers, directors, and actors who had been blacklisted for being "Communists" by the House Un-American Activities Committee (HUAC). In a way, I guess it was all of us accused Communists together.

I nicknamed this group the Joe McCarthy Refugees, a reference to the obsessed U.S. senator from Wisconsin who had convened HUAC to root out Communists in radio, television, and films.

Dalton Trumbo, the Oscar-winning screenwriter, had refused to answer questions and betray friends before HUAC in 1947 and as a result, he had to serve ten months in a federal prison. He was kicked out of the Screenwriters Guild and blacklisted. He wrote 30 scripts under pseudonyms, using "fronts," including the 1957 Oscar-winning film *Roman Holiday*. And his script for *The Brave One* won an Academy Award for Best Story. I met this screenwriting genius during a visit to London. What a kind, intelligent, impressive man! And what an impressive mind and sensibility! Other writers who were living in London were Abe Polonsky, Ring Lardner, and Jules Dassin, who wrote and directed *Rififi*, a heist thriller that remains the benchmark film of the genre to this day. Though banned in Hollywood, they were all able to work in London under pseudonyms. A good friend of mine, Reuben Ship, was the head writer of a very successful TV series in the '50s called *The Life of Riley* starring William Bendix. He wrote many episodes but was blacklisted and had to leave Hollywood. He came to London where he wrote for British sitcoms.

What a terrible, shameful time it was! America at its worst!

My situation was clearly different, though it felt every bit as constrained. My reputation and career hadn't been ruined. I had been labeled a Communist by U.S. Immigration, but no one had made that public. Nevertheless, I was in London because it was the only vital film community where I could work — just like the black-listed artists. Their anger was also greater than mine, as I was much younger and they had established careers pulled out from under them.

But still, I was furious at the film business, at the distributors, and the guilds and unions who cowardly went along with that asshole Joe McCarthy and their complicity in his horrendous destruction of careers and lives.

Tensions ran high when it came to the Hollywood refugees. One night I was having dinner in the show-business hot spot the White Elephant with Zero Mostel, whom I had met working in the theater. Elia Kazan had given Zero's name and several others to HUAC as Communists. Kazan was known as much for directing such classics as *A Streetcar Named Desire* and *On the Waterfront* as he was for turning Judas on his friends. As a result, Zero was unable to work for ten years. So you can imagine the anger he felt toward Kazan.

In the middle of our dinner, Elia Kazan walked into the restaurant with his wife. Zero spotted him across the room and went totally crazy. In an incredible booming voice, Zero attacked Kazan verbally. The whole restaurant, filled with show-business people, heard Zero berating Kazan as a rat shit traitor and calling him the lowest of the low of human kind, and every abusive name under the sun. Kazan sat silent, he didn't engage Zero; he rose from his table and walked out with his wife.

I certainly understood Zero's rage. His career and livelihood had been taken away from him for a decade because Kazan had named him as a Communist. Personally, I find it difficult to judge a person. Had Kazan not testified as a friendly witness, HUAC would have nailed Kazan himself — and he would be the one who was unemployed. The temptation to save himself was just too great, but there was no question that he was also culpable for damaging many careers. Later, Kazan repented, though many understandably never forgave him.

It was the worst of times for people in the entertainment business, and for American political life as well. Not only was HUAC responsible for the loss of careers, but it was also responsible for the loss of lives. Many actors, directors, writers, and producers who could not get work committed suicide. In that regard, I guess I was lucky.

"

After I had been directing *Armchair Theatre* for about a year, Howard Thomas, the head of ABC TV, asked me about Sydney Newman, my boss and mentor at the CBC. Thomas had seen Sydney's producorial work on the CBC *General Motors Theater* episodes that had been aired on

Directing an Armchair Theatre *play for ABC-TV in 1958.*

the BBC. Thomas said that he was considering bringing Sydney to England to replace the existing producer on *Armchair Theatre*, which was an anthology drama series of one-hour plays.

I gave Sydney a glowing report; I said Sydney was one of the best TV producers in the business. Sydney, of course, had started my directing career, so I was really happy to be able to pay him back. Thomas hired Sydney in 1958 to produce *Armchair Theatre*. I now had a place to work any time I wanted.

When Sydney arrived, *Armchair Theatre* was mired in mothballs and mediocrity. They were only doing tired English stage plays and secondhand American television plays. All the directors complained about the subpar material. My first production for them was a 1934 West End hit play *The Shining Hour.* Critics routinely butchered the productions as suffering from the biggest sin of them all: they were boring.

Sydney immediately shook things up. The philosophy he developed in Canada concerning TV drama was what he now pushed in England — that is, that TV was not film, nor was it theater. It was ideally designed to immediately reflect what was going on in the society and culture at that very moment. He didn't want to do American TV plays that weren't relevant to what was going on in present-day London, and he didn't want to do out-of-date theater plays like *The Shining Hour* that dealt with a British world long gone by. So Sydney commissioned a whole pile of original plays on subjects that had relevance to British current events.

At first, those new plays were uneven and crudely done. But an undaunted Sydney persisted in the face of some opposition to his approach. And then suddenly, out of the woodwork came fresh voices, incredibly talented unknown dramatists like Harold Pinter, Clive Exton, and Alun Owen. They were all creative giants.

People sometimes forget that Harold Pinter, the major British stage playwright, started with great success in television, whose mass audience, having no preconceptions, accepted his unusual, idiosyncratic style. It was only then that theatrical audiences took note of him.

I directed five plays by Alun Owen and seven plays by Clive Exton, all gems! I directed the first play delivered by Alun Owen, a writer of a Liverpool, Welsh, working-class background. The play was entitled *No Trams to Lime Street.* It was set in Liverpool and was the story of three young Scouse sailors recently landed home in Liverpool. They are searching for themselves, two of them having to get over their fathers before they can live their own lives.

Alun said that rather than me reading the play, he would read it to me so I could hear it with a Liverpool accent, which he described as a mixture of part Irish, part Welsh, part catarrh.

The play was a knockout. It would be a great debut for Sydney's approach, and for me! Besides the three wonderfully delineated sailors, Alun depicted a tough working-class girl in great depth and believability. It was beautifully performed by Billie Whitelaw, who became one of my favorite actresses.

In my experience, not many male writers are capable of creating such believable and interesting women. Alun was unique in this. But after Alun finished reading it, I said I wasn't going to direct it. Alun, taken aback, asked, "Why?"

"Well, what do I, a Canadian, know about Liverpool working-class life?"

Alun replied, "Ted, you don't know this country! By virtue of you hearing my play, you know more about Liverpool and its working-class inhabitants than 99.99 percent of this country. They know nothing of what goes on beyond the suburbs of London."

He persuaded me.

The play was a revelation for the British TV audience. No other dramatist, be they in TV or theater, had ever delved into this world. It got spectacular reviews, and has become a classic.

For my readers who would like to see his work, Alun Owen wrote the Beatles' film, *A Hard Day's Night*. As you probably know, all of the Beatles came from Liverpool, so getting Alun to write their film was an easy call. I watched them filming several times with Alun and had a chance to meet all of them.

With Sydney in command, *Armchair Theatre* took on a renewed sense of urgency. And visually, the shows broke the old mold. Rather than static two-shots of actors reciting their lines for five minutes or longer, the other directors and I moved the cameras fluidly — Canadian style. The result was that commercially and critically the series took off, and *Armchair Theatre* became the cultural icon of television in its day.

I had seen a play on Granada Television called *No Fixed Abode* by Clive Exton. I recognized his ability and got to meet him through a girlfriend of his wife Mara. I asked Sydney to commission a play from him and that was the beginning of a life-long creative and personal friendship, almost rivaling the one I had with Mordecai.

Clive was a dramatic genius. The first plays of his that I directed, *Where I Live* and *I'll Have You to Remember*, were deeply emotional and profoundly moving. These plays established him as one of the leading talents of his generation, as one critic put it.

Then he changed gears and wrote two dark, savage satires, which further enhanced his reputation. They revealed an unexpected side of Clive, a very black humor. I directed both of them, *The Big Eat* and *The Trial of Doctor Fancy*. Howard Thomas, ABC's chief, and Sydney Newman thought the subject matter of *The Big Eat* was too grim and shocking and, making no bones about it, inappropriate for a TV company whose chief income was from commercial advertising. *The Big Eat* was a caustic assault on the gross, materialistic advertising ethos of our society; "Buy — buy — buy! Consume — consume — consume!" being its relentless message.

The play took the form of an eating competition organized by a large food corporation for lavish prizes: money,
cars, houses, a lifetime supply of the company's food. The
contestants have to eat competitively, and the central character, a Mr. Britten (get it), the most sympathetic of the
contestants, eats himself to death before the guffaws of a
cretinous audience of numbskulls. There are other repel-
lent sequences with the chef's account of a new "freezi-
squeeze" method of the slaughtering of animals (abattoir
echoes in my head).

Howard Thomas and Sydney Newman did not hesitate
to pass on it, but the BBC grabbed it. Being a government-
financed network, and so, commercial free, they had no
inhibitions in attacking the crassness of advertising. I
directed it with great critical success for both Clive and
myself.

Clive's other darkly satiric opus, *The Trial of Doctor
Fancy*, also had severe marketing problems. When I finished shooting it, Howard Thomas thought it was too way
out, too grim, and tasteless, and that it would be unacceptable to *Armchair Theatre* audiences. He ordered Sydney to
shelve it.

The story is a wild satire on man's need for conformity,
the desire of human beings to be like everyone else and
not stick out. The play concerns a conspiracy between a
trouser manufacturer and a fashionable surgeon, Dr. Fancy,
who persuades people they are too tall, causing them terrible neuroses that can only be cured by the amputation
of both legs at the knees. Dr. Fancy makes a handsome
living from these operations, the trouser maker supplies
the amputees with appropriate apparel, and happiness
ensues for everyone. Charges are brought against Fancy.
But the urge to conformity is too great. Fancy is praised

as a humanitarian and a benefactor, and is acquitted by a jury, who, as they file out of the jury box, prove to all be amputees. *The Trial of Doctor Fancy* was a corrosive parable showing the lengths people will go not to be noticeably different from their fellow human beings. Both of Clive's plays were brilliant and deeply disturbing. But my exciting production of this brilliant play was ordered to be shelved.

I was not going to take this lying down. I secretly invited the television critics of every major London newspaper and weekly periodicals to a clandestine screening of *Dr. Fancy*. They universally raved about it in their papers and criticized ABC's pusillanimity in not broadcasting it. I thought Howard Thomas was going to fire me for screening it without permission. He was very angry at me and my ploy that now forced him to air *Dr. Fancy*. But when he did so, all the pre-publicity hullabaloo surrounding it earned *Dr. Fancy* astronomical ratings. And the critics went on heaping accolades, saying it was a jewel in the crown of British television.

Howard forgave me and my trickery.

From 1958 to 1964, I directed 28 different plays. But none matched the drama of the production of *Underground* in 1958.

99

Underground was an apocalyptic tale that told the story of a hydrogen bomb hitting London and destroying the entire city. The play began with London being H-bombed, with the only survivors deep in the Underground (the subway). The story follows six survivors as they struggle through the web of subway tunnels with their only sustenance being sweets and peanuts from the candy machines. One of the six was played by the 33-year-old Gareth Jones, who turned out to be the villain in the piece.

For the shoot, the greater part of the studio had been converted into a bombed-out subway station with piles of rubble everywhere and long tunnels. The great production designer Timothy O'Brien, who designed so many of my TV shows so brilliantly, was in charge of this very complicated set. We always remained close. The camera choreography was elaborate and tricky, with cameras hiding behind piles of wreckage. They would pop out, grab a shot, and immediately hide themselves again, as another camera was about to photograph their concealing rubble.

Halfway through act 2, in the background of one of the sets, I saw a body being carried by two men. I cried out to the assistant director to clear the set. The make-up girl came running into our control room where I was, crying out to me that while she was applying black smudges to Gareth Jones's face, he had fainted and fallen face forward onto her makeup tray. He had been taken backstage, and a doctor was coming.

We were still live on the air. On camera, the five other survivors arrived at the mouth of a subway tunnel expecting to meet up with Gareth. Not finding him there and having no idea of what had occurred, there was a tense moment of indecision. Then the lead actor quick-wittedly ad-libbed as a cue to me: "Let's go down this tunnel. Carl must be waiting for us further down."

I rushed a camera, fortunately nearby, to the far end of the tunnel and photographed them as they made their way down it. They finally arrived at another large subway station, filled with survivors, where a dictatorial fanatic was organizing them into a neo-fascist society. Somehow, we stumbled to the end of act 2.

As we were fading to black, I yelled at the floor manager, "Get all the actors together!" The make-up girl rushed into the control room. "It's Gareth . . . The doctor declared him dead . . . heart attack," she whispered.

What?! In the middle of the show? But he's only 33! Momentarily I was stunned. I turned to Verity Lambert, and told her to contact master control and tell them to have a two-reeler Charlie Chaplin film standing by, in case we ground to a halt and had to fade to black.

Then I grabbed the script and rushed out of the control room to talk to the actors. I didn't tell them that Gareth had died. I said that he had fainted and was out of action. "Now, here's what we're going to do . . ." I said, making it up on the fly. Quickly, I began reassigning his lines and giving them new stage actions for the upcoming Act 3. The commercial break lasted just three minutes. I rewrote the whole of the remaining story at warp speed.

"Two minutes, Ted . . ."

The main problem was that in act 3, Gareth became the Judas figure who betrayed his group to the fascist henchman.

"One minute, Ted . . ."

So I had to re-assign his character and all his many lines to one of the other actors — in just three minutes.

"Thirty seconds, Ted!"

I ran back into the control room as the countdown started, "Ten, nine, eight . . ." and told Verity that she should call out the shots to the cameramen and direct the opening section of act 3. Meanwhile, I was going to figure out what problems would arise as we moved forward because of the untimely death of the villain, and how I could find a pictorial solution to them so we could finish the live broadcast.

The show would go on.

We somehow got through act 3. The whole thing was a feverish dream with me yelling at the cameras as they improvised shot after shot, as the actors improvised line after line.

As the closing credits started, an exhausted and hoarse Ted walked out into the studio. By this time, everyone knew the truth of what had happened to Gareth. No one was moving. It was total silence, broken only by the deep, gasping sobs coming from the star of the show, Donald Houston, who was Gareth's dear friend. The other actors stood immobile, disbelieving.

I tried to comfort Donald as tears streamed down his face. He told me that Gareth was going to be married in two weeks. Oh my god! His wife-to-be had to be given the tragic news. She would undoubtedly be very anxious, because with Gareth's disappearance from the play, she would know something untoward must have occurred. He begged me to speak to the fiancée, Gwenda. He just couldn't do it. He pleaded, and I reluctantly agreed to perform this dolorous duty, the least I could do, I felt, for this man that I had come to know, admire, and befriend.

It was one of the most painful things I've ever had to do in my entire life. I phoned her and said a lot but cannot remember a single word of it. Gwenda was devastated. I knew that there was nothing I could possibly say that could console her.

I returned to the studio. Everyone was still frozen in disbelief. I asked Donald to lead us in prayer for Gareth, all of us still overcome by this tragedy.

News of Gareth's death made headlines. People were shocked that we had finished the show. But what else were we supposed to do? It was a snap judgment on my part.

One TV critic, would you believe, thought it was a brilliant narrative device of mine to eliminate the character! To this day, the story of "Underground" remains legendary in British television lore.

"

There was one additional bonus in having moved to England: I had always wanted to work in the theater as well as film. At one point, I wasn't sure whether I wanted to spend my life in the theater or in film. But in America, that dilemma would have been logistically impossible because film was in Hollywood and theater was in New York. In England, both were in London. So for the next 12 years, I would alternate between directing films, directing TV, and directing stage plays. I felt so lucky to be able to do this! It provided me with endless creative excitement and satisfaction.

It was a turbulent time in the West End, as the British theater district is known. After World War II, the theater was still the playwright's domain — particularly that of middle-class playwrights like Noël Coward and Terence Rattigan, whose *Separate Tables* was still running when I arrived in London. That kind of theater was about to be turned upside down.

It all started with *Look Back in Anger*, written by John Osborne, the first play of the "angry young men" movement. It was a huge success resulting in a revolutionary breakthrough of the new drama into British theater. Soon, it was followed by a flood of new unknown young dramatists, the great majority of whom were provincial working-class playwrights like Shelagh Delaney (*A Taste of Honey*), Brendan Behan (*The Hostage*), Harold Pinter (*The Caretaker*), and Arnold Wesker (*Chips with Everything*). On this list belonged my friend, the Liverpool playwright Alun Owen.

His play was entitled *Progress to the Park*; it was directed by this "angry young man." It was my first foray into the British theater. The play was a dramedy set in Liverpool, a *Romeo and Juliet* story about a Catholic girl and a Protestant boy falling in love in the face of numerous oppositions. And to star in it, I used my favorite actress, Billie Whitelaw. It earned outstandingly good critical attention and did fairly well at the box office. Theatrically I was launched.

The next play that I directed was by Doris Lessing, the Nobel Prize–winning novelist, described by the Swedish Academy as "that epicist of the female experience." *Play with a Tiger* dramatized certain aspects of her mammoth novel *The Golden Notebook*. This book led to Doris becoming a goddess in the pantheon of feminism. She was certainly worshipped as such by American activists in the women's movement, striving on behalf of women's rights and interests.

The Golden Notebook is a daring story in which the many selves of contemporary womanhood were delineated in amazing verisimilitude. Anna Wulf, the central character, is a projection of Doris, as she attempts to free herself from the chains of identity thrust upon a woman and live like a man.

I grew up in a very masculine-dominated culture, where one of my uncles, Fat Stavro, whom I admired and loved in all other respects, would clap his hands and his wife (my aunt) would come running out of the kitchen to see what he wanted. "Woman! Two Turkish coffees!" and off she would run. On one occasion, when I, a snot-nosed 12-year-old, was having dinner with them, my aunt interrupted me as I was telling a story. My uncle turned on her, "Shut up, woman! A man is talking!" I was embarrassed and appalled. When I was 14, I read Simone de Beauvoir's *The Second Sex*. "Yes!" I said to myself, "Yes!!" I became an ardent supporter of the theory of the political, economic, and social equality of the sexes.

So obviously I was very much in sympathy with what *Play with a Tiger* was saying. When we were working together on *Play with a Tiger* at her home, strange men would emerge from her bedroom late in the morning, and, from their demeanor, I could see that they wanted to take the next step and engage with her. But Doris would kick them out, saying she was busy working on a play with me and there was a taxi rank on the corner down the road. Doris loved men's sense of sovereignty. That's what she wanted for herself and all women.

The play opened at the Comedy Theatre in London in March 1962. I gathered a great cast: Siobhán McKenna, the marvelous Irish actress, and the American actor Alex Viespi (a.k.a. Alex Cord) were the two leads. Also in the cast were William Russell, Maureen Pryor, Anne Lawson, and Godfrey Quigley, all fine performers. I feel that *Play with a Tiger* was Doris's best play, focusing on people who have thrown over conventional morality, and I was very enthusiastic about the play's style — part realism and part expressionism.

Doris truly was an amazing woman. I adored her and we became lifelong friends.

"

I directed a play that was part of the Dublin Theatre Festival, *The Au Pair Man* by the Irish playwright Hugh Leonard. He was best known for *Da*, which had a long run in New York. *The Au Pair Man* was a two-character play.

It's about a socially graceless young Irishman who comes to the crumbling house belonging to an impoverished British upper-class lady to repossess a piece of furniture. The house is filled with memorabilia of the British Empire. He is inveigled by her to be her au pair man in exchange for a polishing of his crude and socially awkward ways, which she proceeds to do. Rapidly you discern that the play is a very amusing allegory about the relationship of England and Ireland.

It starred one of the finest Irish actors, Donal McCann, and the comedic English actress, Joan Greenwood, well known for her roles in the British Ealing film comedies like *Kind Hearts and Coronets* with Alec Guinness, and famous for her deep, purring, sexy, plummy voice.

I loved working in Ireland. The Irish are truly the custodians of the English language — they speak it so beautifully and imagistically. I remember, early on, going into a pub by myself. It was darkish inside, so I stood for a moment at its entry, accustoming my eyes to the gloom. It was obviously a pub for locals, for a man's voice said, "There's a cuckoo in the nest." (Who talks like this? Who else but an Irishman.) I retorted, "I may be a cuckoo, but I'm a thirsty cuckoo and I have no intention of going to some other nest!" He rose from his friends, "Ah, sir, ah, sir, I didn't mean to offend you. Will you let me buy you a forgiving drink?" We crossed to the bar. "Would you like one of the specialties here — a 'mother-in-law'?"

"What, pray, is that?"

"A mixture of stout and bitter." He ordered two "mother-in-laws," then he said, "You're off the ice, aren't you?"

I paused. "Yes, I'm a Canadian."

"I'm a merchant seaman, often entering Montreal. As soon as you spoke, I recognized your accent."

Getting back to *The Au Pair Man*, it was staged at the Gate Theatre, where both Orson Welles and James Mason started their careers.

We rehearsed intensely, and the two actors were in fine fettle. Soon, it was the nervous-making opening night. Five minutes before curtain up, I peered through a crack in the curtains and was taken aback to see that the audience was almost 100 percent women! I whispered loudly to the nearby assistant stage manager, "Celine, Celine, come here!"

She rushed over, "What is it, Mr. Ted? What can I do for you, Mr. Ted?"

"Our audience, it's completely women!"

"Yes."

"What do you mean, yes? Where are their husbands, their lovers, their sons, fathers, uncles?"

"Well, they're in the pubs, of course. You do know the Irish definition of a homosexual?"

"No, what is it?"

"A man who prefers women to drink!"

Ah, those Irish!

After its Dublin run, the play moved to London's West End and was enjoyed by many — of both genders.

But my biggest and most ambitious theatrical undertaking was Lionel Bart's musical *Maggie May*, based on a book by Alun Owen. If you recall, I directed Alun Owen's play *Progress to the Park*. Alun, of course, was the one who invited me to be *Maggie May*'s director and persuaded Lionel Bart to accept this total novice.

So as you can imagine, I approached it rather gingerly. Stage musicals are always difficult for any director, let alone a first timer like me. I didn't know what I was getting myself into, but I found out soon enough.

CHAPTER ELEVEN

Playing Musical Chairs with Rex Harrison

Maggie May was a fast moving, hard-hitting, gritty story of life in the docklands of Liverpool, unusual in that it had a tragic ending. Liverpool, of course, was Alun Owen's authorial home turf. So his book for the musical was Alun at his best, full of local color, comedy, drama, and romance.

Lionel Bart's score and lyrics were on par with his brilliant *Oliver!* The songs were strong emotionally with a befitting earthiness, and there were some comedic songs that were very witty. When it came to musicals, Lionel really knew what he was doing. I felt, at times, from the way Lionel watched me working, that he was not entirely sure that I knew what I was doing.

I was thrilled to have Sean Kenny working for me. This delightful Irishman was one of the greatest theatrical designers ever. His sets for Lionel's previous musical, *Oliver!*, were absolutely astonishing. The great Paddy

Stone was to be my choreographer. Surrounded by such talent, some of my qualms evaporated. But only some! For now, it was up to me to deliver a great production.

I got down to work, casting and creating the sets for *Maggie May*. I had endless singing and acting auditions. I cast Kenneth Haigh in the male lead, a dock worker named Patrick Casey. Kenneth had been the star of *Look Back in Anger* where he had made his name. He also had become a chum of mine.

I cast Rachel Roberts in the lead role of Maggie May. Rachel starred in a successful British movie, *This Sporting Life*. Lionel wanted Georgia Brown, that great voice, to play the part, but she was contractually unavailable for a long time playing Nancy in Lionel's *Oliver!* on Broadway. He was very upset about this. Selecting the rest of the huge cast took me some time.

Sean Kenny had a studio in Soho. He had a large model theatre where he showed me his ideas for the sets, lighting and all in 3D. I knew exactly what I was going to get. And *wow*, did I get it! There were two 30-foot functioning cranes lifting freight from the hold of a freighter at a dockside bay. There was the whole side of a ship with wide ramps leading up into it. There was a fairground with appropriate rides that worked! There were Liverpool street scenes, pubs, Chinese restaurants! They were all fabulous. They took my breath away. This musical was going to be epic.

Rehearsals commenced!

Rachel Roberts was married to the famous British film star, Rex Harrison. Rex had just finished the film of the Lerner and Loewe hit musical *My Fair Lady*, in which he played the starring part of Professor Henry Higgins with co-star Audrey Hepburn as Eliza Doolittle.

Rex came to the theater where I was staging the musical and asked me if it was okay for him to watch. "You want to watch the master at work," I joked. "Sure, any time."

One day, with Rex present, I was staging a climactic scene in dockland, where the dock workers, led by Kenneth Haigh, are going on strike, singing. Maggie is present, singing her unhappiness with what is occurring. I put the chorus of 20 strikers on the left half of the stage frame, and Maggie in the wide empty space on the right half.

This had a double function for Maggie: she was alone, frail, vulnerable in her space; but at the same time, because in the proscenium frame she balanced 20 men, it gave her power and stature. What a woman, equal to 20 men! It also reflected the structure of the music: a male chorus singing "Strike! Strike!" counterpointing Maggie's moving solo. I thought it worked thrillingly.

As Rachel sang, she slowly drifted toward center stage and I had to stop the pianist and told her to return to where I had staged her.

I was in about row five in the stalls when suddenly from behind me, Rex, in his resonant voice cried out, "Rachel is the star of this show! This is an important scene for her! She should be singing center stage, not off to the right. Kotcheff, you're diminishing her! Belittling her!"

He missed the point of my choreography totally. Had she stood center stage, she would have strikers behind her, muddying the composition. And far from strengthening her, as Rex thought, the opposite would have been the result.

I ignored Rex, I told Rachel to go back where I had originally staged her. She did.

At lunch break, I went back to where Rex was seated. "Rex, I have to say, this is a very lucky day for you and me." He looked at me quizzically. "You were sitting twelve rows back of me when you interrupted. Had you been sitting behind me, your handsome face would have been re-arranged and I'd have been arrested for grievous bodily harm." I tried to mitigate the harshness of what I was saying with a bantering tone. He got the message. "Rex, I'm no egomaniac. I love suggestions, but next time, please, in private."

Lionel heard of my altercation with Rex. He approached me and shook my hand. "Don't listen to that a-hole. Your staging of that scene is brilliant."

While we were on tour, I spoke to Lionel about giving the Kenneth Haigh character another song, a God song in the fairground scene. (A God song is one in which the character sings alone and pours out his heart to the heavens.)

Lionel agreed and went off to write it — two days later, he came back and sang the new God song for me. When he finished singing it, I said tentatively, "Lionel, note for note that's the 'Limehouse Blues.'" He was thunderstruck for a moment! Then, "Oh my God, Ted, you're right!" After that moment, my musical stock went up significantly with Lionel. For the last thing Lionel wanted was to add to the jokes about his previous musicals like "Lionel Bart musicals are the only ones where you hum its tunes going into the theater!" He tried again and wrote a really fine song for Kenneth Haigh. Then I suggested that we cut one of Maggie May's nine songs, as it was of a lesser quality. He agreed.

I informed Rachel of the cut of her song, then girded my loins for another Rex Harrison onslaught. Sure enough, he barged aggressively into my dressing-room office. "Kotcheff! I hear you cut one of Rachel's songs and added a song to Kenneth Haigh. This musical is called *Maggie May*, not the *Kenneth Haigh Road Show!*"

"I know you're an actor, Rex, but will you stop dramatizing for a moment. Rachel still has eight great songs, and now Kenneth has four. She has twice as many!" He then insinuated that I was playing favorites. That I was doing this because Kenneth and I were friends. "Listen, Rex! There's only one criterion under which I operate — to make this the best possible show that I can. Nothing else motivates me. Nothing!" I shouted. "If you don't know this about me by now, you're totally blind! Now excuse me, I have work to do making further improvements!"

Opening night!

In September 1964, *Maggie May* premiered at the Adelphi Theatre in London. The performance went exceptionally well, and we received a multitude of curtain calls. The entire cast and crew had a wild celebration of relief and joy. I didn't celebrate that night as I waited nervously for the reviews. I got the very first editions of practically every British newspaper.

Universally, we received reviews that one only dreams about. *The Telegraph* called *Maggie May* "the most vigorous musical since *West Side Story*" and "a swaggering compendium of spectacle and song that triumphs over its own flaws by sheer drive and powers." *The Sunday Citizen* called it "a musical winner, it's great!" and *The Observer* said it was "big, bold, and energetic." One newspaper, I forget which, came out with this memorable image: "There were five separate talents working on *Maggie May*. They were five fingers of an extraordinary creative hand. Lionel Bart, songs, Alun Owen, book, Ted Kotcheff, director, Paddy Stone, choreography, Sean Kenny, sets. Where the work of one finished and another began was totally invisible. The musical was seamless and flowed effortlessly to greatness."

Sean Kenny and I met in the lobby of the Adelphi the next morning to discuss some production changes and were out of our minds with joy, reveling in our excitement. The box office manager rushed up to us, "We've sold out the first two weeks and it's only 10:30!" We were a success! Then a grim-faced Lionel came in and stormed over to Sean and me. He waved some newspapers in my face, "Kotcheff, look at all these reviews — they all refer to *Maggie May* as a great musical drama. It is not a musical drama! It is a musical! You made it into a drama with music. And you spent much of our prep time rehearsing Alun's scenes at the expense of my songs!" I replied, "Sorry, Lionel, I thought you wanted a powerful theatrical experience with affecting character conflicts, striking dramatic action interspersed, with emotional songs. Now you tell me you wanted *Maggie May* to be a concert of all your songs." Lionel went puce. "Ted, did anyone ever tell you that you can be an insufferable prick, you smart aleck bastard?" He stormed out. Later, Alun Owen's reaction to some of the reviews seemed lukewarm. Paddy Stone's pleasure was also somewhat muffled. Sean and I looked at each other. I was completely uncomprehending. Sean said, "I guess, Ted, that they didn't want to be fingers. They wanted to be the whole hand." What a carnival of egos!

During its long run, part of my job was to surreptitiously show up for a performance every nine or ten days. I would enter the theater as the curtain was going up and sit at the back of the stalls so that the actors didn't know I was there. The purpose was to ensure that the performances hadn't become slack and were still of the highest caliber, and that the staging hadn't been detrimentally compromised. You'd be surprised how often this happens.

Of course, within a short time I discovered, because of the way they were performing, that all the cast knew I was there. I asked the stage manager after the show how they found out I was there so quickly. He replied, "They can hear the irate scratching of your pen on your pad."

One night, Lionel phoned me and said, "I'm going in tonight. Will you join me? I'm going to show my musical off to my new boyfriend. I'm sure you know him — Sal Mineo." Yes, I knew Sal Mineo as he was a minor film star who had featured in *Rebel without a Cause* with James Dean, *Giant*, and *Exodus*. I joined them for an evening performance of *Maggie May* after a matinée that afternoon.

That performance, Rachel Roberts came out slightly inebriated. This had happened once or twice before. I always knew when she'd had one drink too many before a show because it distorted her fine performance. All her emotions were exaggerated: when she was angry, it came out shrill like a fishwife; when she was romantic, it came out sappy and sentimental; when she was serious and sincere, it came out stilted.

I couldn't stand it. I leaned over, told Lionel I was leaving but would return to speak to Rachel after the show. He refused to join me and masochistically watched in anger, humiliated because of the presence of his new love.

I went to the pub next door to the theater and made notes. The pub and the theater had a common wall, so I could hear loud exchanges and applause, and knew exactly where they were in the show. After a few drinks, I heard the final applause. Quickly I exited the pub, went up a side alley to the stage door at the back of the theater, and rushed up the stairs to Rachel's dressing room. Lionel had beat me there.

It was like a scene from a bad movie. At the end of the hallway, I saw Lionel backing out of her dressing room. He was shouting, "I hate you in my musical, you drunk! I never wanted you for Maggie, I wanted Georgia Brown." I could hear Rachel weeping and screaming, and throwing things at him that were smashing behind Lionel onto the back wall of the corridor outside her door — bottles, a vanity set, a small lamp, books. Lionel charged down the corridor and passed me wordlessly.

I went into Rachel's dressing room. She was sobbing hysterically. I tried to calm her down. She told me she'd had only a small amount of sherry to soothe her sore throat after the matinée. I felt it had to be more than that, but I let it pass. Her whole being was shaking. Her self-regard was in pieces as she continued sobbing deeply. How would she perform the next day? I spent the next hour reassuring her about her performance, trying to put her fractured self back together again.

Rex was in New York for the opening of his film, *My Fair Lady*. Later that night, after the premiere, he phoned Lionel, "Look here, you little homosexual cunt —"

"I'm not little —"

"How dare you attack and humiliate my wife. I'm placing the matter in the hands of my solicitors."

"Rex, you can place it in their hands, or in any other part of their anatomy. Would you like some suggestions?"

"Clever dick. I'm suing you!" and Rex slammed the phone down.

After Rachel Roberts completed her six-month contract, I threw a farewell party for her which the whole cast attended. Rachel was in their midst, hugging, kissing, uttering goodbyes. I was chatting with Rex. Lionel entered. Rex saw Lionel making a beeline for him and stood on guard for an anticipated attack. But Lionel opened with "I can't tell you how much I admire you, Rex. I admire the way you stood up for your mate, defending her, helping her, protecting her. You're a real man, the genuine article." Then he snuggled up to Rex, and in a low, intimate voice said, "Listen, Rex, if anything should go wrong, God forbid, between you and Rachel — I'm available." Rex, for a moment, didn't know how to respond. Then he burst out laughing, laughed his ass off. That Lionel was a real wag. They made up. Peace was restored.

And Lionel got his wish. After Rachel's departure, Georgia Brown took over the part of Maggie May and played it until the end of its West End run.

"

Maggie May played to sold-out audiences for 501 performances. The musical won the Novello Award for the Outstanding Score of the Year and the Critics' Poll as Best New British Musical. The famous Broadway producer, David Merrick, wanted to bring the musical to Broadway with me as its director, raving in *Variety* what a great job I had done staging it. It never happened, nor could it with me because I was still banned from the U.S.

Maggie May gave me a tremendous professional boost. My theater successes added to my reputation established in TV. In 1959, I had been named drama director of the year by the Society of Film and Television Arts. The press I received was also helpful. One British critic wrote, "We know what to expect of his productions: we expect an intuitive feeling for the flavor of the character, the shape of a

With my Best Drama Director Award, from the Guild of TV Producers and Directors, in 1959.

*Alongside Sydney Newman, Hollywood stars John Ireland, Constance Cummings,
and Betta St. John give me a pretend Oscar for directing them in F. Scott
Fitzgerald's* The Last Tycoon *in season three of* Armchair Theatre.

scene, the focus of dramatic interest at any particular point,
and we expect a complete grasp of the sheer technique of
the medium."

The combination of my TV and theater credentials led
to my first feature film job. A producer named Ivan Foxwell
saw *Progress to the Park* and felt as a director I had great
comedic abilities that would be perfect for his upcoming
social comedy, *Tiara Tahiti*. The film, released in 1962,
starred James Mason as a profligate military officer who
is removed from his platoon by his commanding officer,
played by John Mills. Living in exile in Tahiti, Mason's
character later ends up running into his former nemesis.
The story is a clash of two personalities, the upper-class

Mason who's become a beachcomber and the lower-class Mills who's become a multi-millionaire.

During those years in England, I also worked with a commercial company doing various spots to earn extra money between directing gigs. Though I enjoyed them, they weren't necessarily creatively satisfying — until I did the series of British Airways commercials. The concept was unusual for a company run by ascot-wearing executives. BA hired the major star actor Robert Morley, who was known for his bushy eyebrows, his sagging face, and his humorous tut-tut aura of British condescension.

I would take Robert to famous places, such as Hadrian's Wall, Shakespeare's first house, and many castles and stately homes. We shot the British Airways commercials in all the famous tourist places in Great Britain. The BA people would give me some basic information that needed to be conveyed — fly to Rome for 49 pounds — and then let me create a funny situation around it.

We did one commercial while Robert Morley played golf at the famous St. Andrews golf course in Scotland. At one point, while he's furiously hacking away trying to free his golf ball from a sand trap, producing clouds of sand, he accompanies this by extolling the virtues of British Airways. Then Robert takes a colossal swing at a teed-up ball and then quickly looks into the distance with hand-shaded eyes to watch where the ball went. But the audience can see he's missed the ball totally. And other such classic golf jokes.

We shot Hadrian's Wall, that long defensive fortification built by the Romans in the north of England from sea to sea, designed to keep out the Barbarians. A portly, overweight Robert Morley waddles on the top of Hadrian's Wall chasing his hat that a blast of wind has blown off and keeps rolling it away just out of his reach, and breathlessly delivers his pitch for British Airways.

All the commercials were staged in this unconventional and amusing way. The ad agency would give me the text they wanted Robert to say and leave me to stage them any way I wanted. The commercials were hugely successful. British Airways absolutely decimated all the other airlines on the transatlantic route. People making phone reservations would ask to speak to Robert Morley to assist them with their flight. BA had Robert record his voice for incoming calls. His messages were in line with the comedic tone of the commercials. For instance, he would say, "Welcome to British Airways reservations. This is Robert Morley. I'd love to help you, but unfortunately I'm off shooting a film, so one of my trusty assistants will be on the line to help you in two shakes of a lamb's tail. Toodle-oo!" I used Robert Morley in my films twice, once in a smallish part in *Life at the Top* and once in a large part in *Who's Killing the Great Chefs of Europe*, where he created a marvelously funny character. My commercials with him became cult classics.

United Airlines, in an attempt to compete, imitated us using Peter Sellers. Didn't work.

"

My time in England represented a chance to become a director and explore creativity. I really loved working in the theater: just me and the actors, with no 100-man film crew waiting for me to make up the rumpled bed of my mind. There was time for me to experiment with performances, try different things, and I felt I learned a lot about eliciting good performances from talented actors. Over the 17 years I was there, London became a tremendous petri dish for creativity. All eyes had turned to the city, which *Vogue* editor Diana Vreeland had called "the most swinging city in the world at the moment."

In the early '60s, I fell in love with an actress named Sylvia Kay. I had first noticed her when she took over Vivien Leigh's role in the play *Duel of Angels*. I had cast her in an Alun Owen TV drama I directed in 1959, and we began dating shortly thereafter. We got married in 1963. We ended up having three children together — Aaron, Kate, and Joshua — all of whom spent their formative years in London and two of them still remain there.

The creative people I met and worked with in London stayed with me throughout my whole career.

JAMES MASON

In the first feature film I directed, *Tiara Tahiti*, I experienced what it was like to work with and get to know a world-class actor. I also had my first insight into the idiosyncrasies and quirks of a world-class actor.

James Mason was cast in the lead. It was a heady thing for a 31-year-old rookie director to be working with an actor of that caliber. One of the biggest stars of the time, James had toplined some 50 movies, including such classics as Alfred Hitchcock's *North by Northwest* and *20,000 Leagues Under the Sea*. I wasn't intimidated by him per se, but rather by the fact that I was a callow, untried, green-as-grass tenderfoot.

The film was shot in 1961 on location in the South Pacific island of Tahiti. How do you like that as a location for one's first film?! James and I both rented ocean-front houses outside of the capital city of Papeete. By happenstance, our houses were close to each other. One night, early in production, James invited me to have dinner at his place prepared by his cook. I gladly accepted.

We sat down to dinner. I started talking nervously, about what I can't remember, but I talked all the way through the first course. I realized that an hour had gone by and James hadn't said a thing. Finally, by the middle of the meal, James began to loosen up, and by the end of the evening he was talking somewhat freely. Once the ice was broken, we had a pleasant evening of social intercourse.

I invited him to dinner the following night at my place, as I too had a Tahitian cook. We sat down, and again I started talking. About an hour into the meal, I realized he had barely uttered a word. We were back to square one. But like the preceding evening, he eventually relaxed, and we had an engaging and freewheeling conversation.

A few nights later, we were back at his house for dinner. The exact same thing occurred! He was virtually mute for the first hour, and then he slowly became his animated self. I decided to say something.

"James," I said gingerly, "I don't understand how you start off every dinner completely locked up, but by the end of the evening, we seem to be talking very freely about our loves and hates and experiences. But then the next day, we are right back to where we started as if we had never met."

James threw up his arms in a pronounced gesture of surrender. "Ted, I suffer this fucking English reserve that freezes my soul, and I can't shake it," he said. "It was part of my upbringing. It follows me like a ghost wherever I go."

From then on, though, our dinners were interactive from the moment we sat down.

Not only was he a lovely man, we enjoyed working together and became friends. He also starred in another film for me, *Dare I Weep, Dare I Mourn?* One night on that shoot, he gave me a wonderful compliment: "I love being around you Ted, because you are one of the few people who can get me to break down my wall of reserve."

One of James's curious eccentricities was that he never came to watch dailies to see his performance. For most actors, it's impossible to keep them away from attending dailies. I'm not sure, but I think that James never even saw any of his completed films, even when they were in theaters. I wanted to ask him why he didn't attend dailies, but I refrained because I thought it was an impertinence to ask him about such a private matter.

Later, in a moment of uncharacteristic candor, James confessed to me that he couldn't stand seeing himself, and he especially disliked his voice, that wonderful, distinctive tambour of speech that I and many others adored. I was a bit stunned when he told me this. I would have liked to argue with him, but I didn't. I have a deep and abiding affection for this intelligent, considerate, decent, good-humored, gentle man.

There is one last mystery I want to share with you that I first encountered with James Mason. John Mills, the other lead in *Tiara Tahiti*, was also a major British film actor who featured in films like *A Tale of Two Cities*, *Goodbye, Mr. Chips*, *Great Expectations*, *Around the World in 80 Days*, and 127 other significant credits to his name. There was a scene in *Tiara Tahiti* where the lower-class John Mills is bragging to upper-class James Mason about how rich he's become and how now, as a result, he's been invited to exclusive men's clubs in London, usually only open to the upper classes. John Mills is drinking as he expounds and boasts on this subject, getting drunker and drunker.

I did John Mills's long, five-minute speech in one shot.

We dollied back on a crane from the living room out onto the exterior balcony of James's unpretentious Tahitian seaside shanty. Both men are in the frame all the time. John Mills gave a bravura performance. Playing drunk convincingly is never easy, especially getting more and more drunk, but he did it brilliantly. At the end of the first take, the whole crew spontaneously burst into applause.

We did the shot once more. Again, an incredible display of acting virtuosity. The crew clapped again. And British film crews are not noted for demonstrativeness.

James Mason is always in the shot, saying nothing, just standing and listening to the riveting speech given by John Mills. But the next day at dailies, you couldn't get your eyes off James Mason. What caused this reaction, not only in me but in several of us in the screening room, was beyond comprehension. Was this the magical "star quality" in operation?

It was a baffling, inexplicable mystery. But I've never forgotten it. Big stars have this uncanny connection with the camera. They are effortlessly magnified by it to larger-than-life proportions. Not moving, not speaking, but the camera made it James Mason's moment, not John Mills's. I thought to myself, "Ted, there's a lot you have to learn about the nature of filmic stardom."

MICHELANGELO
ANTONIONI

It all started with a phone call from a producer named Pierre Rouve. Like me, he had Bulgarian roots. He had changed his name to Rouve from the less refined Roueff en route to becoming a European intellectual, an art critic of some repute, and a film producer. As two of the only Bulgarians (probably) living in London, we had had a few social encounters. Pierre explained to me that he and the well-known Italian producer Carlo Ponti had produced a movie called *Blow-Up*.

"Please," I said, interrupting him. "Everybody in London knows about *Blow-Up*. It is made by the great master director Michelangelo Antonioni."

The papers had been full of stories about the production. One of the best was that because the leaves in Hyde Park weren't the right color for him, Antonioni had them all painted by the art department.

The problem, Pierre explained, was that he and Carlo Ponti both felt the film was 20 minutes too long. And Antonioni himself also agreed that the film ran 20 minutes too long, but he was so close to it he couldn't figure out where to make the necessary cuts.

"Michelangelo loved your film *Life at the Top*, and he told me that you would be perfect to suggest where he should make cuts," Pierre explained.

I laughed out loud and took a stand for my fellow director. "Come on, Pierre, I know the slimy tricks you producers get up to. Michelangelo hasn't agreed to make any cuts and you are going behind his back. Well, you're not going to sucker me into cutting the film of one of the greatest directors of all time."

"Dear Ted, for one so young, you are so cynical," he said.

I had called his bluff. But to my surprise, he didn't back down. He asked how he could convince me that he was telling the truth. "It's very simple," I told him. "If Michelangelo wants me to help him cut his film, have him phone me." I hung up.

Not a half hour later the phone rang. "Michelangelo here!" said the cheery voice on the other end of the line. I was thrilled to be talking to such a distinguished filmmaker.

One of the undisputed masters of cinema explained to me that he was desperate for a new pair of eyes to look at *Blow-Up*. "I want somebody young with a fresh outlook like you to help, not some old fart director, his head full of tired clichés," he said in a thick Italian accent.

What an opportunity! Of course I immediately agreed to screen the film and make my suggestions. The plot involves a fashion photographer, played by David Hemmings, who believes that he has accidentally photographed a murder.

Directing, on a camera crane.

On one level, the film, which takes place in a single day, examines reality seen and interpreted through a camera lens. On a higher plane, it is an existential examination of the watching and making of movies.

Because the film was a cinematic masterpiece, it was difficult to suggest cuts. In the end, I gave him about 18 minutes of possible cuts that I felt tightened and clarified the narrative without damaging its structure.

Somewhat surprisingly, but very flatteringly, Michelangelo Antonioni ended up using practically all of my suggestions. He told me that he was eternally grateful and insisted on taking me to dinner when I was next in Rome.

About a year later, I found myself in Rome. Producer Carlo Ponti flew me in to discuss a film based on the novel *L'Attenzione* by Alberto Moravia. I phoned Michelangelo and we had a fabulous dinner just off the Via Veneto, the kind of Italian feast that makes you feel lucky to be alive.

Ever the student of film, and one can never learn too much as I've discovered, I pressed Michelangelo on why Italian films always have so many writers. I had noticed that *Blow-Up* listed eight writers in the credits.

"Here is why, Ted," he said. "You see, unlike you English-speaking directors, we consider dialogue to be sound effects. We believe that films are pictorial creations. You must tell the story in pictures. For example, a wife slams a door in her husband's face. Of course, you must hear a *slam*, but it's not the *slam* that is important, but what is important is this picture of a barrier created between them, that may never be overcome. Dialogue is like that *slam*. It has to be there, but it is not important. So I sit down with my chief writer and together we write the film as if it is a silent film."

I was slightly puzzled. "You mean like doing a treatment?"

"No, no, no," he said, waving his hands. "We write it like a full silent film, 100 pages sometimes, with all the action but no dialogue at all. It is all pictures. If we were in the silent film era, the script would be immediately produced. At this stage, my chief writer's work is finished, and he departs."

Michelangelo then explained the process of adding the dialogue. He would look at each scene with the producer. For example, there might be scenes of matrimonial discord. "So we will ask, 'Which writer do we know who is good at writing matrimonial dialogue?' 'So and so, he's great at husband and wife scenes.' So we would hire him to write those scenes."

There might be action sequences. Michelangelo and

the producer would discuss who is the best action writer to salt those scenes with interesting dialogue. In the end, all the dialogue added to his "silent film" script was done by several writers best at what the various scenes called for.

"Films are pictures; dialogue is for the theater," he said.

Hearing Michelangelo's process had a profound influence on me. It changed my whole thinking about filmmaking. Rather than trying to make the film understood through the dialogue, I looked at the film pictorially first and then used the dialogue to enhance what the pictures were communicating.

"

Movies were certainly a bigger puzzle than I had ever imagined. Though outwardly I was very confident and building a résumé to back it up, I did wonder if I would ever be able to achieve the mastery of the filmmaking craft like Michelangelo. What kind of film director would I become? Would I become a workmanlike director or a master craftsman? Would I even have a choice? There were so many obstacles in my path — not the least of which I was still banned from America and Hollywood, the world capital of cinema.

At the time, I studied the films of the great masters. I loved Billy Wilder's social comedies and Alfred Hitchcock's taut and brilliant thrillers, and all of the films of Federico Fellini, who really was brilliant at staging for the camera. I was also captivated by the *Nouvelle Vague* (New Wave) directors of French cinema, the works of François Truffaut, Jean-Luc Godard, and Éric Rohmer. The French, as I said before, had the perfect word for director: *réalisateur*, a realizer.

That was what I wanted to be.

INGRID BERGMAN

Howard Hawks once said that the most important element in an actor's performance is confidence. I couldn't agree more. Much has been written about how actors need to work in a protective cocoon and have absolute trust in their director to overcome their insecurities. Very early on in my career, I learned this firsthand when I worked with the incomparable Ingrid Bergman.

The opportunity was given to me in 1966 by David Susskind, one of my early champions. Because I had directed a stage play by Doris Lessing, I had earned the reputation of being a woman's director. David approached me about directing a TV movie based on the one-woman French play *The Human Voice* by Jean Cocteau. It required a tour de force performance from an actor. The entire play consists of a woman talking on the phone to her lover the night before he will consummate an advantageous marriage to a woman who comes from a rich and important family. The woman is being dumped for this marriage of convenience.

I was a bit hesitant at first about doing it; it sounded like a very difficult artistic challenge. One woman on the phone for an hour. Then David told me he had cast Ingrid Bergman. I said, "Where do I sign?" I loved Ingrid Bergman; I had seen almost all of her films.

Ingrid, who was 50 at the time, was a big-screen legend with two Academy Awards, for *Gaslight* and *Anastasia*. And, of course, she had played Ilsa in *Casablanca*. She was also one of the most beautiful women in the world. In short, there was much to intimidate a young Canadian director.

I had the great English television and stage playwright, and a good friend, Clive Exton, do a brand new translation to make the language of the play more demotic and less stilted. I then went to meet Ingrid Bergman at a farm south of Paris where she lived with her third husband, the Swedish shipping tycoon Lars Schmidt.

It was a lovely summer day. We had a long lunch on her terrace and discussed the script. She loved all the changes that Clive and I had made. She talked very intelligently about the part and was clear on how she would play it. We got along famously and couldn't wait to start rehearsals in London. Then I made a crucial mistake.

I always have a read-through at the very beginning of rehearsals to see how long a show is, so I can trim it if it's long, or add things if it's short. Since it was to play on commercial television, it had to be precisely 50 minutes.

Because it was Ingrid Bergman, the executives of Associated Television, the English company co-financing the production with David Susskind, asked to be present at the read-through, and I okayed their request. That was my mistake. On the day of the reading, three executives turned up. They stood stiffly behind me with their eyes fixed on the great star as Ingrid began to read the play.

Suddenly, for Ingrid, it was not just her and me and the stage manager. The guys in suits who were writing the checks were also watching. She became very rattled and nervous. Suddenly she felt her isolation; everybody watching her. She had a panicked realization that she had to carry this film all by herself; there were no other actors. Whereas at her home in France, she thought every line was great, now she was stopping and quarreling with practically every line. She would say that she didn't like this speech or that speech, and she complained that her character would never say such a thing, that this phrase was awkward and badly written, and so on.

I tried to calm her down by telling her that we were just reading the script for timing and that we could discuss editorial concerns later. I promised that I would attend to all her worries about the script. But that didn't calm her at all. She actually grew increasingly more rattled and edgy. I continued to try to reassure her, but to no avail. She kept quarreling with the script, getting more and more out of control.

Finally I lost my temper. "Ingrid, you are behaving like an hysterical child," I shouted, scolding her. "I told you what we are doing here. This reading is strictly for timing. Now stop behaving like some immature juvenile, and read the material as it is written on the page. Nothing is written in stone! We can resolve any problems with the script in the coming weeks of rehearsal. Now, read!"

A dead silence fell over the room. Ingrid then read the rest of the script without a hitch.

After she finished, the reading broke up without anyone saying anything else. I left quickly and went to my office.

I picked up the phone and called David Susskind in New York. I told him that I wanted to be taken off the show. He was shocked! He asked why.

I explained that I had done the unforgivable and yelled at Ingrid during the read-through. "I've yelled at crew members before when they were too noisy or not focused but never, never have I yelled at an actor. Their psyches are understandably just too fragile and easily shattered, and you can obliterate their self-confidence by vociferating at them."

David begged me not to quit.

"I have to," I told him. "This is a one-woman show, there are no other actors, and I've totally ruined the relationship between the director and its solitary star. Now the show will never work because it will be impossible for me to elicit a great performance from her."

David refused to accept my resignation until he spoke to Ingrid.

A half hour later he called me back. "Ingrid loves you. She wouldn't hear of having anybody else direct her," he said.

Needless to say I didn't believe him. "Don't be up to your slimy producorial tricks and lie to me so brazenly," I said.

"Phone her if you don't believe me," he said. "She can't wait to get back to work with you and start rehearsing tomorrow."

So the next day, I showed up at rehearsal not knowing what to expect. Ingrid greeted me warmly and there was nary a mention of the previous day's traumatic events.

I had an inspired idea: I had Clive Exton write out what was being said to Ingrid by her lover so she didn't have to imagine it. In the rehearsals, the stage manager read the lines. Ingrid was overcome with gratitude; she thought it was a brilliant idea that would help her achieve even greater heights of thespian glory. It cemented our relationship totally: we were as one. For the following days, we worked perfectly together, nuancing the material and having a laugh every now and then.

Her husband, Lars, who was the executive producer, showed up at rehearsal one day. At the end, he came up to me. "Ted," he said, "you are a very, very clever man."

"What prompted this observation, Lars?" I asked.

"On that first read-through, had you let her get away with that unspeakable behavior, *you* would have been fired that evening because you would have lost control of the production," Lars said. "After the read-through, Ingrid came home and said, 'I've got good news, Lars. Ted yelled at me. He must know what he's doing and exactly what he wants. I am safe in his hands!'"

It was a classic lesson that I kept with me my entire career. The one thing a director must understand is that all actors are insecure. In Ingrid's case, she was facing a situation where she saw a young Canadian director whom no one had ever heard of, and she thought, *Oh my God, my career is in his hands. Would he be able to evoke the best from me and recognize it when he sees it? Would he photograph me in a fresh and interesting way?* But by my showing her that I was secure, her own insecurities dissolved.

No matter how big the star is, they have to be made to feel secure, that their careers will be safe in the director's hands.

There were, however, things that Ingrid was quite secure about — namely her appearance. She was Scandinavian and, as such, totally unselfconscious about her body. The play takes place at 2 a.m. so I had her wear a nightgown. She chose a very short one. In between set-ups, I would go to her dressing room to give her notes on the upcoming scene.

Most of the time she was resting on a sofa with her short nighty having fallen open. Of course, if she was going to leave it open, I was going to look. Finally, I said to her while making a dividing line gesture at her waist, "Ingrid, from here up you're fifty, but from here down, you're nineteen."

She laughed and laughed. She loved racy comments like that.

Another day, I told her that my father had taken me to see all her films. I was obsessed with *Notorious*, particularly the scene in which she delivers a series of hot, open-mouthed kisses all over Cary Grant's face when he's on the telephone to Washington. "I hope you won't be embarrassed if I tell you this," I said to Ingrid, "but I was thirteen when I saw that provocative scene and I had my first adolescent sexual experience." Ingrid hooted with laughter. She thought it was one of the funniest things she'd ever heard. She loved that story. She kept saying to me, "I gave you your first sexual experience!"

After the shoot was over, we had an obligatory dinner with all the suits from the companies that had financed the movie, including David Susskind who had flown over from New York. Everybody was very happy with the show; the mood was celebratory. At one point, there was a lull in the conversation. Ingrid perked up and said, "It's a little known fact, but I gave Ted his first sexual experience."

All eyes turned to me. I gave Ingrid a wide Cheshire cat grin. I never told them what it was about.

The performance that Ingrid gave, the emotional depth she plumbed, her anguish and tragic despair was so real, so powerful, so moving that it's almost painful to watch. It is one of the greatest pieces of acting that I, as a director, have ever received from a performer.

CHAPTER TWELVE
Coming to America

The success and creative stimulation that I was enjoying in London did not mask the fact that I would one day need to figure out how to work in America if I were to have a big career. My immigration problem remained, shadowing me like a ghost that both dared me to ignore it and reminded me that it had to be dealt with. In the absence of any urgency, I simply waited until circumstances forced me to act, which they eventually did.

In 1967, some ten years into my London sojourn, David Susskind approached me to direct three TV shows to be shot in New York: *Of Mice and Men*, starring George Segal and Nicol Williamson; *At the Drop of Another Hat*, a show with the comedy duo Flanders and Swann; and *The Desperate Hours*, also with George Segal and Arthur Hill.

I told David nothing of my immigration problems. I thought I would merely give it a go. McCarthyism had become totally discredited. And surely, the American government would have forgotten a small fish like me who had tried to cross the border in Vermont, now more than a decade ago. I reasoned that I would swim through a hole in the immigration net — or at least I hoped I would.

So I accepted the job and flew to New York, getting more and more nervous as we approached the United States. But upon arrival, I breezed through immigration and customs without incident. Wow, what a relief! I assumed that my banishment had been long forgotten. Thank goodness!

I dug in and started rehearsing *Of Mice and Men*. One day, I was handed a form to fill out by David's lawyer, Justin Feldman. Because I was a foreigner, I had to apply for a work permit. At the bottom of the form, the last question was "Have you ever been barred from entering the United States?" I couldn't evade it. I had to answer truthfully. Because I knew that if I were caught lying, I would be immediately deported and would never be able to return to the U.S. again under any circumstances for the rest of my life.

I went to David Susskind and sheepishly fessed up. He was very sympathetic. David thought my disbarment was disgusting. He wanted me to go on his TV talk show and tell my story.

David sent me to Justin Feldman, his very powerful attorney. He was also sympathetic but instructed me that under no circumstances should I take on the American government on David's popular late-night talk show. My appearance might be provocative viewing, but it would certainly make things much worse for me with the authorities. The immediate issue was obtaining a waiver so I could direct the three shows.

Feldman was able to secure the waiver, but because there was a slight conflict of interest between David and me, he could not represent me personally. He recommended an immigration lawyer named Abba Schwartz. When I was finished directing the three episodes, the waiver expired, and I had to leave the United States and return to London.

I couldn't have asked for a better lawyer than Abba Schwartz. Abba had written the law on immigration matters concerning entry to the country. He had served as Assistant Secretary of State for Security and Consular Affairs in the Kennedy administration. He had been a vociferous advocate for more liberal and practical immigration policies. After leaving the State Department, he had returned to private practice and had written a book entitled *The Open Society*.

However, even Abba was stymied over my disbarment case, because many years previously, I had appealed to a three-judge panel. The three-judge Eisenhower panel that I had appealed to and been rejected by was non-existent now, as the original members had died and not been replaced. Therefore, there was no official body to undo their original decision. This could only happen in a government bureaucracy. And so, because the ban could not be overturned, it was reinforced.

"

Abba went to work on my case, but he hit one roadblock after another. That damn Left Wing Book Club had really done me in. Ironically, appealing my banishment while in England years earlier — the absolute right in the American judicial system — had made things even worse.

Because Abba represented an oil company in Saudi Arabia and often connected through London, where I was still living, we met regularly to discuss my situation. My case became his cause célèbre.

During the time that Abba was fighting through the bureaucracy, I hit a few stumbling blocks that made Abba's job even more difficult.

The first came in 1968.

At that time, I directed and produced charity shows for the anti-apartheid movement in England. My first show was held at the Prince of Wales Theatre, courtesy of the wonderful impresario Bernard Delfont. Practically every well-known British actor, singer, and comedian participated in the show. It was a huge success that raised a ton of money for the cause. We wanted the second show to be even bigger. We booked the Royal Albert Hall, which had many more seats. I contacted Marlon Brando to be the MC and was thrilled when he agreed to do it.

I asked Dick Gregory, the famous black comedian to MC along with Marlon and provide the comedy. He also agreed to be part of the fundraiser. And again, I added a star-studded roster of British talent from film, TV, and music.

Tickets were 100 pounds each — the equivalent of 1,000 pounds today. The show sold out in three days. We were all excited, as everything was set for a great, entertaining evening.

But less than a week before the show, Dick Gregory was arrested in some midwestern state for illegally protesting the violation of a North American Indian sacred site and interfering with the building company and workers who were destroying it. As a result, he was incarcerated.

I phoned the state's governor in hopes of springing Dick from jail. I explained the imperatives of my situation, but the governor was not sympathetic and totally immovable. He adamantly refused to let Dick come to London.

Well, I thought, at least I had Marlon.

Then two days before the big show, I received a telegram from Marlon that read:

> There is a time to render unto Caesar
> That which belongs to Caesar,
> Sorry, have to withdraw,
> Have accepted a film.
>
> Regards, Marlon.

I was screwed, really screwed. People had paid 100 pounds to see Marlon Brando and Dick Gregory. Now I had neither of them. These patrons would surely string me up from the rafters of the Royal Albert Hall.

I began scrambling. I had 48 hours to put the show together and save myself. I persuaded Marty Feldman, a very well-known English comedian, to perform the daunting task of being the MC. But I needed a big star for the show. I needed a marquee name to replace Marlon Brando.

As it happened, Sammy Davis Jr. was in town playing at the London Palladium Theatre in a production of a musical version of *Golden Boy*. The night before the fundraiser, with my stomach churning, I arranged to go backstage after Sammy's show to speak to him about rushing over the next night to the Royal Albert Hall and making a late appearance in my charity show after the curtain came down on his.

I met him in his dressing room. The place was packed with friends, agents, and hangers-on. Sammy was sweating and exhausted, having just finished his closing number. I talked and talked, but he demurred. I told him I wanted him to sing only three songs . . . just three I promised.

Sammy considered my request and begged off. "Please, Ted, my voice at the end of my show is worn and exhausted. I won't physically be able to do it."

I dropped down on my bended knee before him in front of his coterie. I actually did. Everybody in the dressing room turned to watch this drama play out.

"Sammy, you have to do this," I pleaded. "Think of your enslaved, black brothers in South Africa. They are now in the same situation your forefathers were in the South before Emancipation. They want freedom, the same freedom you have now. Do it for them, Sammy, do it for them!"

Embarrassing, yes. Shameful, most definitely. But also successful. Reluctantly, Sammy agreed to perform.

When the show opened, we announced no Marlon Brando. This news was greeted with expected tut-tutting and even a few indecorous boos from the high-paying, star-demanding crowd. But they were somewhat pacified when Marty Feldman took the stage and promised them someone equally famous was going to participate, though he didn't provide any further details.

Marty was brilliantly funny. He loosened up the audience, which was further mollified by the array of terrific British performers that followed.

Then Sammy Davis, still in the wardrobe from *Golden Boy*, bounded on stage near the end of the show. The normally reserved, buttoned-down audience went bananas. Sammy performed the agreed-upon three songs.

The audience clapped. They shouted, "More! More!" Sammy, like all famous, popular entertainers, could not resist the adulation. He kept singing and singing. In all, he sang an unbelievable 12 songs, giving a fabulous performance and blowing the audience away.

I was cock-a-hoop with self-congratulation. But then, suddenly, triumph turned to trauma. A pop group performed the closing number of my show, a bravura performance of "America" from *West Side Story*. They even used the Albert Hall's pipe organ. The instrument's passion shook the entire building. And then the tour de force: they unrolled a large piece of white cardboard on a stand. As the music of this famous song played, one of the musicians, with spray paint cans in both hands, created the American stars and stripes flag. It was brilliant. The audience went wild. What a tremendous statement!

I had already seen this done in the dress rehearsal, but it played far better before the audience — that is, until the musician who was painting the flag pulled out a lighter and lit the paper on fire. The American flag went up in flames. It was the time of the Vietnam War, and the band was clearly lodging a protest in the biggest arena they could.

I went nuts. I wanted to kill the guy. Aside from the anti-American politics, he had set a fire in the Royal Albert Hall, which was constructed entirely of wood. The venerable concert hall, which had opened in 1871, had been renovated many times, but it remained basically a building of wood. As such, it had strict fire restrictions. The fire was extinguished before it could set fire to the building or harm any of the patrons. But I was singed — badly.

I was dressed down by the Royal Albert Hall manager and immediately banned from doing anything at the hall ever again, because I endangered the lives of the paying public. The next day, the *Variety* headline was *TED KOTCHEFF BANNED FOR LIFE FROM ROYAL*

ALBERT HALL. The Hollywood trade magazine ran a detailed report of the incident.

The American Embassy in London got ahold of a copy of *Variety* and contacted Abba. He and I had visited them several times to assist us with my problem. But now I was obviously an anti-American, left-wing troublemaker who richly deserved to be kept out of the United States. First a Communist and now a flag burner!

Abba was pulling his hair out, but he swung into action. First, he arranged for me to sign an affidavit swearing that I knew nothing of the flag-burning plan in advance. Fortunately, a lot of the embassy officials were Abba's friends because, when he worked in the Kennedy administration, he had appointed many of them to their posts in London. Abba flew over from Washington, met with them, personally handed them my affidavit, and convinced them of my innocence in the affair.

The Royal Albert Hall fire was metaphorically extinguished. But not the Brits: they have never lifted the ban on me. Nevertheless, with the American authorities, we were back to square one. It had been many years since my original experience of disbarment in St. Albans, Vermont. Abba saw me when he could over the passing years, but there was never any real progress. I was giving up hope. I guessed I would never be able to enter the United States again.

During this time, I also participated in an anti-apartheid protest. The rally received significant press coverage. Bringing attention to myself as a protestor wasn't the best thing to help my plight, but what difference did it make? I didn't care if the U.S. Immigration officials found out. I was going to participate in any march for freedom that I so pleased.

At the protest, I ran into my friend Robert Morley from the British Airways commercials. I was surprised to see him, firstly because Robert always looked like the ultimate British Tory, and secondly because socialist activism can be a risk to an actor's career. When I asked what he was doing there, he turned the question back on me.

"Have you ever worked in South Africa?" he asked.

"No . . ."

"That's because you haven't been asked!" he said. "I've been asked, and I turned them down flat."

Fortunately, there were no repercussions from the American Embassy to my attending the rally.

"

Years flew by. It was now 21 years since my original disbarment in St. Albans, Vermont. On one of Abba's trips through London in 1974, he arrived at my house in Highgate. He told me that he had a plan to have my disbarment rescinded. I was all ears.

"Ted, there is only one way we can solve this," Abba said. "I think you had better sit down, because you are going to take offense at what I am going to say, but I promise you, I have examined in minute detail every possible avenue and this is the only way."

My pulse quickened. "What is it, Abba? Spit it out!"

"You have to come in as a defector," he mumbled.

"A what?!" I shouted.

"A defector," he repeated softly. "I know it's an ugly word, but it's the only way."

I couldn't believe what I was hearing. "You mean, for over 20 years, I have sworn to the American authorities that I wasn't a Communist, and now, I'm saying, 'You know, sorry, I was lying. I was a Communist. But now I've seen the light of the superiority of American democracy . . .'"

"Ted, it's the only way."

"And where am I defecting from? England? Canada?!"

"Ted, it's just a bureaucratic term. It has no reality in fact," he said, forcefully.

It took me quite a while to calm down, but once I did, I realized he was right, I had no choice. I asked him what the procedure for this was. Abba told me that I needed to provide two public utterances of my "newfound" anti-Communist position.

By happenstance, I had directed two shows that fit the bill, one of which I had also written. *Dare I Weep, Dare I Mourn?*, a film thriller for ABC in the U.S., starred James Mason as a man smuggling his father out of Communist East Germany into West Berlin. Obviously, it was damningly critical of the Communist regime in East Germany. So there was one checkmark.

The second show I directed was *The Trial of Sinyavsky and Daniel*, which I also wrote. It was a story for the CBC about two dissident Soviet writers who were secretly tried on charges of anti-Soviet writing — talk about echoes of me disseminating anti-American material. Someone had smuggled a transcript of the secret trial out of Russia, which was the basis for the show. Again, it was a damning portrayal of the total lack of freedom of expression in Communist Russia. Checkmark number two.

Abba scheduled a hearing at the American Embassy in London. I arrived armed with videotapes and scripts of my anti-Communist shows and a written speech renouncing my supposed-once-loved Communism.

It worked! The hearing lasted all of five minutes. The ban was lifted! After 21 years, Kotcheff was finally free to enter and work in America. Hurrah! I kissed Abba!

"

One often thinks, as I did, what might have been? What would my life have been like if there were no ban? But all one can do in this life is play the hand dealt by fate, circumstances, and other things beyond one's control, and just hope for the best. The main, bitter residue of the whole disbarment experience was a deep disgust with the Royal Canadian Mounted Police, for it was painfully obvious to me that they were trying to cull favor with America by providing the FBI information about Canadian citizens. I was sure I was not the only person that suffered the same punishment. My feelings for the Mounties took some time to overcome.

Though I had never been a Communist, or even a sympathizer, some file buried deep in the American Embassy still says I was. But I couldn't have cared less. The most important thing for me was that after 21 years of being prohibited from directing films in the U.S., I could now work there any time I wanted. I was deeply grateful to Abba for seeing my case through. Without him, it's likely I never would have gotten out from under the ban and been able to direct the films I have.

CHAPTER THIRTEEN

Walking with Edna

Back in 1969, when I was still stuck in London, my reputation as a director grew to the point that a BBC executive called me in for a meeting and said that she would finance any idea that I had. She wanted me to make a movie for the BBC series *Play for Today*. "Great," I said. "Do you have any scripts?"

"No, we were hoping you might have something you want to make."

"I'm afraid I have nothing at the present moment," I said honestly.

But that wasn't going to stop me from taking advantage of this fantastic opportunity. I gazed out the window. Looking down from the fifth floor, I saw a bag lady wrapped up in three overcoats, with a crumpled, sexless hat, carrying all her earthly possessions in two shopping bags. She walked at a snail's pace up Wood Lane in the drizzling rain, as she certainly had nowhere to go to seek shelter from the elements.

I don't know what possessed me, but I pointed her out to the BBC executive and said, "I'd like to make a film about her."

The BBC executive nodded and said she thought it was a wonderful idea. "How much money do you need to make it?"

Though I hadn't the slightest idea how much the film would cost, I said, "Half a million pounds."

"Smashing," she replied, "Let's make a film."

It was the quickest film deal I've ever made.

I knew just the writer for the job: playwright Jeremy Sandford. Jeremy and I had worked on a film script about the homeless in London that I ended up not directing because of other commitments. Jeremy was an odd duck. Despite being from an upper-class family, and a graduate of Eton and Oxford, Jeremy lived like a homeless person, dressed like a tramp, and wandered around London in bare feet! All year round! So Jeremy was perfect for the job, twice over — a wonderful writer who lived like a derelict.

I conceived the film as a drama in the guise of a documentary, a form I had never done before. So, of course, as usual, I needed to do my "research." In this case, because of the subject matter and the documentary style, absolutely obligatory.

First, I followed a destitute woman surreptitiously for a whole day. I couldn't walk slowly enough. Since she had nowhere to go, nothing to do, she merely wandered. Occasionally, she would stop, lost in thought, then she would wander again. People were always passing her, for they walked with a purpose: going to lunch, to a meeting, to see a friend, a lover, whatever. She was purposeless.

To further my investigations, I had the BBC wardrobe department provide me with authentic tramp's clothing: a disgusting, thick, hairy overcoat and a hat made of the same material. Of course, they were cleaned and deloused. I didn't shave for a couple of weeks, left my hair disheveled. Then one night, dressed in my costume, looking my worst, I went undercover to the Sally Ann shelter for men, off Hanover Square.

The shelter had several hundred beds, and there was a huge mess hall where, for sixpence (about a dime), you could have a hot cup of tea and a slice of bread with marge smeared on it. The place was jammed with some 600 men, derelicts and tramps — the homeless, the desperate, the depressed, and the mentally disturbed. I fetched a cup of tea and sat down, taking it all in. After a few minutes, one of its denizens approached me and stood over me, staring accusingly.

"You're a copper, aren't you?"

"No, I'm not a policeman."

"Oh yes, you are, you're a copper pretending to be one of us."

"I'm not a copper, I told you. Now sit down," I said, emphatically, "I'll buy you a tea; I'd like to talk to you."

He sat, puzzled. I brought over a tea and told him that I was writing about down and out life in England. What I discovered from him was that practically all derelict men and women had committed some truly minor theft — say, in hungry desperation stealing an apple from the stands outside a greengrocer — and they then think they are on a wanted list, and the police are looking for them. This is exactly what my new acquaintance had done: filched an apple.

Thinking my tramp disguise was very good, I asked him why he thought I was a copper. "Because you looked around with curiosity."

This was spot on. Of course, everyone in the hall was not looking around at all. Some had their depressed heads in their hands, almost all were looking down at the ground or into their tea. They were so absorbed in their own pain, they didn't make eye contact or attempt to engage with anyone. Meanwhile, I was looking around, scanning wardrobe, attitudes, mannerisms, and traits, making me an easy stand-out.

Furthering my research, I was going to sleep upstairs in the vast, multi-bed dormitory. I walked to the bed reserved for me, listening to the snoring and farting, the air redolent with the unwashed. I looked at the pillowcase, gray and grimy, and decided there was no way I could put my face to it. Research be damned, I left.

Another great assistance to me in my research was going out with London's St. Stephen's Society every night for a couple of weeks. We brought hot soups and bread to the homeless all over London the whole night through, served from the back of a long paneled truck. There were places where the homeless always gathered to sleep: under Charing Cross Bridge, Waterloo, Victoria Embankment Gardens, a church in Covent Garden, and many others. That's where we went, and that's where the derelicts awaited us. So every night I encountered every variety of destitution. And, unlike the Sally Ann, there were both genders to observe.

There are certain things I think every man and woman should have to do before they get their license to be a human being. Two of them are: work at an abattoir for one day, and go out with the St. Stephen's Society every night for a week. I met and befriended an extraordinary variety of people on these nightly trips, and saw some touching things like an indigent middle-aged couple sleeping in a cardboard box in a damp churchyard. The man lovingly drew up a long piece of cardboard like a blanket, covering his beloved up to her neck. Her gaze at him was filled with such love.

Another night, I met a man, filthy in shabby charity clothes, who, in a few sentences, as he received his soup, revealed himself to be a very intelligent and articulate man. I asked one of the St. Stephen's people if they knew his story. I was told that he was a full professor of philosophy at a major English university. His wife had dumped him, taken his two young children, and disappeared with them somewhere in the United States, never to be seen again. He had a nervous breakdown. He fell apart totally and became this derelict that I met nightly.

What a piece of luck! I obviously wanted to talk to him about the derelict world that I was going to make a film about, as I was sure he would have some interesting and useful observations. I invited him to have dinner with me at a good restaurant that I frequented. I had alerted the headwaiter of the restaurant ahead of time. Even so, upon our entrance he gave me an alarmed look and sat us at a table hidden in a back corner next to the toilets. We looked at the menus, and I noticed they had meatloaf as a special that night, so I said, "I love meatloaf, that's for me."

The professor said, "I wouldn't have that if I were you."

I said, "Why not?"

"It's not very good here."

"How would you know?"

"Well, I eat their garbage regularly, don't I?"

Besides his culinary advice, the professor provided me with other invaluable information. The best places to panhandle for money and when to do it: payday Friday afternoon near a cash machine. He filled me in on the everyday life of a homeless mendicant: where you go to eat, relieve yourself, the best parks to sleep in not to be hassled by the police (I've seen the police approach tramps sleeping on park benches and forcefully smack the soles of their feet with truncheons to drive them off), and where you sleep in bad weather, which was an abandoned subway station way out in the suburbs. And always, a vagabond's life involves walking great distances having no money even for public transportation — walking mile after mile for food and rest, for no one would ever give a derelict a lift, not even a garbage truck.

I went to that abandoned subway station that the prof had told me about. I ultimately shot some of the scenes in my film there. The only fluttering light came from several small camp fires scattered around the abandoned, run-down station. It was full of ghostlike figures, some huddled, some wandering.

Hunched over a sputtering fire, bundled in the obligatory profusion of various overcoats, was a bearded man. His eyes, reflecting the fire he was warming himself over, gave him a kind of Satanic look. I was freezing, so I asked him if I could share his fire. He motioned for me to squat down. I asked his name; he told me he was God. I inquired how he knew that. He said that he had been praying to God for a very long time, talking to Him, asking Him questions, pleading with Him, when he suddenly realized he was talking to himself. "So I must be God, mustn't I?" It was hard to argue with his logic. I asked for his blessing. He gave it.

Since the leading character of my film to be was a woman, and since I couldn't spend a night in a homeless women's hostel, I persuaded my wife, Sylvia, to do it for me and give me a report. There was a large women's hostel in the suburbs of Nottingham, near a freeway. We drove up, then I pulled over. It was getting dark. I let Sylvia out, and she walked the mile to the hostel. She knocked, and the woman in charge opened the door and looked at this well-dressed woman, slightly baffled. Sylvia told her she needed a bed for the night.

"Why, what happened to you?" the woman asked.

"My husband and I had a violent argument driving up the freeway," she said. "He pulled over suddenly onto the shoulder, opened the door, kicked me out of the car, and drove off taking my handbag with him."

"The bastard!" said the manager. "Of course you can stay here."

Sylvia was a bit apprehensive about her bed-to-be, but she was astonished how clean and orderly the dorm was. In the bed next to her, a homeless woman had picked up a tin can, filled it with water, placed a wild flower in it, and set it on her bedside table. How different from the male dormitory at London's Sally Ann.

There is no question that women are mentally stronger than men. When men become derelict, they disintegrate, become total wrecks. They don't wash, they don't take their toe-jam filled shoes off for weeks, and they lose complete control over every aspect of their lives. Women never sink so low, neither in their personal hygiene nor their emotional behavior. And they still keep some semblance of their life heretofore. They never lose it completely. With men, little or nothing of their previous life is visible. All the middle-class social characteristics, all the bourgeois virtues and values evaporate. There is no question in my mind that men are the weaker sex.

Jeremy Sandford's script was absolutely brilliant. It was entitled *Edna, the Inebriate Woman*. And what made the film really work was the amazing performance of the woman I so luckily cast in the role of Edna, the homeless wandering vagabond, the actress Patricia Hayes. The only thing I had ever seen her do was a feed for Benny Hill in his comedy show. Her performance set the style of the film, for it was quirky, poignant, funny, lovable, irascible, daring, explosive, and her resiliency was never crushed by her endless setbacks.

There were two idiosyncrasies Jeremy gave Edna, which were absolutely wonderful. One was she hated being referred to by social workers as "the vagrant." She would not be dehumanized and reduced to that bureaucratic category and always went wild when she was called that. "I am not the vagrant!" The other touchingly funny quirk Jeremy gave Edna, whenever she was within earshot of a ringing telephone, be it at a social security office or a hostel, she would cry out, "That's for me!" It was very moving that she so desperately wanted for someone, anyone to be calling her. No one, of course, ever did.

There was one amusing incident that occurred during the shooting of the film. The scene was Edna walking away from the camera down a wide sidewalk begging for money from anyone she encountered. Not actors, but real people. I placed my camera smack in the middle of the wide sidewalk in the Victoria section of London. There is a law in England that does not exist in the United States: if a film camera is in full sight, whatever it photographs is in the public domain. Therefore, whatever ordinary passersby are accidentally caught on camera, you don't need their permission to use them in the film, and you cannot be sued later for invasion of privacy, or defamation, or for any other reason.

I line up a shot for Edna, the Inebriate Woman, *filming on a London street in 1968.*

As Edna went down the street, holding out her hat, some people gave her a shilling or two, but one disgusted gentleman said, as he turned his whole body sharply away from Edna, "Get away from me!" He said it in a very callous way. Obviously, we used that shot in the film, as it's a perfect example of the typical, unfeeling attitude of the general public toward vagabonds.

The day after *Edna, the Inebriate Woman* was broadcast, I received a call from Scotland Yard! From a woman (secretary, detective?) who told me that the man who so uncaringly refused Edna the pittance she asked for was one of the heads of Scotland Yard. The scene in the film had made his life a total misery by his family and his colleagues. Everyone was razzing and taunting him about how he could've been so heartless to that lovable Edna — and she was lovable; the show was a huge hit mostly because the audience loved Edna.

The caller was asking for a favor. She heard that the show, being so hugely popular, was going to be repeated shortly. "Could you spare this man further embarrassment and teasing by excising the scene he appears in?" she asked. Of course, I agreed, and I hope it was a salutary lesson for him to be more charitable in the future.

"

When I screened *Edna, the Inebriate Woman* for myself to write about it in this book, I had not seen it for 40 years. I was bowled over by it, which surprised me. I don't always feel that way when reviewing my early work. The creation of a huge panoply of characters, the graphically eloquent faces of those that dwell in an invisible netherworld and are always with us, the rejected, the hurt, the damaged, the wretched who live a life of endless wandering in perpetual quest for the next meal, the next bed.

Although some clips of *Edna* are on YouTube, you'll probably never get to see it in its totality, so you'll have to take my word for how good it is. If my word is not good enough, then you'll have to listen to the word of my professional industry colleagues. The British Academy of Film and Television Awards (BAFTA) are a British version of the Emmys and Oscars combined. In 1971, *Edna, the Inebriate*

Woman swept the BAFTAs, winning best single play, best director, best script, and best actress.

Then in the year 2000, further honors. The British Film Institute organized a group of industry professionals to determine what were the 100 greatest TV programs ever screened in the U.K. in the 20th century, covering all genres. Out of a list of 650 possible shows, *Edna, the Inebriate Woman* was selected as one of the 100 greatest.

Yes, to have a film achieve artistic recognition always gives me a tremendous boost. But there is nothing more gratifying to a filmmaker than seeing one of his films having a deep and positive social impact. *Edna, the Inebriate Woman* is a frightening depiction of what it was like at that time to live at the mercy of society's day-to-day rescue services. It moved and affected a lot of people.

For many years after *Edna* first came out, it was constantly circulating in schools and social science organizations under the auspices of Christian Action and other charitable groups. As a result, more and better hostels were established, and a more humane, compassionate attitude toward the single homeless was engendered. For that, I still feel proud.

CHAPTER FOURTEEN

Realizing *Wake in Fright*

During the 1960s, my immigration situation had me worried about my career. When I was not allowed to film in the U.S., it seemed like a massive impediment that would interfere with my developing filmic abilities. But looking back, the restrictions forced upon my career had the opposite result; some artists do their best work when they are constrained. I am one of those. Being boxed in and bottled up brought out the best of who I was at the time. Hollywood being out of the question, my attention turned away from my hero, Billy Wilder, to great European filmmakers like Fellini, De Sica, Olmi, and Truffaut.

Aside from England, the only other English-speaking country with any film industry to speak of in the early 1970s was Australia. Luckily for me, my résumé was strong enough to attract a feature-film-directing opportunity in Australia.

It was 1970 — keep in mind that I would not have my immigration hearing until 1974. I was feeling awfully depressed about the human and political situation at that time. Personally, of course, I had been banned from the U.S. over a stupid political game that stemmed from the Canadian authorities wanting to suck up to the U.S. authorities. I had watched the world come so close to committing global suicide in a nuclear war, as President Kennedy and Soviet Premier Khrushchev stared each other down in the Cuban Missile Crisis. The Vietnam War seemed without end and certainly without purpose. Even in England, where I was living, there was a massive pro-test movement against what had become a senseless war. Overall, I was in a very dark and despairing mood, which permeated the film I was about to make.

My directing stock was at its highest to date due to the kudos received by *Edna, the Inebriate Woman*. By this time, two Hollywood directors that had risen to prominence had come out of directing live television drama, Sidney Lumet and John Frankenheimer. Lumet had made *12 Angry Men*, *The Pawnbroker*, and *Long Day's Journey into Night*, and Frankenheimer had directed *Birdman of Alcatraz* and *The Manchurian Candidate*. Because of their success, my expe-rience in directing live television drama was deemed a real plus, as producers are always certain that lightning in a bottle can be repeated.

The Australian project was *Wake in Fright*. It came to me from a writer named Evan Jones. We had worked together on my film *Two Gentlemen Sharing*, about the racial situation in London in the 1960s, and had become close friends. Evan told me that he had been hired to adapt an Australian novel of the same title written by Kenneth Cook. (By the way that title, *Wake in Fright* comes from an

Australian adage: "You dream of the Devil and you wake in fright.") Evan handed me the book and said, "I know you Ted; this subject matter is right up your alley." I read it and Evan was right. I loved it.

Evan recommended me to the two financing production companies: an American company based in London, Westinghouse Group W. Films, headed by Peter Katz, and NLT Productions in Australia. Peter Katz hired me to direct the film. Evan and I worked on the script in London, but unfortunately, there was no money in the budget to bring Evan to Australia. So I would have to do the final polish of the script myself after seeing the reality of the Outback. Make no mistake though, Evan Jones wrote the screenplay, and a brilliant job it was.

My then-wife, Sylvia, and our three children, Aaron, Katrina, and Joshua, arrived in Sydney in November 1969. We moved into a rental house in an area of Sydney called Vaucluse somewhere near Nelson Bay, where at Christmas we enjoyed watching people have their flaming Christmas puddings on the beach.

Wake in Fright tells the story of a young, self-righteous schoolteacher in the Outback named John Grant who leaves for a trip to Sydney during the school's Christmas break. But his plans are waylaid when he stops over in an Outback town and loses all of his money gambling. He ends up stuck there, lodging with a nihilistic, alcoholic, defrocked doctor named Doc Tydon. Consequently, his life falls into a world of drunkenness and moral turpitude, one man's descent into hell.

I responded very strongly to the novel's theme — that of hyper-masculinity — and its intense atmosphere and subject matter. At the core, I saw the story as a voyage of self-discovery. John Grant, the school teacher, starts off believing that he is better than all the people around him, but he finds out that he isn't and that we are all in the same existential boat. He discovers bitter truths about himself and mankind that he never contemplated.

As a filmmaker, I have always been attracted to characters who know nothing about themselves like John Grant and Duddy Kravitz, perhaps because I often feel purblind and groping about what motivates some of my own behavior. I'm also drawn to characters who are outsiders I think because, as a foreigner of Bulgarian descent, I always felt like an outsider growing up in Anglo-Saxon Canada. Of course, the situation of man versus his community is naturally full of interesting conflicts; it's the bread and butter of drama.

Initially, I was a bit worried about making a film depicting a world whose customs and mores I knew very little about. It is getting the behavioral details right that is the essence of filmmaking. However, when I arrived in Australia, I discovered the Outback was not dissimilar to northern Canada — the same vast empty spaces that, paradoxically, instead of being liberating are imprisoning. I used to describe Canada as "Australia on the rocks." It boasted the same hyper-masculine society, the same separation of the sexes.

I remember early on, Sylvia and I went to a swanky party in Sydney's Point Piper. The women were congregated at one end of the room and all the men at the other. Sylvia grew tired of talking about salads and hats and wandered over to our male group, hoping for more interesting chat. She reported to me later that all the men looked at her as if she was a tart. She quickly got the message and returned to the women's group, where she received steely eyed looks reserved for husband-stealers.

I understood and admired the men of the Outback: their fortitude, their camaraderie, their generosity, their support of each other in the most inhospitable world in which they worked and lived. I had met such men in the north of Canada.

The film was budgeted at $800,000. Gary Bond, a British theatrical actor described as a young Peter O'Toole, was cast as the schoolteacher, Grant. I first offered Michael York the part of Grant, but he passed. (Years later, I bumped into Michael, who told me it was the worst mistake of his career.) I cast Donald Pleasence as the bizarre Doc Tydon. I had seen Donald give an amazing performance in Harold Pinter's *The Caretaker* and had cast him in one of my first *Armchair Theatre* dramas playing the president of the United States. My wife, Sylvia Kay, who was a very accomplished stage and television actor, was also in the film.

I remember when I was casting the other parts of the film in Sydney and Melbourne, many of the male actors who came in for auditions would squeeze my hand very hard during the handshake. One actor crushed my hand so much, I yelped in pain. When I asked him what the hell this was all about, he told me apologetically that in Australia, you tell someone you're an actor, he automatically thinks you're a "poofter." The hand crushing is supposedly an expression of manliness.

I remember meeting an actress who talked to me with an unexpected and obvious note of contempt for me during her interview. In the course of the audition, she mentioned that she had seen a wonderful film two days ago called *Two Gentlemen Sharing*. When I told her that I had directed it, she was incredulous. She then went on to explain her earlier attitude — that only failures, hacks, and the dregs of the American and British film industry would come to

Australia to make a film. Australia, seemingly, at that time was the last refuge of the untalented and the unsuccessful.

"

When you wish to learn anything and everything about a town in which you will be filming, take the editor of the local newspaper out to dinner. They know everything that's gone on, going on, and is going to go on. They know where all the bodies are buried, as the saying goes. The editor of Broken Hill's local newspaper, *The Barrier Daily Truth*, came out with a startling fact: the men in the town outnumber the women three to one.

"Three to one!" I said, "Where are the brothels?"

"There aren't any."

"Is there a lot of homosexuality?"

"Homosexuality?! Certainly not! This is Australia, mate."

"Well, what do they do for human contact?"

"They fight." I discovered the truth of this observation subsequently, and I'll expand upon it later.

I felt for these men, outnumbering the women so distressingly. I remember a time when I was looking for locations in China in 1979. I had broken up with my girlfriend at the time, and my only companion was my producer, John Kemeny. I was missing feminine company oh so acutely. I said to John, "You're a very nice man, John, a pleasure to be with, but if I don't speak to something soft soon, I think I'm going to lose my mind." Perhaps this was the reason that so many of the men I encountered later in Broken Hill had already lost theirs.

The editor, at the conclusion of our dinner, suddenly displayed the same inferiority complex that plagues

Canadians, saying, "You've come here to rubbish us, haven't you?" Provoked, I was tempted to reply sardonically, "My sole and only purpose." But my good sense prevailed, "No, I don't condemn and criticize; I observe and empathize. I'm never the judge of people, I am their best witness." He seemed a bit bemused by this high falutin' explanation.

I then set out to do my necessary research. I always do this on my films, but in this particular instance it was imperative. In spite of some superficial similarities to northern Canada, I had to get the details of life in the Outback totally right. Three things are done for recreation in Broken Hill: drinking gallons of beer in pubs, or "hotels" as the locals call them; playing the slot machines in the Returned Serviceman's League Club; and gambling in the Two-Up School. So these were where I started.

With the assistance of my location manager, John Shaw, I searched for a very specific location: a pub in the middle of nowhere in the Outback, surrounded by hundreds of miles of nothing in every direction.

I loved the Outback. It seemed like a different planet. Everything had unusual colors and shapes. The earth was orange, the leaves on the trees were blue, and the vegetation was deep purple. D.H. Lawrence described it perfectly in his novel *Kangaroo*: "the Outback was like some vast creature, always watching you." At times, standing in total emptiness, I felt as if someone was watching me. I'd snap my head around to catch who it was. Of course, there was only empty space.

As we drove through the Outback, looking for the aforementioned location, on dirt roads full of sharp, flinty stones, our vehicle blew a tire. Soon after, we blew our spare tire. We were stuck in the sweltering heat. Remember, there were no cell phones then. As I escaped the sun in the vehicle, John Shaw lay under it.

We waited.

After a while, we saw a vehicle's dust in the distance, perhaps 20 miles away. It took an eternity to reach us. The driver gave us his spare tire! I offered to pay him, but he refused money. He said, "You'll help me next time. With these dirt roads, I'm sure to find myself in the same pickle," and drove off. I found this often, men supporting each other generously in the difficult circumstances of living and working out there.

Finally, I saw exactly what I was hunting for: a pub completely isolated in the surrounding desert. As an added attraction for me, it had a 30-foot beer bottle on its roof. We turned off the road, bounced and bumped our way across the open desert, and arrived at the pub.

The place was perfect. It was a Sunday, and the pub had about 30 cars parked around it. Each car had a woman inside it with a beehive hairdo, cooking in the extreme heat. They were waiting for their men, with the odd woman popping into another car for a gossip. Women were not allowed into pubs. *Boy*, I thought, *does this country ever need more feminists like Germaine Greer*.

From inside, I could hear loud, raucous laughter. I said to my location manager, John, "Wow, the exterior is great, absolutely perfect for our film! Let's go inside and see if its interior is also good for us to shoot."

John demurred. "Let's come back tomorrow when all the men inside are back down the mines and on the sheep ranches."

"What, drive forty miles out here from Broken Hill tomorrow and lose another two tires? Why? We're right here!"

"Ted, they're not crazy about outsiders around here, and they are especially not crazy about outsiders who look like you."

John was referring to the fact that, at the time, I resembled a hippie. I had hair down to the middle of my back and a long, droopy handlebar mustache.

"Let's go in," I prodded him. "They're never going to hit charming Ted Kotcheff."

"If you want to go in, it's your funeral; I ain't going in with you."

"Well, I'm going in."

Full of bravado, I left the car, but as I did so I thought to myself, *John Shaw looks like a rugby player, built like a brick shit house. If he's afraid to go into the pub, what the hell are you doing, Kotcheff?* But, as I was committed, I kept going. So, I lose a few teeth . . .

I entered the pub. It was like a scene from a John Ford western. All the talking and laughter in the pub ceased as 40 pairs of drunken eyes watched me cross to the bar in total, unnerving silence.

I asked for a schooner of ale, by this time I knew the local lingo. Conversations resumed. Then a drunken man standing right next to me, leaned toward me and examined my long hair. He growled a drawn out "Shiiiiiiiiiiiiiiiiiit." Then he leaned toward me once more and scrutinized my handlebar mustache and growled again, "Shiiiiiiiiiiiiiiiiiiiiiii iiiiiiiit."

I just kept drinking and smiling, saying nothing. Then, shoving his face aggressively toward me, his chin up, he said, "Hello, Stalin!"

I remained silent, raised my glass toasting him, and drank.

In a very loud voice that quietened the whole pub,

jutting his chin even closer, he repeated, "I said, hello *Stalin*!!"

He was inviting the reply, "Who the fuck are you calling Stalin?!" Biff! Right on his chin! All eyes were upon me, awaiting my reaction. I smiled and said, "I'd love to talk to you, but I'm dead."

For three seconds, no one got it. Then it sunk in. They all laughed uproariously, including my interlocutor.

He yelled out, "I love a bloke with a sense of humor! Publican, give this man another schooner of ale!"

Soon, I was surrounded by a group of men. They bought me drinks; I bought them drinks. In no time at all, I was six pints behind. They poured their beers down their gullets with such incredible rapidity, I couldn't keep up with them. An Australian once told me that every day eight pints of beer are consumed by every man, woman, and *child* in Australia. These men were making up for the children and the women.

We drank together for hours, and about a half-dozen of these men became my mates and protectors. The entire time, John Shaw was outside in the car cooking. No guts, no glory.

Subsequently, still pursuing my "research," I would go out at night into some crowded pub, order a drink, and, inevitably, someone would want to fight me. A voice would cry out from someone hidden in the crowd, "Burt, leave Ted alone! He's my mate." The voice belonged to one of the men that I had befriended in the "Stalin pub." Burt replied, "Oh, sorry Jack! Hey Ted, let me buy you a beer." I don't know how they did it, but wherever I went in my explorations, there was always one of them looking after me, protecting me. Their stewardship continued all the many weeks that I shot in Broken Hill. I now understood the concept of "mateship."

The other thing I began to understand was that all the men who wanted to fight with me didn't want to hit me, they wanted me to hit them. I grew up in the Cabbagetown streets of Toronto. I learned at a young age the answer to the question: how do you win a street fight? You start it. You punch first, he goes down, then you put the boot in, kicking his nuts so hard he's immobilized. Fight over.

All the men who wanted to fight me in Broken Hill would stick their jaws forward. One swift punch from me, I could have broken their jaw in three pieces. I remembered what the newspaper editor told me, they were all yearning for human contact, someone to put his hands on their flesh.

I used this insight in a fight sequence in the film where Donald Pleasence and the two kangaroo hunters are rolling around on the ground furiously, wrestling with each other, but it's in a close embrace. I wanted to reveal that desperation for human touch that I witnessed repeatedly. Everywhere I went in Broken Hill, I felt the men's corrosive loneliness.

"

A very important sequence in the film, a turning point, is where the schoolteacher loses all of his money gambling in a Two-Up School and becomes stuck in a town that he loathes. John Grant hates being a teacher in the Outback, but the government needs teachers out there, so to ensure a steady flow of qualified candidates, the government requires that aspiring pedagogues must spend three years teaching in the Outback in order to get a full teaching license. To be sure that you fulfill your term, you must also post a bond of 1,000 dollars.

When John sees the money being won in the Two-Up gambling game, he can't resist participating to win the 1,000 dollars that will buy him his freedom.

Two-Up is a very uncomplicated game. John Grant snobbishly refers to it as a "simple-minded game." In a space about 30 feet by 12 feet, groups of men sit, stand, and squat all around its perimeter, taking turns throwing two old-fashioned, large Australian pennies, each about an inch in diameter, that are placed on a wooden tablet. The thrower stands in the center of the space, hurls them up into the air, and they come down on the floor. Two heads wins, two tails loses; any other result, you throw again.

Before the throw, the bettor lays down his wager. Once it is covered, everybody loudly makes side bets on the outcome, many times yelling across the room, "I got ten dollars on heads!" Somebody on the other side would yell back, "You're on, mate! I've got tails." The betting is noisy and rowdy. I was always surprised that there was never any cheating. If you won, the loser would cross the space to your side and hand you your winnings. You have to throw the pennies over your head. If you just drop them, as the schoolteacher does in the film, the throw is invalid, whatever the result, and you have to throw again.

Wanting to experience it myself, I began to play. I soon became addicted to Two-Up in Broken Hill, as there's nothing much else to do there on a Saturday night. The associate producer of the film, Maurice Singer, joined me, and he became addicted too.

One night, Maurice threw 21 straight pairs of heads. The odds against doing this are astronomical. He threw and, squatting on the floor, I controlled the betting. I cried

out, "I'll take any tails, any tails!" (Pronounced "tiles.")
After each pair of heads that Maurice threw, everyone
thought he's bound to throw a pair of tails now, so tons of
money were being thrown at me. Soon, I had a huge pile
of cash on the floor before me.

Maurice and I won about $12,000. The owner of the
Two-Up school locked the doors, came to us, and said,
"Boys, you've got a ten minute headstart before I unlock
these doors." He let us out, and we ran like hell through
the dark streets of Broken Hill, back to the motel where we
were staying and hid the money.

However, after the euphoria of winning had dissipated,
I felt really bad. I said, "Maurice, these poor guys, sheep
ranchers, opal miners, zinc miners, we stripped them all
of their whole weekly pay. We can't hand them back their
money, it would insult their manhood."

But I had an idea, to which Maurice agreed. We threw
the biggest bash in the history of Broken Hill, inviting all
the Two-Up players. All you could eat, all you could drink,
and dancing! With the lack of women, men were dancing
with men.

When we got back to Sydney for the remains of the
shoot, I couldn't give up my Two-Up habit and went to a
game pretty regularly, somewhere in Paddington. This is
the game that I shot in the film, and I used all its regular
players as extras in the Two-Up scenes. The extroverted
Aussies were all natural actors.

We had printed a lot of money to be used in the scene,
and the property people went a bit overboard in the look
of the money. It was tantamount to counterfeiting. The
Two-Up scene took five days to shoot, and each night
the prop people would come to me and say, "Ted, some of
the money is disappearing."

I stage the Two-Up game in Wake in Fright *with all my Australian gambling pals.*

I was forced to address it. "Listen, I love gambling with you," I told the players. "You've become my good friends, and I don't want anything bad to happen to you. Keep the money as souvenirs only, but please don't try to pass this fake money as real — you know it's a very serious offence and you'll go to jail for a long time. I beg you, don't try it."

Of course, two men did. They tried to pass the money at a racetrack and got caught, much to my distress. And I almost got busted myself, for aiding and abetting.

It is worth mentioning here that the Two-Up Schools themselves were highly illegal, but no sheriff in his right mind would enforce that law and close them down. The miners in Broken Hill would send him packing with a black eye, or worse.

"

We shot the film in the heart of the Australian Outback. The conditions were brutal. It was perpetually 110 degrees in the shade — and there was no shade. There was endless dust swirling from the dry, desert floor, and there were flies everywhere. To ward off the flies, I had a hat with small corks hanging on threads from its brim, and as I moved my head, the corks would swing back and forth hoping to keep the flies out of my eyes and mouth. Still, every time I yelled "Action," a fly would pop into my mouth. I figured that every day of the shoot I consumed at least a dozen flies. I can assure you, it is not a gourmet dish.

One of the things I wanted to do in my film was make the audience feel what it was like to be out there in the Outback: experience the heat, the dust, the sweat, the flies. I used what the German philosopher Leibniz called *petite aperceptions* — small apperceptions. Translating this concept to film, *petite aperceptions* are the small details that you put in every frame that have a subconscious effect on the audience.

For instance, if I shoot a close-up of an actor, the frame also captures what is behind the actor, such as the things hanging on the wall or sitting on a shelf or the color of the wallpaper. Even though the viewer is concentrating on the actor's face, subconsciously what is behind the actor will affect the viewer's reaction to the actor himself. By contrast, if I shoot the actor against a white wall, the viewer's perception will be entirely different.

I set up a shot in Broken Hill.

Before filming began, I met with the production designer and the wardrobe supervisor, and told them that I did not want to see one cool color in the film. "I never want to see blue or green in the wardrobe or in the wallpaper, or anywhere else. I want only hot colors — yellow, red, orange, brown, and burnt sienna. I want the intense heat of the Outback to be omnipresent, keep the audience sweating in their seats throughout the whole film."

Something else I did when we filmed the interior shots was that I ordered an insecticide squirter and a barrel of Fuller's earth, a fine dust used for special effects. I had the dust tinted the color of the Outback desert. Before every

My Australian crew for Wake in Fright.

take, I squirted it over everything in the frame, covering it with a fine layer of dust, and pumped it into the air, so motes of dust would be hanging there.

I also ordered hundreds of sterilized flies from a lab in Sydney. Before rolling the camera on the indoor shots, I would release 20 or so flies, so they were buzzing around and crawling all over the furniture. Though the audience would not focus on the flies, the dust, or the hot colors, these small apperceptions would register on that part of their eye that would obliquely sense these things and affect their subconscious.

One of the things I am proudest of in my film is how

powerful an atmosphere of oppressive heat, discomfort, and dust was created by my attention to these minute details. After viewing the film, one of my friends said, "I've got to get home and have a shower."

"

The most controversial part of my film was the climatic kangaroo hunt. In the hunting sequence, the teacher ends up participating in a brutal kangaroo slaughter. The yahoo in him, who unfortunately exists in all of us, takes over. It climaxes with one of the hunters engaging in hand-to-hand combat with a kangaroo.

There is no way in the world that I would ever hurt an animal. Not only would I not kill or hurt an animal in the normal course of life, I wouldn't sacrifice one hair on its body for a scene in a movie.

As a young man, I had seen a film that horrified me. The film is about three World War I veterans who return to their awful, provincial French town, totally dehumanized by their experience of the war. They don't know what to do with themselves; so for amusement, they pour gasoline on a stray dog and ignite him. It was painfully obvious from the length of the shot of the burning dog that they had done this for real. The director had actually set fire to a dog to show man's inhumanity. For me, the only cruel and inhuman person in the mix was that fucking director.

I had no idea how I was going to do this climactic sequence, this kangaroo massacre, without hurting a kangaroo, as this was well before the days of computer-generated images. The scene was critically important to the film, but I was not going to kill or harm kangaroos to realize it. While I was puzzling over my dilemma, a member of the crew who lived in the Outback told me that hundreds of kangaroos were killed every night there.

When I expressed surprise, he explained the reality to me. "It's a big, lucrative business," he said. "They kill them for the American pet food industry."

"You mean, American cats and dogs are fed on kangaroo meat?" I said, outraged.

"That's right, but not only that, they skin the kangaroos and use the pelts to make those nice, cuddly Koala bears you give your kids for Christmas."

I was furious and disgusted.

The crew member told me how it all worked. There was a large refrigeration truck that would act as a kind of base from which six stake trucks, each one having two hunters in its cabin, would go off in different directions looking for kangaroos. After killing the kangaroos, they would decapitate them and skin them. After killing about 16 kangaroos and hanging their bodies on butcher's hooks around the edge of their stake truck, they would return to the refrigeration truck to unload them, then go back out to get more kangaroos. Once the refrigeration truck was full, it would drive a long-distance haul to the docks to ship the meat off to America.

The stake trucks were outfitted with large spotlights on the top of the cabin, operated from within, which when shone on the kangaroos hypnotized them, causing them to freeze in place, thus making them very easy to shoot. My crew member suggested that maybe I could persuade a pair of these hunters to let me ride along and film the hunt like I was shooting a documentary.

That was exactly what I did.

It was a harrowing experience for me and my British producer, George Willoughby. We started out at 8 p.m.

We rode standing in the bed of one of the trucks with a camera mounted on the top of the cabin next to the light. The two hunters sat in the cabin down below, which had a retractable windshield; when it was raised, it allowed them to rest their guns on the dashboard and kill from their seats. The men were quite proud of their jobs and their knowledge and expertise in killing kangaroos.

One of the hunters asked me where I would like them to shoot the kangaroos. He explained that they could shoot them in the kidneys, in the heart, or in the brain.

"What's the difference?" I cringed.

"Big difference, mate," he said. "If you shoot them in the kidneys, they drop dead right on the spot. If you shoot them in the brain, they take one enormous leap into the air, then they die. But if you shoot them in the heart, they take three huge hops and then die."

I shuddered and told the hunters, "Please don't do anything special for me. Please, please, just get on with the job that you do every night."

They did just that. They shot kangaroo after kangaroo. Suddenly, I heard a thump behind me, I turned around, my producer had fainted from the barbarity and horror of it. We returned to the refrigeration truck with a full truck-load of corpses and an unconscious producer. While we were there, one of the older men told me, "All hunters have a saying: you must never look into the eyes of a kangaroo. If you do, you'll never be able to kill another one again."

We returned to the hunt minus one producer. After shooting several dozen kangaroos, I noticed at around 2 a.m. their bullets were hitting the kangaroos but not killing them. The truck would then have to try and chase the animals down to put them out of their misery. I can't tell you how upsetting it was to see this happen. The wounded kangaroos would be bleeding and trying to flee to safety. Fountains of blood would be spurting out of their nostrils. Some escaped, disappearing into the darkness, to a death that would be protracted and painful.

I couldn't understand what was happening. Why were they missing? For the first five hours, they were incredible marksmen, dropping the kangaroos with expert accuracy. After seeing this horrible butchery happen several times, I leaned over to look into the truck cab below to see what was happening with the hunters. On the dashboard was a half-empty bottle of whiskey. That was why they were missing and torturing these poor kangaroos. I almost vomited.

Everything I did with animals on my film was under the auspices of the Royal Australian Society for the Prevention of Cruelty to Animals. When they saw the footage I shot from 2 a.m. to 5 a.m., they told me that I had to use it in the film to show the world the inhumane treatment of the animals. "Ted, you don't understand, no one in the big cities like Sydney, Melbourne, Adelaide knows that this is going on in the Outback," the representative told me. "We have to show it to them."

I told them that I completely sympathized with what they were trying to achieve, but I couldn't show that footage. It would be hard enough for the audience to stomach kangaroos being slaughtered with a single bullet, but to show them suffering horribly and bleeding to death would send people running up the aisles and out of the theater. Instead of showing it in the film, I told them that I would give them all the footage I did not use. They could do with it what they wished as ammunition for their cause.

"

During the film shoot, I felt a real kinship with the kangaroos. For some reason, the kangaroos gravitated to me. On one occasion, when I was filming with them in a fenced-in area, they were lounged at the foot of my director's chair, resting their heads on their hands in a very human fashion.

In fact, kangaroos are the most anthropomorphic creatures I have ever met. I tell people that they were like the character Nick Bottom in *A Midsummer Night's Dream*, who wore a donkey's head over his head. I felt that a kangaroo was going to lift off his head and say, "Ted, it's me . . . Bottom." Now I understood what that old hunter meant, why, if you look in to their eyes, you could never kill one again. The look in their eyes is so unbelievably human.

I developed an extraordinary relationship with the kangaroos that is hard to explain. I hope you won't think that I'm delusional when I say I could communicate with them telepathically. We came upon a "mob" of kangaroos in the wild, and I quickly set up the camera for an establishing shot. The lead kangaroo was 20 feet away and I needed him to move to the left. I would think, "Jump left now," and the kangaroo would do it. If I wanted him to move toward me, I'd think, "Take three hops toward the camera." And the kangaroo would respond with three hops. It was uncanny.

But when it came time for the hand-to-hand fight scene between a kangaroo and the actor Peter Whittle, I could not get any of them to fight. I would joke that they were followers of Gandhi. They are brave creatures, but when they felt that the odds were too heavily against them, they would just lay down in a relaxed fashion around me and my director's chair and refuse to fight. Even the University of Sydney zoologist on set could not make them engage.

I turned to the kangaroo wrangler for help. We had built a huge pen the size of a football field, with a high fence covered with muslin the color of the desert, so that one could not see it by day, let alone at night. I told the wrangler to set free the six kangaroos lying around me and go find six more. He headed into the Outback and returned, herding six fresh kangaroos into the pen.

One of the kangaroos was eight feet tall and had only one eye. From the look of where the other eye had been, we surmised it had been shot out by a hunter. I nicknamed him Lord Nelson, after the British naval commander who was blinded in one eye early in his military career. This kangaroo was the Moby Dick of kangaroos. Having had his eye shot out, he vehemently hated all human beings. He was ferociously angry and wanted to rip us all to shreds — which was exactly what I needed for the fight scene.

In the scene, Peter Whittle's character gets into a mano a mano with the kangaroo, hoping to cut its throat with a knife that he has in his hand. Before I filmed the scene, the zoologist explained to me that in self-defense, the kangaroo uses its arms to lock anyone threatening it in a close embrace. They have a prehensile tail, which means they can lean on it like an extra limb, allowing them to lift their powerful legs inside that embrace, kick you, and break every bone in your body.

The fight scene was scheduled for three whole nights, but I filmed it in three hours because Lord Nelson was so relentless, he kept going after Peter time and time again. He never stopped. How Peter was able to act in the face of this eight-foot tower of animosity, I'll never know. There could be no stunt man. To keep himself from being mauled, Peter's character gets behind Lord Nelson and lifts up the kangaroo's tail off the ground. The kangaroo is now helpless. Peter pretends to slit his throat.

The expenditure of energy by both combatants was

Herculean. After we had completed the sequence, something strange happened: Lord Nelson and Peter, both totally exhausted, had bonded. Lord Nelson realized Peter meant him no harm and rested his tired head on Peter's shoulder. It was a very moving sight.

We had been turning four cameras to cover all the action. I spoke to my camera operators, "Did we get everything?"

"We got fantastic material," they all said.

I told the crew, "Let's give Lord Nelson a big hand!"

The entire crew applauded him. The kangaroo looked around puzzled, wondering what these human beings that he despised so much were doing.

I then ordered the gates open. "Lord Nelson, you did a terrific acting job. You can now go back to your friends and family in the Outback." He wasn't sure about this, coming from an untrustworthy human being. He took four exploratory hops to see if anything untoward was going to happen. He stopped and looked back at me. "I mean it, Lord Nelson, you are free; have a wonderful life." He turned and hopped off into the darkness.

The truth is, you always need luck on a film. And Lord Nelson was a really huge piece of good fortune. I never would have gotten that sequence without him.

"

The film, which was being distributed by United Artists, was shown at the Cannes Film Festival in 1971. For a filmmaker, this is the ultimate accolade. I was thrilled. I flew to Cannes for the screening.

It was a magical experience. I dressed up in my tuxedo and walked up the sweeping red-carpeted steps of the grand Palais. Here is where all the great film auteurs that

I so admired, like Truffaut, Godard, and Fellini, had come to present their masterworks at the most prestigious film festival in the world. I took my seat front row center on the first balcony, the customary place for directors whose films are being shown. The festival jury walked out to their seats, bowed to me, then the screening commenced.

The balcony where I sat was reserved for people in the film industry: writers, directors, and producers, most of them from European countries. But there was one American seated immediately behind me who kept voicing his feelings all though the film. He would say, "Wow, what a scene!" or "This is terrific." He made continual comments of approbation — music to a director's ear.

Some people were shushing him, but he didn't seem to care. He carried on with his observations. When the climactic, homosexual rape scene came on, he resorted to play-by-play. "This director is going to go all the way ... I think he's going to go all the way ... oh my god, he went ALL THE WAY! Fucking fantastic! Absolutely BRILLIANT!"

I kept wondering to myself, *Who is this guy?*

When the lights came up, the audience applauded. I stood and gave an appreciative wave. I then glanced over my shoulder to see where this running critique was coming from. He was a young man, no older than 25, wearing horn-rimmed glasses. Because of where he was sitting, he had to be in the business, but I had no idea who he was.

Outside the theater, I pointed him out and asked the two United Artists publicists working on my film who he was.

"Eh, he's a nobody," one publicist said. "A young American director who has only made one film, and it flopped."

"Well, I'd like to know his name," I said.

"You wouldn't have heard of him," the second publicist countered dismissively.

"What's his name?" I insisted.

"Uh — it's kind of an Italian name . . . Score-something . . . Oh yeah, Scorsese. Martin Scorsese."

"You're right, I've never heard of him," I said.

Dissolve to 40 years later. A further accolade, *Wake in Fright* was declared a Cannes Classic and was going to be screened once more at the festival. Guess who was in charge of selecting the Cannes Classics? Yes, Martin Scorsese, who unbelievably remembered my film after 40 years. That kid director, of course, had become one of the greatest American film directors of his generation.

At that time, only one film had ever been screened twice at Cannes, Michelangelo Antonioni's *L'Avventura*, and now mine was going to be the second. I can't tell you how thrilled I was to have one of my films reach the cinematic heights of one of my greatest idols.

In the intervening years, wherever the film was shown, be it in a cinema or festival, Martin Scorsese would generously provide me with quotes to use in the publicity and on the posters. Here's one example from 2012: "*Wake in Fright* is a deeply — and I mean deeply — unsettling and disturbing movie. I saw it when it premiered at Cannes in 1971, and it left me speechless. Visually, dramatically, atmospherically, and psychologically, it's beautifully calibrated and it gets under your skin one encounter at a time, right along with the protagonist played by Gary Bond."

Although I often wrote to him to thank him for all his incredible assistance, I had still never met him in person. Finally, I spotted him at an Oscar party held at the Beverly Hills Hotel. He was huddled with Robert De Niro. I went over and introduced myself and thanked him for his endless praise of *Wake in Fright*. I regaled De Niro with the story of how, way back in 1971, Martin had talked through the whole screening in Cannes.

De Niro laughed. "Ted, he talks through everybody's films. But you're one of the lucky ones. He *liked* yours."

Back to 1971: Because of my film's success at that year's Cannes Film Festival where both critics and audiences loved it, *Wake in Fright* ended up playing in Paris for nine months. The French love films showing men under existential stress. However, France was the only country where *Wake in Fright* succeeded.

When the film was released in Australia, in spite of a very strong critical response, the popular reaction was lukewarm. I think people there were a bit affronted by the depiction of the Aussie male as a drunken, brawling kangaroo hunter. Jack Thompson, one of the Australian stars of the film, told me that at one cinema, a man rose, pointed to the screen, and yelled out, "This is not us!" Another voice cried out, "Sit down, you fool; it is us."

United Artists, the U.S. distributor, did not believe in the film at all. The head of distribution said, "Americans are not going to come out to see this film. It's far too tough." They wanted to change the film's title to *Outback*. I argued with them, "You make it sound like a National Geographic documentary. What's the matter with *Wake in Fright*?"

"Sounds like a Hitchcock film."

"That's bad?!"

"Yes, especially when you don't deliver Hitchcock."

Many years ago, at a dinner following a screening of my second film, *Life at the Top*, I sat next to a guest of the screening, Julius Epstein, one of the writers of *Casablanca*. He said to me, "Ted, you're a wonderful director. You're young and you've got a great career ahead of you. I'm sure you'll fight like hell to preserve the integrity of your work, but there's two areas you can save your energies in your fight with the distributors because you'll never win: titles and endings."

I lost the argument; the film was released under the bland title, *Outback*. Despite the fact that the film received many positive reviews — the influential critic, Rex Reed, named it one of the 10 best films of 1971 — United Artists abandoned the picture. They opened it in a small art house theater in New York with no advanced publicity whatsoever on a Sunday night in a heavy blizzard. No one saw it except for the projectionist. The United Artists executive turned to me, "Told you nobody would come." Distributors are very good at self-fulfilling prophecies.

It was shown nowhere else, and that was that. As time passed, the prints slowly disappeared out of circulation. The film was never released on video or DVD, so no one was able to see it again. *Wake in Fright* seemed to be one of those films that was lost and forgotten.

Cut to 1996, 25 years later. One of the Australian producers, Bobby Limb, began making inquiries on what had happened to the original print and the negative of *Wake in Fright*. The canisters containing the negative of the film could not be found in Sydney, where the production company was based, nor in London, where the film had been processed. The film had seemingly vanished. Bobby Limb hyperbolically declared it to be a national disaster.

Then the editor of the film, Tony Buckley, took up the challenge. He loved *Wake in Fright*, believing it to be an Australian masterpiece, and spent the next 13 years trying to track down the negative. Between jobs, he traveled from Australia to London, Dublin, and New York searching for it, all at his own expense. He was incredibly persistent and, in 2007, finally found the film in a warehouse in Pittsburgh of all places — over 200 cans of negative, dialogue tracks, music tracks, interpositives, and internegatives in two large wooden containers. On the outside of the containers was written in big red letters *FOR DESTRUCTION*. Had Tony arrived but one week later, the negative would have been incinerated and my film gone forever.

The Australian National Film and Sound Archives immediately stepped in. Two women from the archives, their handbags full of cash for outstanding storage charges, flew to Pittsburgh and arranged for the negative to be shipped to Australia.

Negatives need looking after, frequent waxing to protect them. *Wake in Fright*'s negative, ignored for over 25 years, was torn, damaged, and hopelessly faded, meaning that a traditional photochemical print could not be made from it. Another fan of the film, Anthos Simon of Deluxe Labs in Sydney, volunteered to help on his own time. Using the latest digital techniques, he spent two years restoring the film, frame by frame by frame. The result is absolutely stunning. There are colors, details, and patterns in the restored film that I had never even seen in the original. The brilliant, exotic colors of the Outback — along with all the *petite aperceptions* that I had worked so hard to put in my film — are captured with amazing fidelity. I was deeply touched that my film was saved by two people who truly love it.

What happened to *Wake in Fright* was not some singular occurrence. Unfortunately, as I discovered, it happens all the time. If a film is perceived a failure, it's deemed worthless and not even worth the cost of storing the film cans. It's dumped and destroyed.

Fortunately, *Wake in Fright* was given a new life. The film was re-released in theaters in the U.S., Australia, and Canada in 2009 and later in Great Britain. The reviews were outstanding everywhere. Australian musician and screenwriter Nick Cave said the film is "the best and most terrifying film about Australia in existence." In 2009, *Filmlink* in Australia declared it the best Australian film ever and said it was "a ball-tearing, long unseen masterpiece." This time, the film was a huge success in its home country.

Roger Ebert called the film "still powerful and crushing," and wrote that "Kotcheff's film is raw and uncompromised, well acted, brilliantly photographed, and edited. It's rare to find a film that goes for broke and says to hell with the consequences."

Perhaps even more satisfying was that the film had a lasting impact on the lives of kangaroos. About 15 years after the film was first released, a woman from the Royal Australian Society for the Prevention of Cruelty to Animals called me and told me that, as a result of my film and the additional footage that I had shot and turned over to them, a law had been passed forbidding the killing of kangaroos for the pet food industry. I was so exhilarated. It's very rare that a film can have such a profound social impact.

Then, as mentioned, the Cannes Film Festival, under Martin's guidance, heard that the film had been rescued and asked to see the new print. Nearly 40 years after its premiere there, the festival declared *Wake in Fright* a Cannes Classic. And so, in 2009, I returned to Cannes for the black-tie screening of a film I consider to be one of my best works.

I truly felt like I had become a *réalisateur.*

GREGORY PECK

Gregory Peck had a magnetic persona that was omni-present on screen. He was exactly what everyone should be: a committed humanist. He displayed this quality in films like *Gentleman's Agreement*, decrying anti-Semitism, and *To Kill a Mockingbird*, attacking racism. What you saw onscreen was what he was. Gregory had a natural heroic dignity, being both morally and physically courageous.

My first meeting with Gregory Peck was certainly unforgettable. Gregory had a gorgeous classic villa on the Côte d'Azur in the south of France. He invited Norman Jewison, my producer, and me to come down from London and spend some time together with him so we could get to know each other, discuss the script for the project we were working on together, *Billy Two Hats*, and so on. Of course, Norman and I readily agreed. Not only was Gregory perfect for the part, if we could get a top star like him to agree to play the lead in the film, it would be an automatic green light for its financing and production.

For our first night in France, we were invited to come to his villa for dinner. Gregory was a warm, easy, amiable host. He told us that he hoped we wouldn't mind that he had asked his neighbor David Niven, the well-known British film star, to join us at dinner. Mind? Norman and I were thrilled. David Niven turned out to be a very witty man and, at dinner, he regaled us with an anecdote of something that had happened to him recently, which had us laughing for days.

It was a common practice in those days for the studios to arrange dates for their upcoming stars with their big, existing stars. They would go to restaurants that were the haunts of the rich and famous, like Romanoff's. Photographers would be alerted, they would stand outside the restaurant awaiting the star's limo, pictures would be taken of the arriving couple that would appear in all the film magazines. They would be an item in all the tabloids' gossip columns. The studio's own PR people would churn out coverage of the event, sending it to all the big newspapers in New York and other major cities. The relatively upcoming star would become better known with much speculation about a romance in the making.

In keeping with this ploy, the studio had arranged for the young David Niven, recently over from Great Britain, to have a date with the glittering Joan Crawford. He arrived all spruced up to pick her up at her sumptuous home in Beverly Hills.

The butler let him in. David entered its grand hallway with its impressive, winding staircase up to the second floor. Ushering David into the living room, big as a playing field, the butler informed him that Miss Crawford was not

On the set of Billy Two Hats: *Gregory Peck on his horse.*
Seated next to me are Desi Arnaz Jr. and Jack Warden.

quite ready but would be down shortly. Meanwhile, would he like a drink?

After waiting about 15 minutes, he thought he should phone the restaurant that the studio had arranged for them to say they would be a bit tardy. The butler said he could use the phone that was directly under the top of the staircase. While he was talking to the restaurant, he suddenly felt drops of water, like rain falling all over him, even splashing into his drink. He looked up to see where the water was coming from: it was Joan Crawford at the top of the stairs.

Joan Crawford had her skirt up and, panty-less, was peeing all over him!

Gregory, Norman, and I laughed for five minutes at this fantastically funny picture. Finally, I asked David, "What did you say to her?"

"Well, being an English gentleman, I said, 'It's very nice to make your acquaintance, Ms. Crawford. And thanks for opening yourself up so generously.' Drops were still falling on my upturned face."

More gales of laughter!

"Of course, I had a perfect view of the delicious private parts of her anatomy, and I had been christened by her perfumed pee all over my jacket," he added. "Why, we achieved immediate intimacy, perhaps the propitious beginning of a romantic entanglement."

I asked him, "Did you at least finish your whiskey?"

"Ted," he said, "I did draw the line at finishing my single malt *au pissoire*. But my perfumed jacket and all, she and I had an enjoyable evening out. And I had several scotches *sans pisse*."

There is nothing like shared laughter to weld people together. Gregory had a good sense of humor and a winning, boisterous laugh. I knew we would get along. I've never cared for humorless people. And I don't like humorless art. As I said before, life, for me, is a strange admixture of tragedy and farce.

The following day we strolled through his beautiful gardens discussing the script and his character. Gregory said he liked the script very much, and he told Norman, my producer, that he liked me and what I had to say about the film. Norman and I looked at each other triumphantly; we were in business.

We came to shoot *Billy Two Hats* in Israel of all places. You might well ask what in the world we were doing making an American western in Israel. Well, everybody's heard of spaghetti westerns, I guess this was going to be a kosher western.

United Artists, the film's distributor, wanted *Billy Two Hats* to be made outside the United States. They had made a lot of money with their films abroad, and they did not wish to bring these profits into the United States where a big chunk of them would be gobbled up by American taxes. United Artists said they would only finance the film if it was not shot in the U.S., so they could use their foreign assets. So I began scouting locations abroad.

I went to Spain. They had a western town there, but it and its surrounding landscapes had been photographed endlessly by the Italian directors. Nothing would be fresh.

Norman asked me if I would consider Israel, primarily because if I chose it, he would be shooting *Jesus Christ Superstar* in northern Israel at the same time that I would be shooting *Billy Two Hats* in southern Israel. This would allow him to be able to visit the production on weekends. Norman Jewison's film *In the Heat of the Night* had won the Academy Award for Best Picture in 1967, so you can imagine how great his assistance would be to me.

So I scouted Israel. I went out into the Negev desert. It was spectacularly photographable and it looked exactly like the Mexican–New Mexico borderlands, where my film was set. It had the same unforgiving, bleak, barren beauty, perfect for my story. Because it was a story of my two central characters being pursued by the law, one was able to see someone coming from ten miles away. And, surprise, a rich Israeli-American had hired a top Hollywood production designer to design and build an entire period western town just outside of Tel Aviv in hopes of having the same success in attracting filmmakers as Spain had with the spaghetti western producers and directors. The town had never been used. I would be the first to film in it. Directors love virgin sets and locations. Israel it was.

Two months later, the line producer, Pat Palmer, and I were working very late in our production offices located in a Tel Aviv motel. We were buried in a ton of production problems. We were scheduled to start shooting in ten days. Gregory Peck was to arrive from California in three days, as I like to rehearse the script for a week to iron out any script problems beforehand and not on the shooting set where time is so expensive.

A knock came on our motel door. I yelled out, "Come in!"

Two burly men walked in wearing raincoats and sunglasses. At midnight? In the desert? I said, "What are you two cops doing out so late?"

"How did you know that?" one guy asked.

"It was my perceptive director's eye. What's up boys?"

"We're agents from the Mossad," the guy replied. "I'm afraid we have some unfortunate news for you. We have received some intelligence that a group of terrorists are planning to assassinate Gregory Peck when he comes here.

He's the first major Hollywood star to come to Israel in years. So, can you imagine the attention it would receive all over the world if they pull it off? That's what they're after."

Pat and I just sat there stunned, speechless. "What do you suggest we do?" I asked.

The agent replied, "Well, we have a very experienced agent, name of Harry, who can be his bodyguard."

"He'll take a bullet for Gregory if anything happens?"

The agent steeled his gaze at me. "Yes. Of course."

After a lot of discussion and planning, the Mossad agents left.

Pat and I sat dead still for a seeming eternity. What the hell were we going to do? Then I reached for the phone and started dialing. "Who are you calling?"

"Gregory, of course; let him know what's going on," I said. "I talked to him earlier and he's in his Beverly Hills home."

Pat got up and pressed down hard on the telephone, cutting me off. "You'll do nothing of the kind."

"What do you mean?"

"Ted, if he learns about this, how's he supposed to act when he thinks that at any moment some crazed terrorist is going to leap out from behind some bush and take a pot shot? And if we phone him, Gregory might withdraw from the project and we'd be in the toilet."

"Pat, it's his *life* we're talking about."

"He's got the bodyguard protecting him who will take the bullet. We will see to it that he is well guarded all the time. He'll be okay. Anyway, how reliable is this 'intelligence'?"

I demurred. The argument went on back and forth vociferously for hours.

Finally, Pat lost his patience with me. "Ted, I am ordering you, as the producer of this film and United Artists representative, not to contact Gregory."

"Okay Pat, on your head be it."

The following day, I met Harry, the proposed body-guard for Gregory. To this day, I cannot tell you what he looks like. He was totally featureless to the point of invisibility. I used to say that when Harry entered a room, you felt that someone had left. When Gregory, Harry, and I were in the same room together, Harry disappeared into the wallpaper. Later I would remember this encounter as an intimate tête-à-tête with Gregory, just the two of us.

Harry had been handcuffed to Adolf Eichmann for nine months during his trial in Israel for his horrendous crimes against humanity, for being a major organizer of the Holocaust and the extermination camps. In case a surviving concentration camp victim tried to kill Eichmann, Harry was ready to protect him. I was incredulous: he would take the bullet for Eichmann?!

Gregory Peck arrived in Israel. We had a warm reunion. I told him we were a bit behind with our filmic preparations, so I was postponing our rehearsal for three days. Why didn't he visit some of the sights? I suggested the Wailing Wall, the Via Dolorosa, and the Dome of the Rock.

I introduced him to Harry, his "driver," and off they went. At the end of the first day of touring, Gregory came to me and told me about his day. "Harry's wonderful, so attentive, always by my side. At lunch, Harry went into the kitchen to see if my lunch was being well prepared." (I knew that he was tasting it for poison.) The second day, the same. The third day, Gregory stormed into the production office. "Why didn't you tell me that Harry's not just my chauffeur, he's my bodyguard?"

I apologized, saying we didn't want to worry him.

"Ted, you think I'm a fool?" Gregory said. "When I was at home in Beverly Hills, didn't you imagine I'd have thought about this and knew that I might be a target? But it wasn't going to stop me. I wasn't going to have my life run by some Middle Eastern crazies."

"God Gregory, what guts. You're like the hero in one of your movies." I hugged him.

"And Ted, I'm so glad I have Harry to take the bullet for me," he said.

"How did you find out that Harry was a Mossad agent and a bodyguard?"

"We were going through the Arab quarter in Jerusalem," he said. "When people recognized me, they were all clapping and cheering. A young girl, ten or twelve, came toward me, offering me a bouquet of flowers. This being the traditional way of assassinating someone, with a gun hidden in the flowers, Harry immediately responded instinctively. He walloped the girl, knocking her to the ground, and quickly searched through the flowers to see if there was a gun. There wasn't. I picked her up and took her to her family. I apologized, and they accepted me, laughing and welcoming me into their abode. That is how I found out that Harry is not merely my chauffeur, but also my bodyguard."

Every film is an adventure. Not necessarily as adventurous as this one, but an adventure all the same. You have to be on your toes, ready to deal with the unforeseen and the unexpected, for there are surprises galore. I love it.

Finally, after all this pre-production excitement, Gregory and I started shooting our film. Gregory Peck was one of the most sweet-tempered men that I have ever met. He had not a trace of meanness or pettiness, and there was no insistent ego whatsoever.

But no actor is without his distinctive, personal idiosyncrasies. One day, I was shooting one of his lines as he sat on a travois and the production manager brought a visitor onto the set just as I yelled "Action." Gregory glimpsed the stranger out of the corner of his eye, and he flubbed his line, totally uncharacteristically. I told him to start again, gave him my "Action." Again, he flubbed the line. I told Gregory to do the speech again, and he flubbed it once more. A fourth go on his part, and he flubbed it again.

There was something puzzling going on here that I didn't understand. Soon after, he stumbled again. I said, "It's almost the end of the day, let's just shoot Gregory getting up from the travois to exit the shot. We'll pick up this scene tomorrow."

At dinner that night, I asked Gregory what happened. Gregory explained the situation. "Well, I see this total stranger, and I stumble on a line. Having flubbed once, I flub again. Then I think what that stranger must be saying to himself, 'Boy, look at the great Gregory Peck. Can't even get a simple line out!' I flub again. 'They're paying him all that money, thousands of dollars, look what you get!' I stumble again. 'He must be physically or mentally damaged.' It's over, I can't get the line out."

Of course, from then on in, I banned visitors from coming to set.

He had one other minor peculiarity. He was obsessed with his acting being real and never being fake. Once I had a close-up of Gregory, and I told him, "You see this Indian on horseback riding across the top of the mountain from left to right." I said, "Action."

But instead of doing the scene, Gregory stopped. He said, "Excuse me, Ted, where's the Indian on the horse?"

I said, "Come on, Gregory, you can pretend. That's acting, pretending."

"Ted," he said quite seriously, "I feel fake if I'm pretending to see the Indian. It's so much easier to respond with authenticity, seeing the real thing. Can you have an Indian ride across the mountain please?"

It was late in the day. I was worried about the time, but I didn't want to argue with him. I turned to the AD and said, "Howard, get one of our Indians, put him on a horse, and have him ride across the top of the mountain."

Fortunately, I had brought to Israel Apache tribespeople; the governor of New Mexico's wife had helped me cast the roles. So we waited while the real Apache man rode his real horse to the top of the real mountain. We waited quite a while, patience not being one of my virtues. Finally, the actor was ready for action on his walkie-talkie. The sun was going down. "Action!" Gregory gave a very convincing performance of someone watching an Apache man riding across the top of a mountain. From then on, whenever I asked him to look at something off-camera, I made sure it was there. I consider it a very small price to pay for the performance Gregory gave me.

But aside from these two minor peccadillos of his, Gregory was a consummate actor. He had to play the part with a subtle Scottish accent, indicating he was an immigrant to America, and he mastered it perfectly, listening endlessly to his language recording.

Each day was a revelation working with him. As I pointed out earlier, both of us were students of the Michael Chekhov method of acting, and Gregory Peck wrote an introduction to Michael Chekhov's book *To the Actor*. This allowed me to use Chekhov's approach and terminology when I was directing him. It made it so easy to communicate to Gregory the subtle shades of performance I was pursuing. He understood what I was after and provided it so immediately and so brilliantly.

CHAPTER FIFTEEN

Duddy and Me

The Apprenticeship of Duddy Kravitz changed my life — not instantly, mind you. It took 15 years.

When I moved in with Mordecai to share his flat on the top floor of a condemned house in Swiss Cottage with decor by Charles Dickens, he had just started writing the novel, his fourth. It took him two years to complete. The novel was hilariously picaresque, yet a heartfelt tale of a third-generation immigrant who lived in the St. Urbain Street Jewish ghetto in Montreal. He was the consummate schemer who desperately desired and ruthlessly aspired to be a somebody. The basic question of the novel was posed to Duddy Kravitz by a gangster: "Kravitz, why do you always run around like you've got a red hot poker up your ass?"

Upon completion of its creation, Mordecai literally lifted its last page from his hot typewriter and asked me to read the novel. I finished in one sitting, all 350 pages.

"Not only is this the best Canadian novel ever written," I declared, "but one day I am going to go back to Canada and make a film out of it."

We then both laughed at the absurdity of the idea because, of course, there was no Canadian film industry whatsoever at that time. And though one realistic side of me saw that no British or American company was going to finance a film about a Canadian Jewish Sammy Glick, another part hoped that I might find the exception.

In the meantime, I was able to convince *Armchair Theatre* to let me do a few chapters of the novel. Mordecai and I made a one-hour TV play of the part that takes place at a Jewish summer resort hotel where Duddy works as a waiter. But the show didn't turn out very well, because it was difficult to cast Brits as Canadian Yiddish characters. The idea for making it into a feature film seemed even more like the pipe dream of a couple of naïve Canadian expats, but I never let it go. And I always kept envisaging the film.

For years and years, I struggled to find someone who would be interested in financing a film based on *The Apprenticeship of Duddy Kravitz*. From the day that I read the novel in that dingy apartment, whenever I would meet a film producer, I pressed a copy of the book firmly into his hands, telling them with absolute, true conviction what a fantastic movie this book would make.

But after a decade of trying, I still did not have a single taker.

And then, participating in the Venice Film Festival was a film I had directed in England entitled *Two Gentlemen Sharing*, about the racial situation in London in the 1960s. Also in attendance at the festival was an American producer, Sam Arkoff, who was vice-president of a distribution company called American International Pictures (AIP). He purchased *Two Gentlemen Sharing* and distributed the film in the United States in 1969. Sam told me in Venice over lunch how much he liked my films and asked what else I was working on. I gave him the novel, and he responded immediately.

"Ted, I love this book!" he said with the gusto of a true Hollywood producer. "And I want to produce it."

Oh, thank my lucky god, I thought with a sigh of relief. I was unbelievably elated. Never mind that AIP's stock-in-trade was making raucous movies like *Beach Party*, outlaw biker movies, and assorted low-budget horror films. With the stroke of a pen, Sam Arkoff had the power to put *Duddy Kravitz* into production.

". . . but," he paused. I've hated "buts" my entire creative career. "Buts" never bode well. He sipped his wine. "But there's one thing: I don't want Duddy to be Jewish. I want him to be Greek."

"Greek? Greek! But Sam, the story is about this Jewish kid in a small Jewish enclave surrounded by a mammoth Catholic metropolis," I said. "He's staring at a cross at the top of Mount Royal flashing *Christianity* at him all day long. When Mordecai was ten, he witnessed students marching through his Jewish ghetto in Montreal crying, '*À bas les Juifs!* Down with the Jews!" I said. "The students then committed their own version of Nazi Kristallnacht, smashing the windows of Jewish shops. When Mordecai was a kid, French-Canadian kids chanted as they danced around him, 'You killed Jesus Christ! You killed Jesus Christ!' This is what Duddy faces and has to triumph over. This is what has shaped him. That's the point of the film. It's what makes him sympathetic! He has to use his French-Canadian girlfriend to buy the properties he is chasing, because the French-Canadian farmers won't sell their land to a Jew!"

In spite of my diatribe, there was no turning Arkoff around. No matter what I said, either Duddy would be Greek — Dudopholous Kravopolous perhaps — or Arkoff was out, and I was back to beggar's row.

It was an easy decision for me. No matter how badly I wanted to make the film, I couldn't violate the integrity of my best friend's masterpiece. I had watched him slave over the novel for two years. The story was so close to him, and now to me, that there wasn't even a small chance I would make Duddy a Greek.

However, I did understand where Arkoff was coming from in general. He was part of an entire generation of Jews in Hollywood who did not wish to make films about Jews and never did.

I had one other strong nibble from another important producer, but he wanted to set the story in Pittsburgh. His reasoning? Montreal was too parochial. "And Pittsburgh isn't?" I said. "The working-class steel capital of the world where a man's beer gut was a point of pride? No, I'm not setting it in Pittsburgh." And then he said, "No, I'm not doing the film."

Was this to be my fate with this project? It seemed to have insuperable obstacles to it ever being made.

More time flew by.

"

Not only was *The Apprenticeship of Duddy Kravitz* a brilliant novel written by my dearest friend, but also I had become obsessed with the lead character. I felt I knew him well and the world he inhabited. He was an outcast, as I had been growing up. Colorful, shady characters populated Duddy's world as they populated mine.

When I was 15, I worked at my dad's restaurant that he had recently purchased, Norm's, a small diner in a run-down area of Toronto. As I said, the place was populated by colorful characters, some on the fringes of the underworld: bookies, pimps and prostitutes, blind pig owners, drug dealers, con men, and artists — you name it, they hung out there for breakfast, lunch, and dinner. I came to know them all very well.

One of the bookies came to me and said, "Ted, I've got a hot tip for you. There's a big fix on the sixth race today. Put everything you've got on it." He gave me the name of the horse. I was always getting these kinds of tips, but this one somehow convinced me. He told me it would put me through university. So I put $20 on the nose, which was a lot of money for me those days. He won at 15 to 1. With the $300 in winnings, I paid for my first year at the University of Toronto.

One small-time crook that came to Norm's was called German Johnny. He was the black sheep of a prominent family that owned a brewing company back in the beerland of Milwaukee. Johnny would dress up in an expensive suit and take a well-dressed woman with him to a jewelry store. They would pretend to shop for a wedding ring. The salesman would bring out a tray of diamond rings and, when he turned his back, German Johnny would quickly swap a real ring with a zirconium copy. Although he came under suspicion, the jewelry stores couldn't prove it. Still, he did it so often, he was banned from all jewelry stores. These guys were very much like the characters in the town at the beginning of *Duddy Kravitz*.

The summer when I was 14, I worked at the Old Mill Restaurant as a busboy. It was one of the top restaurants in Toronto, similar in feeling to the one at the resort where

Duddy works. I told Mordecai some of my experiences there and he incorporated them in his novel.

The food at the Old Mill was wonderful, but the waiters never got to eat a bite of it. At 5:30, before the patrons arrived, all the waiters and busboys sat down to our dinner and we were served what could be called, at best, "second-hand food" brought in from god knows where. The dessert was the same every night: stale apple and cherry turnovers. They tasted like cardboard.

One day, the dessert chef called me over to his station and solved that problem. "Hey kid," he said surreptitiously, "when people order wine with their dinner they rarely drink it all, these Canadians; bring the bottle back to me and I'll put aside some good desserts for you."

Done deal. I watched all the patrons who ordered wine, and I had many corks in the pocket of my white busboy's jacket. The second the guests left the table, I would whisk away the leftover wine, jam a cork back in, lay it on my busboy's tray, cover it with used napkins, head for the dessert chef's station, and slip it to him. I was slipping bottles to him all night long.

The dessert chef, mind you, wasn't picky. Red, white, rosé, he liked them all — and he liked them all mixed together. He would pop the cork out and pour all the varietals into the same gallon jug he kept below his pastry workspace. When the restaurant closed, we would sit out back, and as he drank his blended wine, I'd savor one of my wonderful desserts.

One evening at the staff's 5:30 pre-opening dinner, I was enjoying an exquisite Napoleon topped off with a dollop of homemade ice cream. The other waiters, who were French and German, were gagging on their stale apple and cherry turnovers. A stoic German guy eyed me with disgust.

"Alright, Kotcheff," he said, disapprovingly, "what Jew tricks did you get up to for that dessert?"

"I'm not Jewish," I replied.

"Yes you are!" he insisted. "You're a Jew and you're pulling Jew tricks for that dessert."

I felt as if I were back in my childhood, asking my father if we were Jewish and him saying, "Almost . . ." As poor Bulgarians, we were only a half step above the Jews.

There I was, a victim of anti-Semitism, and yet I wasn't Jewish. I got to feel what every Jew must endure. I didn't mind, I used it directorially later.

The whole "wine story" had literary value. I told Mordecai the story, and he threw in a wonderful line about Duddy, who was able to cajole the cook into giving him his orders quickly: "The gift of a bottle of rum insured the cook's goodwill — Duddy had no trouble getting his orders."

When I finally made *The Apprenticeship of Duddy Kravtiz*, I built this up in the film.

In one scene, Duddy is in the kitchen, waiting impatiently for his entrees. The chef shuns him and gives the entrees to another waiter. Duddy realizes that the other waiter is somehow paying off the chef.

So, one night after the restaurant closes, Duddy gives the chef a bottle of whiskey as a "present." The chef, in return, begins giving Duddy his orders quicker than the other waiters, ensuring him bigger tips.

One night while working at the Old Mill, I had the most extraordinary experience. I observed a couple in their mid-20s. They smelled like money. I felt certain I would get a big tip. Like Duddy in the novel, I kissed ass — but instead got a piece of something else.

Shortly after the couple ordered, they started arguing. They were angrily whispering and gesturing harshly at one another. While cleaning up a nearby table, I could read their lips: "You cunt," he said. Her reply, "Don't call me that, you piece of shit."

The argument grew even more heated. In a moment of anger, the woman swung her hand and accidentally knocked over the bottle, sending red wine all over the table. *Shit*, I thought, *there goes my dessert!*

The headwaiter rushed over to me and told me to change the tablecloth immediately.

Changing the tablecloth required great dexterity. We busboys had been warned never to reveal the top of any table because they were all so unpleasantly scarred. We were taught to roll the new tablecloth on as we rolled the old one off. While I was engaged in this tricky process, I put my hand below the tabletop to smooth out the new cloth. The wife grabbed my hand and put it between her legs — right on her minge!

I was 14. I was confused and embarrassed. I struggled, but she wouldn't let go. The husband was scowling at me. He wanted me to get the hell away so they could resume their argument. Little did he know! Finally, I pulled my hand away. I rolled up the stained tablecloth and slid away as gracefully as I could.

I glanced back at the woman. She was smiling triumphantly at her husband, as if to say, *You don't know it, but I had my way with that 14-year-old boy!*

Wow, Ted, I thought, *you have a lot to learn about women.*

99

The natives finally came through for Duddy Kravitz.

In 1967, the Canadian government set up a funding organization called the Canadian Film Development

Corporation. The CFDC was run by a lovely man named Michael Spencer. Once things were up and running, I sent him the novel and the script.

I had a pretty fair script from a young Jewish writer from Montreal, Lionel Chetwynd, who was working for a film company in London. The adaptation was a difficult one, for Mordecai's novel is long and complex. Mordecai didn't want to write the script. He was in the middle of another novel, and he said to script *Duddy* would take him back to a state of mind that would interfere with what he was doing creatively in his new novel.

Michael Spencer loved the story but thought the script needed work. Mordecai said, "Get the structure right, Ted, and I'll polish up the dialogue afterward." Lionel and I streamlined the structure, then, as agreed, Mordecai took over and did the final draft.

Michael Spencer had one proviso: the film had to be produced by a Canadian. He gave me three names and their credits. I objected vociferously, "Come on, Michael, I've made five films, these guys are raw amateurs, inexperienced novices, their credits are risible," and he said to me, "Exactly, but I want to develop Canadian producers, so if you want government money, that's the deal." So I met with them.

The first guy wanted to own the film and pay me a small fee. I told him he was out of his mind. "You're going to pay *me* a small fee?! I've directed five films, what the fuck have you done?" I said. "I have lived with his book deep in my soul for a decade. And I developed it! And furthermore, you are being thrust on me, because I'm supposed to be giving you an education in producing! I don't even fucking want you!" Obviously, he was excised from the list.

The second was John Kemeny. He was very deferential to me. We hit it off so well that I never met with the third guy. Right away, I saw that John would be able to squeeze the most out of every dollar, which he did. He budgeted the film at a remarkable $750,000. Remember, this was a period film with period cars, period wardrobe, and period hair. Not cheap. The CFDC agreed to put up half the money. And we raised the other half from a real estate developer in Montreal named Gerry Snyder.

We were ready to go, except for two key ingredients to the filmic stew. We needed a great Duddy — no, an *unbelievable* Duddy — and we needed the most beautiful lake that God had ever created. After an eternity of aching for the opportunity to realize the novel as a film, I found myself only two weeks away from the commencement of shooting, but missing its two most important elements.

I had been auditioning endlessly for the role of Duddy Kravitz in Canada, but I could not find anyone that I thought could carry this difficult film. Finally, I phoned Lynn Stalmaster in Hollywood. Lynn had cast my Gregory Peck western, *Billy Two Hats*. He was the most brilliant, sharp-eyed casting director in the business. He had cast dozens of movies at that time, classics like *Harold and Maude*, *Fiddler on the Roof*, *Deliverance*, and many others, and he went on to cast more than 300 films in his long professional career.

But there was one problem: on a budget of $750,000, I couldn't afford him. When I talked to Lynn, I said, "Lynn, I desperately need your help, but I haven't got the money to pay you." Lynn replied, "Ted, don't worry about the money; you're going to be making many films. We will be working together again, and you'll pay me a little extra on your next big project. Send me the script pronto!" I couriered it to him. He read it immediately and phoned me, "Ted, this is one of the best scripts I've read in years, and I've got just the actor to play Duddy. You won't have heard of him. Young guy named Richard Dreyfuss. He's playing one of the leading roles in a film right now, *American Graffiti*. He played Baby Face Nelson in the recent Dillinger film."

"I'll check it out," I said.

"No, no, I don't want you to watch it; he overacts in the film."

"Lynn, are you kidding! Are you recommending someone who overacts for the part of Duddy Kravitz?!"

"Ted, I'll bring the ten best, most promising young actors in Hollywood to read for you, but I'll bet you anything you'll end up with Richard Dreyfuss. He was born to play this part."

I flew to Los Angeles for the readings, tingling with anticipation.

I had lived with my vision of Duddy for a dozen years. A man with Slavic looks, brown eyes, dark hair, slim body. Into the casting office, Lynn brought in Richard: blue eyes! Light hair! Pear shaped body! Had Lynn flipped his wig? He had aroused such high expectations about Richard in me. My heart sank — two weeks to go, and still no Duddy. I told Richard to start his reading.

As soon as Richard opened his mouth, it was electric! He had Duddy's manic energy. You understood him, felt for him, you saw his needs. He grabbed you by the lapels and demanded your attention, your feelings, your sympathy. It was an extraordinary reading.

One of the great things about Lynn Stalmaster was if there were two actors who were equal in the audition, he would say, "Take B, the camera will magnify and enhance his performance." And that's what he said about Richard. He said, "As brilliant as his reading is now, it will reach even greater heights in front of the camera. And his performance

In a Montreal street shooting The Apprenticeship of Duddy Kravitz.
Mordecai Richler, Richard Dreyfuss, and me.

will be more complex and grow in unexpected directions."
How right he was.

I remembered my time at Camp Naivelt. There were
mostly dark Polish Jews, but there were two boys who
were red headed! And Mordecai said German Jews were
often blonde and blue-eyed. In any case, Richard made me
forget any hesitations I had about his appearance with his
electrifying performance. He was Duddy Kravitz.

The other important role was Duddy's French-Canadian
girlfriend. That spring, Mordecai and I were in the south
of France. During the Cannes Film Festival, Mordecai
said there was a French-Canadian film in the festival and

suggested we see it. The film was Gille Carle's *Le Vraie Nature de Bernadette*. Bernadette was played by an actress unknown to me, Micheline Lanctôt. Halfway through the film, I whispered to Mordecai, "There's Duddy's girlfriend, Yvette." Little did I know, she would end up being my girlfriend as well.

Now I needed a lake that looked like a Monet painting come to life.

The film was being shot in Quebec, the land of a thousand lakes. How hard could it be to find a lake that fit the bill? The lake was the most important location in my film. The first shot of the lake had to be arresting. The audience's response to it had to be visceral; they had to be as overpowered as Duddy was by its beauty.

Duddy's entire goal in the story is to buy the lake and all the land around it. Without land, he is told by his grandfather, a man is nothing. This starts his quixotic quest. The beauty of the lake must justify the nasty, devious things Duddy does to acquire it. The audience has to see that Duddy's reaction to it is not merely acquisitive.

Lyse Venne, the film's location manager, was charged with finding the perfect lake. She looked at some 350 (!) lakes and showed me more than 100 of those. None of them gave me goosebumps. I kept saying no, no, no.

With only two weeks until the cameras rolled, on what was already a very tightly scheduled production, the producer, John Kemeny, was understandably getting nervous because we didn't have our key location, the lake. He said to me, "Ted, what are you doing? A hundred lakes? One lake is like another lake."

I replied, "One lake is not like another lake, this has to be the lake of lakes. It has to be the Platonic lake, the ultimate lake!"

"Ted, you're crazy."

"I may be crazy, but I'm not stupid," I said. "I'm not compromising on this lake. If it's some ordinary, boring fucking lake, we'll never forgive Duddy for some of the things he does to get that dreary body of water."

"Okay, Ted, get on with it."

Finally, a few days later, Lyse came to me and said she had found *the* lake. "If this isn't it, Ted, I'm committing suicide."

We drove to the area and parked. We walked down a short hill. At the bottom was a tall hedge, blocking the view of the lake. I pulled the hedge back and practically had an orgasm. The lake was breathtaking. Its beauty hit me like a hammer. It was a totally virgin lake, with no houses in sight, just a glistening lake surrounded by beautiful autumnal foliage.

"This is it! We found the lake!" I shouted to Lyse.

I turned around and double-timed back to the car. Lyse stayed put. "Come back here, you bastard, and give me some satisfaction! Three hundred and fifty lakes?! Stay with me for ten seconds and look at it!" she yelled.

"No time!" I yelled over my shoulder, "I have to get back to the office, tons of production problems!"

It turned out that it was a private lake owned by two wealthy German environmentalists, who kept the lake in pristine condition. The Germans stipulated that we touch no trees or bushes or alter anything created by nature, and if we moved even a single stone, we put it right back where we found it. And they weren't joking, they were very strict with us. One day, there was a large piece of driftwood that was interfering with my shot. I had it taken out. After the scene was over, one of the German owners tapped me on the shoulder.

"Where's that piece of driftwood that was right there?" he asked.

Dutifully, I retrieved the driftwood and put it back in the water in exactly the same place.

""

The shoot lasted eight weeks. They flew by. Every day was a revelatory experience with Richard. And there was no ego problem ever. He was always in high spirits, full of amusement. Richard and I played a mind-reading game he created and loved to play in front of the crew. A member of the crew would whisper, say, "President Roosevelt" in my ear. I'd say, "Fanny spent one month in London the first time she went." Richard would immediately answer, "President Roosevelt!" to the amazement of the whole crew. See if you can figure out how it was done. If not, the answer is at the end of this chapter.

The film ended up going over budget by about $150,000. We actually had bill collectors show up on set to collect. This is where John Kemeny showed his mettle: he held them at bay, while I stepped on the accelerator to finish the film.

Aside from the past-due invoices, we had another looming deadline. Because it was one of the first films backed by the CFDC, *Duddy Kravitz* was slated to premiere at the Place des Arts, a major performing arts center in Montreal.

The post-production was a short six weeks. I worked my ass off night and day to finish the editing and deliver the film. The night before the premiere, I stayed up all night with the lab technicians color correcting the film.

The next morning, I was still putting the finishing touches on my film. Eventually, I showered, put on my tux, and headed to the premiere.

The crowd was the haute monde of Montreal society. It was a proud moment — the arrival of a truly Canadian film based on a great Canadian novel.

Mordecai and I, standing in the lobby, were nervously sipping cognacs and smoking cigars to keep us going, especially me. Saidye Bronfman, the society doyenne of Canada, surrounded by her entourage, fluttered up to us to say hello. She was the matriarch of the Bronfman family, whose fortune had come from the largest liquor business in North America, Seagrams. The family was also incredibly philanthropic. Her name seemed to be on every third community building.

Saidye eyed Mordecai in his tux. "Well Mordecai, you've come a long way from being a St. Urbain Street slum boy," she said.

"Well Saidye, you've come a long way from being a boot-legger's wife," Mordecai replied, without missing a beat.

Saidye was not amused. She turned on her heels like Queen Victoria and pranced away. No one could trade one-liners like Mordecai Richler, as I had seen quite often.

But the highlight of the night came after the film ended. There was a rousing ovation. As it died down and everyone started to file out, I overheard a man say to his wife, "I can't believe a Canadian made such a great film!"

"

The attention the film received got me noticed by the Hollywood players, for all the reviews were outstanding — with one glaring exception, *The New Yorker*.

At that time, *The New Yorker* was the gold standard of film criticism because of Pauline Kael. A rave from Pauline Kael was a career maker. But, as luck would have it, when *Duddy Kravitz* was screened for the American critics in New York, Pauline was on vacation. Her interim replacement was an English critic named Penelope Gilliatt.

A creative person has to develop a rhinoceros's hide. I've discovered, in my long experience, that no matter how good I believe my film to be, there will be someone who dislikes it, and no matter how mediocre one of my films is, there will be some fool who loves it. Of course, reviews affect the film's box office tremendously, but I have never learned a single thing from a film critic.

Many years ago, I was at the opening night of a play and I was talking to the great Irish playwright Brendan Behan. As we watched the critics arriving, he turned to me and said, "Critics are like eunuchs in a harem. They see the trick being done every night, but they can't do it themselves."

Penelope Gilliatt panned my film in *The New Yorker*. Some of the other critics at the screening conveyed to me that she arrived late and somewhat drunk. But the damage was done — or was it?

Three days after Penelope's review was published, I received a phone call from Pauline Kael herself, who had seen the film. "That bitch!" she said. "I can't believe she gave you that review. She doesn't know what she's talking about. I love your film and I'll do anything to help you with it."

Pauline suggested that she write her own review and allow us to use it in our advertising. Her praise became the centerpiece of our press campaign. It was featured in all our ads. Here it is in all of its wonderful entirety:

No matter how phenomenal Richard Dreyfuss is in other roles, it's not likely that he'll ever top his performance in this teeming, energetic Canadian film. His baby-faced Duddy is a force of nature, a pushy 18-year-old con artist on his way to becoming an entrepreneur. Mordecai Richler's screenplay, based on his exultant, Dickensian 1959 novel, really enables us to understand *What Makes Sammy Run*. Duddy waits on tables, he drives a taxi, he deals in pinball machines, he sets up a company to film weddings and bar mitzvahs. He jiggles impatiently and sweats and scratches himself. His drive for success is a comic passion. We feel with him every step of the way; he's a little monster, yet we share his devastation when his suave uncle (Joseph Wiseman) tells him, "You're a pusherke, a little Jew-boy on the make. Guys like you make me sick and ashamed." The work of the director, Ted Kotcheff, is often crude but it has electricity. And the film has a real wit; it even has visual wit when we see a bar mitzvah film made by a drunken, half-mad blacklistee (Denholm Elliott). With Randy Quaid, Jack Warden, Micheline Lanctôt, Joe Silver, Henry Ramer, and, as the grandfather, Zvee Scooler. (The adaptation is credited to Lionel Chetwynd.) Shot mostly in and around Montreal, on a budget of less than $1 million.

99

As a result of the film's success in its initial release, my agent, Robert Shapiro, who was then head of the William Morris office in London, got several offers for me to direct studio films in Hollywood. But I was not ready to leave Canada for Hollywood yet.

"

As promised, the answer to Richard Dreyfuss's game is: you use the first letter of all proper nouns and any number refers to the vowel: 1-A, 2-E, 3-I, 4-O, 5-U. So in this case, "Fanny spent one month in London the first time she went," the clue for the answer is "Fala," the name of President Roosevelt's dog. You always spell out something associated with the answer, but never spell out the name itself.

CHAPTER SIXTEEN
Oh, Canada

My first three films dealt with life in England. The next, life in Australia, followed by a Western shot in Israel. Though I had lived in Great Britain for years, and continued to do so for 17 years altogether, there was no way I would ever understand English life, or the English character. The strength I had in England, working both in television and in films, was what I call the "man from Mars perspective"; that is, I am an outsider who comes to England and sees what is unusual, strange, peculiar, and idiosyncratic about British society which they themselves cannot see. The Brits were exotic creatures to me. I would never know the minutiae of English life; that knowledge is essential, I think, to filmmaking.

But, always, I was haunted by the feeling that my best work in film would be made at home, in Canada. When Mordecai and I shared that London flat, it was a frequent subject of our conversations. Mordecai's feelings were in line with mine. Mordecai pointed out, "Look at one of my favorite writers, William Faulkner. All his novels and short stories are set in the fictional Yoknapatawpha county based on Lafayette county in Mississippi, where he spent most of his life. That was his authorial turf to which he remained loyal. My authorial turf is Montreal and St. Urbain Street." And my filmic turf was definitely Canada.

With the passing of time, Mordecai was getting more and more antsy about being away from Montreal. He told me, "Ted, I think it's imperative that I return to Canada." If he didn't, he feared that the roots that fed him and inspired his work would dry up. Finally, one day he said to me that *The Apprenticeship of Duddy Kravitz* would be his last novel of four written abroad, that he was selling his London house, and returning to Montreal. It was very hard for his wife, Florence. She loved living in London, the West End theaters, the opera companies, the art shows, and museums. Montreal, by comparison, felt a bit provincial. And she loved the opulent house that she had furnished so beautifully in Kingston, a London suburb.

Mordecai's departure reinforced my own feelings. So in 1974, after an absence of 17 years, I returned to Canada to make *The Apprenticeship of Duddy Kravitz*. I can't tell you how great I felt to be finally making the film I had dreamed about for a decade. At that time, the only slightly discordant note was that I was greeted by the Canadian newspapers with a description of me as "emigré Canadian director, Ted Kotcheff."

I was really annoyed with that epithet "emigré." The newspapers kept using it. I complained to them: "It's as if the moment one leaves Canada, one's Canadian identity, being so slight, quickly evaporates." I said to the reporters, "Ernest

Hemingway and F. Scott Fitzgerald lived and worked in France, writing novels for many years. Did you ever hear anybody in America call him 'emigré American novelist Ernest Hemingway,' or 'emigré American novelist F. Scott Fitzgerald,' or 'emigré American writer Gertrude Stein'?"

I was a bit pissed. "You seem to confirm that old jape about Canadians: 'What is the distinguishing characteristic of a Canadian?' 'That he has no distinguishing characteristics.' So the moment you enter England, you become English."

Well, I make my first Canadian feature film, *The Apprenticeship of Duddy Kravitz*: lo and behold it wins the Golden Bear for best film in the Berlin Film Festival, becoming the first Canadian film to win an international prize; it wins a gold medal at the Atlanta Film Festival. I felt all this proved clearly to me, that my best filmic work would be in Canada. And on top of these awards, the film's investors earned their money back in the first two weeks of the film's exhibition in Canada, and it went on to make huge profits for them. I thought I would be all set in Canada, making films there for the rest of my life. For it achieved the ultimate desideratum for a film director: a fine film artistically that makes a great deal of money. I thought that the Canadian investors would be falling over themselves to give me money for any film I wanted to make from here on out.

To capitalize on the momentum, Mordecai and I quickly finished an adaptation of another one of his novels, *St. Urbain's Horseman*. It was a great script and I set out with high hopes of getting it quickly financed in Canada. But could I get the money for its production in Canada? No. I spent the best part of a year going everywhere with my begging hat outstretched without any success.

Me with the man who changed my life and brought me to Hollywood, Peter Bart.

I don't know if that cautious Scot's syndrome prevailing in the Canadian makeup is the culprit, but Canadians seem to lack that entrepreneurial and buccaneering spirit possessed by Americans in financial and investment matters. Of course, the other side of that coin, Canadians are less aggressive people and, thus, more pleasant to be with.

However, my dreams were shattered and I got really depressed. I was also broke. I had just divorced my wife of 11 years, Sylvia Kay. She remained in England with our three children. *Duddy Kravitz* was made for a very small amount of money, so my fee was proportionately small. With two households to support, and three British children at private schools in England, I became desperate. A year flew by with absolutely no income, and in all that time, I couldn't raise a penny for *St. Urbain's Horseman.*

So, at this moment, two Hollywood producers sent me a script: it was a social comedy about a top executive who loses his job and turns to crime. I loved the script, entitled *Fun with Dick and Jane*. So, Hollywood it was! This was not how my story was meant to play out. But my life was about to have a new American script.

When I arrived in Hollywood to begin work on the film, I had no idea of what to expect from my two producers. But boy! Did I get a surprise! Peter Bart had just left Paramount Pictures where as a top executive, he had initiated *Love Story* and *The Godfather*. *The Godfather*! Yikes! Peter's partner, Max Palevsky, was a brilliant man who had just become the first techie billionaire. *Dick and Jane* was self-financed, courtesy of Max. Firm offers were made to me, and later to George Segal and Jane Fonda in advance of studio acceptance. This accorded me a creative freedom unheard of for a "new director" to Hollywood. What a reception! What a fabulous way to come to Hollywood!

And Peter, I discovered, was a knowledgeable, insightful, witty, supportive man. He and I immediately hit it off, the beginning of a friendship that has lasted over 40 years. And Max treated me with the thoughtfulness and consideration of a true patrician gentleman. Banished were all my memories of the past wasted year, with my perpetually empty begging bowl extended for money for *St. Urbain's Horseman*. This was filmic paradise!

CHAPTER SEVENTEEN
Directing Is Hard,
Comedy Is Harder

Billy Wilder, in my opinion, is the best Hollywood director ever. He was my film hero. I wanted to have his career. I have seen all of his films and, without exception, they are all great. Amazingly, there never seems to be a false moment. But what impressed me most about him when I studied his work was how successful and skilled he was at making different kinds of comedy, while also being able to direct equally brilliant films in other genres. *Love in the Afternoon* was a marvelous romantic comedy. *Sabrina* was the social comedy of its era. *The Apartment* — give me a break! It was a screwball comedy with dramatic social overtones, an overall work of genius. Yet this same filmmaker directed the film noir classics *Sunset Blvd.*, *Double Indemnity*, and *The Lost Weekend*.

I can't say that I learned a lot from watching Wilder's films, only because you can't learn much from watching perfection. That said, the flip side is that you can learn quite a bit from watching bad films because you can see all the things you should not do when directing a film. The one thing I did notice in all his comedies is that jokes never humiliate the central character, as I had learned from Chekov. But other than that, I watched his movies for pure pleasure.

I was in awe of Wilder because comedy is the most difficult genre to execute by far. Every director, writer, and actor always says so — and it's true. Since I don't confine myself directorially to one genre, I am often asked at film schools of the three genres — action, drama, and comedy — which is the hardest to do. I think action is the easiest genre; usually there isn't a great dramatic depth to explore. I can turn a novice filmmaker into an action director in 30 minutes. The key: get a great stunt coordinator like the one I always use, Conrad Palmisano.

Okay, that may be a bit facetious but it's also partly true. Another advantage that an action film has is its ready-made structure. Think of my action film that almost defines the genre, *First Blood*. It has a binary dramatic structure: the pursuers, the pursued. You can cut back and forth between them, generating energy and pace. The tension of the chase is an omnipresent given, and what will happen when the pursuers and the pursued finally confront each other provides you with a climax.

Drama is next easiest. When you are making a drama, you have a point of reference with your own feelings and your own human experiences. Everyone has loved and then broken up. Everyone has suffered the death of a loved one. Everyone has experienced the whole gambit of emotions: hope, sorrow, joy, depression, fury, fear, envy, hatred, ecstasy, and so on. Chances are if something moves you, then it will move other people because we are all basically built the same. You always have a measuring stick with which to appraise an emotional performance for its depth and genuineness. And even if a scene is 80 percent moving, it can still work.

But comedy is an entirely different animal. Oscar Wilde is credited with a great line about comedy. When he was on his death bed, someone supposedly said to him, "Dying must be hard, Oscar." He replied, "No, dying is easy, comedy is hard."

People have said to me, "Comedy is such fun. I don't see why comedy is so difficult." I always respond the same way: "Okay, go ahead, make me laugh. Go on! Say or do something that will make me laugh!" Silence ensues. "So, you see the difficulty." And there's no middle ground of success with comedy. Unlike drama, a joke can't be 80 percent successful; either a joke works 100 percent or it's zip.

For starters, comedy is a total artificial construct and a stylized medium, because it has to carry jokes. That's the director's problem: your jokes can't stand out like raisins in a pastry, and you have to create a filmic texture that allows them to occur naturally. But a warning: you are always walking a tightrope and you have to be careful not to go too far with the humor, or you will fall off.

There are a couple of central rules to comedy. There must, in some way, be an underlying meanness to it. It needs a barb to make the joke stick. Otherwise it doesn't work. And you shouldn't mix different styles. If you're making a social comedy, you can't descend into farce, tempting as that might be. It destroys credibility.

Very early on, Billy Wilder became my inspiration to have a diverse film career, one that did not follow a straight line. I vowed never to confine myself to one type of film.

"

I thought of Billy Wilder while making *Fun with Dick and Jane*. The script was written by two veteran writers, David Giler and Jerry Belson, who wrote for *The Dick Van Dyke Show*. Mordecai Richler also worked on the script, bringing to it his brand of mordant humor.

In the film, Dick and Jane are an upwardly mobile, overextended couple trying to stay ahead of the Joneses. However, when Dick finds himself unemployed, the creditors take away their possessions including their front lawn which a landscape company rolls up and hauls away. Dick and Jane then turn to robbery to support and maintain their affluent lifestyle.

I cast George Segal as Dick and Jane Fonda as his wife, Jane. Jane Fonda was exactly what I wanted for the role of Jane. At that time, Jane Fonda had been active for five years protesting the Vietnam War, even visiting North Vietnam. For this, she had earned the sobriquet, "Hanoi Jane." *Fun with Dick and Jane* was to be her first role after five years of not acting.

When we started pre-production, I went looking for locations, especially a corporate headquarters of which Dick was an executive. The owners were thrilled that we were going to film our comedy in their company. But when they learned that Jane Fonda was to be one of our stars, they angrily refused, saying, "I'm not going to have that traitor on my property." This didn't occur once, but several times. Most of them were typical right-wing warmongering Republicans accusing her of supporting the enemy.

But even some liberal-leaning companies turned us down. Max Palevsky, my wealthy, business smart producer, explained it to me. "Ted, all companies have skeletons in their corporate closets that they don't want investigated. These companies felt that if they let Jane Fonda shoot in

Jane Fonda waits as the focus puller and I line up a shot for Fun with Dick and Jane.

Having fun between shots on Fun with Dick and Jane *with talk show host Merv Griffin, George Segal, and Ed McMahon.*

Singing for a publicity shot: George Segal, Merv Griffin, Jane Fonda; and me.

Staging the modeling scene in Fun with Dick and Jane.

their premises, our Republican president would sic the SEC or some other federal body to investigate their business proceedings."

There were murmurings at Columbia that maybe we should rethink the casting. I said absolutely not. "Jane Fonda is exactly what I want for the role of Jane. And I'm not going to allow these corporate rednecks to interfere with my film." I found a way around the problem by building the company headquarters on a sound stage.

And did Jane ever deliver! A wonderful comedic performance, so engaging and perfectly adjudged. Together with George Segal, they made this film work. You believed their metamorphosis from middle class to criminality.

I filmed a scene in which Dick invites his boss over for lunch and desperately tries to amuse him. In the scene, I needed a transitional gag. I had Dick walk into the living room carrying an ice bucket. He had three ice cubes in his hand and, pretending to pee in the bucket, with his hand at his crotch, he drops the ice cubes into the bucket and says, "Eskimo peeing . . ." and laughs at his own joke. When I later saw that scene on film, I thought to myself, *Billy Wilder would have never done that*. It was too out of character and, worse, not that funny.

I will say that George Segal, with whom I did two comedies (*Fun with Dick and Jane* and *Who's Killing the Great Chefs of Europe?*), is in my opinion one of the finest light comedy actors in the business. He used to tell me that he loved working with me, as I laughed when they did something funny in rehearsal and struggled to stifle my laughter during the take, but George could still half-hear it, or sense it, and it fed him, helped him with his timing. Plus he knew he was on the right track comedically.

I was told that Charlie Chaplin used to bring in people,

laughers, to watch him when he shot his silent film comedies, to react and assist him with his timing — how long to
go on with a comedic gag. When I worked in the theater
in London doing a comedy, on the opening night in the
West End, the management brought in paid, professional
laughers for a dual purpose: firstly, the same as for Charlie
Chaplin and George, to assist the actors in their timing,
but also they sat them next to all the drama critics, who
never laugh, to hopefully influence them in their critiques
on the comedy's humor quotient.

One thing I learned about comedy from doing *Fun with
Dick and Jane* was that the joke is often created in the editing
room once you cut the right shots together; if you play the
joke as one long piece of film, it often isn't as funny.

I found that sometimes the actors don't know what's funny
either. I remember one scene with Jane Fonda where she said
that she needed a funny exit line. I thought for a second and
came up with one. I told her, as you reach the stairs to leave,
you say, "The bank manager phoned today. Know what
he said? 'Madam, you're no longer banking with us; we're
banking with you.'" Though this fit their borrowed-to-the-
limit lifestyle perfectly, Jane didn't think it was funny. I told
her to just say the line and promised it would get a laugh. It
did, owing as much to her delivery as to the line. But to this
day, I don't think she understood why the line is funny.

That said, Jane had a sharp instinct for comedy. In one
scene in a bank, a holdup takes place and, in a flurry, money
gets tossed about. Jane grabs $1,000 and hides it in her
clothing. When Dick and Jane arrive home, Jane is so excited
from stealing the money that she has to pee. The plan was for
Jane to pull Dick into the bathroom to show him the money.

As we were setting up the scene, Jane approached me.
"Why can't I be shown peeing, Ted? They always show

men peeing in films." I couldn't see why not. I told her we would film her peeing while she told George's character what she had done.

"One thing I would do is that when I was done peeing, I would get some toilet paper and wipe myself," she added. I told her to go ahead and do it. After all, good comedy is truth!

The next day, the head of Columbia Pictures called me into his office. He had seen the dailies of Jane peeing and wiping herself.

"How could you, Ted?! You are such a person of great taste and discrimination," he said. "How could you show Jane Fonda wiping herself with a piece of toilet paper?"

This from the studio executive who had supervised the sexually charged *Shampoo*. I shot back. "I will not be lectured on matters of taste by a studio head who approved Julie Christie going under a table and sucking Warren Beatty's cock!"

"That was a ten million dollar scene!" he retorted.

"Oh, so it's not tasteless if it makes money," I said. "Well then, the jury is still out on my scene, isn't it?"

I ended up leaving the scene in the movie. It may not have been a $10 million scene, but as far as I know, it was the first time a female movie star was shown peeing and wiping in a mainstream movie. Years later, Laura Dern emailed and told me that she loved the scene so much, she used it to introduce Jane at an awards banquet. So it did endure!

"

I followed up *Fun with Dick and Jane* with a comedic mystery caper, *Who Is Killing the Great Chefs of Europe?* Having worked in kitchens and restaurants through my teens, mostly at my dad's places, a comedy set in that world came very naturally to me.

When I worked at the Old Mill in Toronto as head busboy, one of my duties was to take down the head chef's dictation of the menu for the day and print it. This man had been head chef in the royal kitchens of King Alfonso of Spain, so he thought of himself as royalty and behaved like it. I had come to know his extensive repertoire of culinary creations.

"What shall we have for soup today?" he would ask.

"May I suggest *potage Saint-Germain*, sir?"

"Perfect, Billy, perfect, put it down. Hmm, now a vegetable —"

"May I suggest *carrottes Vichy*, sir?"

"Brilliant, Billy, put it down."

He behaved like some exalted deity. In the mornings, in the Old Mill's large kitchen, his acolyte sous chefs all waited for him to taste their preparations for the day; the royal head chef, wearing pristine white gloves, never touched anything. The saucier, the chef for all the sauces, for example, would fill large spoons with each of the sauces for the day and then bring one up to the lips of the head chef to taste and criticize. "I think this one needs a touch more thyme."

"Yes sir, yes sir, of course, sir," as he bowed and scraped.

Chefs can be very temperamental, as befits creative artists. I once saw a waiter return a rejected dish from a customer, his tip thus endangered, and utter insulting comments on the chef's abilities. The chef retorted by hurling a large butcher's knife at the waiter, which fortunately only hit him but didn't pierce him. There was always a traditional enmity between chefs and waiters, swearing and cussing at each other. There is a scene in *Great Chefs* where all the French chefs gather in a park to discuss who might be killing all the famous chefs. One of them says, "It's a waiter, of course."

And I was lucky to have as my writer Peter Stone. He had won an Oscar for *Father Goose*, starring Cary Grant, for best writing, and *1776* won a Tony for Best Musical and a Drama Desk Award for Outstanding Book of a Musical. We worked together on the script in his place up in Amagansett in New York State. He was a very witty man, with an acute sense of the foibles and follies of human nature; he was invaluable in writing a comedy.

I was thrilled to have in my star-studded cast, besides George Segal, Jacqueline Bisset, and Robert Morley, the cream of the French film acting community, and stars like the great Philippe Noiret, the fabulously funny Jean Rochefort, the romantic Jean-Pierre Cassel, and the amusing Jacques Marin.

We filmed in Paris. At the end of a shot, when I would utter the magical words, "Cut! Print! On to the next shot," George Segal and Jackie immediately retired to their trailers. My French stars rarely had this treatment. But I arranged a green baize-covered table a short distance behind the camera where they would all sit while awaiting the next shot, sip their black coffees, and exchange funny stories about their past acting experiences. I would often sit with them to enjoy these tales. I remember Jean Rochefort telling us how he had once been in a two-handed stage play, which is always difficult to sustain. It was a turgid drama with a ceaseless examination of a husband and wife's neurotic relationship. At one point, the wife crossed to the window and looked down at the dark street below and said, "Darling, there's a strange man standing under the lamp post." A loud, despairing voice came from the audience, "For God's sake, please invite him up!" When the AD said, "Ted, we're ready," we would all rise laughing and

I show the Great Chefs, Jean-Pierre Cassel and Jackie Bisset, my culinary techniques.

chortling at these stories, creating the perfect atmosphere for performers in a comedy. It was a glorious time for me.

Directing is a very physically demanding activity. Many years ago I had lunch with an outstanding British director, Tony Richardson. Toward the end of it, he said, glancing at his watch, "I have to go, Teddy, I'm late for the gym."

"Go to the gym? Why?"

"You haven't made a film yet, Ted, but you'd better be in good physical condition when you do. You're on your feet twelve hours a day, six days a week for two or three months."

It's true, you're in your director's chair, but quickly you jump out and cross to the camera operator to discuss the framing. Then back to the chair. Then you jump out again to give a direction to the actor. Back to the chair. Out again to speak to the other actor . . . And so on ad nauseam. If you're not lean and in peak condition, you'll quickly exhaust yourself, hindering your work. When I became a film director, I remembered Tony's words and prepared myself accordingly. At the end of a film, I would usually have lost 10 or 12 pounds. Except with *Who's Killing the Great Chefs of Europe?*

We shot in two- and three-Michelin-starred restaurants, and I regularly ate in them, getting special treatment from owners and chefs. Even before shooting started, during the location scouts, I visited the kitchens of many two- and three-star restaurants, which, for one reason or another, didn't quite work for my film. But I would always have a meal there. It was a once in a lifetime opportunity to eat in these fabled restaurants that I didn't wish to miss. Also in this period of prep, Paul Bocuse had agreed to be my technical advisor and to design the four dishes featured in my film. At this time, Paul Bocuse was considered to be one of the greatest chefs in the world.

I direct Jacqueline Bisset and Gigi Proietti in a scene alongside a Venetian canal for 1978's Who's Killing the Great Chefs of Europe?

I went down to meet him in Lyons. Our meetings were held in his three-star restaurant, L'Auberge du Pont de Collonges. On our first encounter, we talked most of the afternoon; then, it being dinner time, I asked for his restaurant's menu. Paul Bocuse was affronted. "No menu! I shall cook for you!!" And cook he did, a great, memorable meal. He would prepare one of his great dishes, then watch me consume it. Then he would return to the kitchen to cook the next course. My meal seemed to have endless courses. His special soup called V.G.D., after then-president of France Valéry Giscard d'Estaing, for whom he had invented it originally, was followed by a fantastic *loup en croûte*, a river fish baked in a pastry crust. And on and on it went. I found myself swelling.

Well, I think by now you've gotten the message. After six weeks of pre-production and 10 weeks of filming, and all that time gluttonously gourmandizing in the finest restaurants in London, Paris, Venice, and Munich, I emerged at the film's conclusion 40 pounds heavier — 40 pounds! My torso had become a pear, and my once-lean face had become a full moon. It took me several years to get back to normal, but never quite.

One thing I loved about shooting in Paris was the well-known "French hours." In every other country, we shot from 7 a.m. to 7 p.m., with an hour break for lunch at 1 p.m. In Paris, we started at 11 a.m. and shot straight through to 8 p.m. These are the French hours. There was no lunch break: a buffet was set up close to the camera, looked after by a cook. It was covered in French delicacies, several plates, a selection of cheeses, soups, salade Niçoise, plates of *asperges*, and wine of course. So whenever you felt peckish, you could wander over to the buffet for a few minutes and satisfy yourself.

The benefit of this arrangement was that, since there was no hour-long lunch break in the middle of your day, the momentum you had going for you was not interrupted. And after the lethargy that followed a substantial lunch, the crew took some time to regain their tempo. So I would get just as much shooting done in the shorter French hours as I would in the usual schedule.

I asked a French producer how this arrangement came about. He told me that, at one time, they had many beautiful actresses starring in their films. Ordinarily, these actresses would rise at 5 a.m., report to hair and makeup at 6 a.m., and be ready to shoot at 7. A week of this and their faces would begin to suffer, requiring more and more concealing cosmetics. So instead, under French hours, the actresses could sleep in until 9 a.m., hair and makeup at 10, ready to start at

11, their faces perfect. My lovely leading lady in *Great Chefs*, Jackie Bisset, loved French hours. So did I.

An interesting by-product of making *Who's Killing the Great Chefs of Europe?* was that I got this reputation of being a distinguished food and wine connoisseur — totally undeserved. Practically every restaurateur and chef in Europe and America had seen the film. So when I made a reservation in a fine restaurant, my name would be recognized and I'd be welcomed by the owner and chef, and given special treatment. The chefs would suggest dishes not on the menu. One chef came out with four different sauces on large spoons for me to taste and savor, to see which I preferred on my main course. This happened in London, New York, Los Angeles. Another byproduct: I was invited to join a club of wine fanciers and collectors in L.A. with some true connoisseurs. I accepted the invitation and have remained a member ever since. We congregate monthly in fine restaurants, each member bringing his greatest wines. The group is called WOW, the World Organization of Wine.

The production was a veritable European travelogue. After filming in Paris, Venice, and London, the final location was in Munich. I was staying in one of Munich's best hotels when I discovered that Billy Wilder, my hero, was staying there too. I was beside myself. Billy was shooting *Fedora*, starring William Holden and Marthe Keller, at the same time that I was shooting *Great Chefs*.

One day, both Billy and I happened to arrive back at the hotel from shooting at the same time. He was standing in the lobby, and I took the opportunity to rush over to my hero and introduce myself. Having done so, I said, "Mr. Wilder, I have to say that I think you are the wittiest . . ."

He interrupted, "I know, I know, I know, I know." He said it four times very rapidly. Then smiling, he said, "Mr.

Kotcheff, I have to tell you that I think *The Apprenticeship of Duddy Kravitz* is one of the funniest . . ."

I quickly interrupted him and, with a tinge of sarcasm that I hoped would land, said, "I know, I know, I know, I know," just as he had done.

Billy laughed. A kinship of sorts had been created. "Say, why don't we have dinner together tonight?"

I was thrilled. I immediately accepted.

We ate in the hotel's plush restaurant. Naturally, we talked about Hollywood and filmmaking. There was a continual flow of Wilder wit.

In the middle of our dinner, an attractive woman approached our table and said, seductively, "Hello, Billy."

Billy looked blankly at her.

Somewhat hurt, she asked, "Billy, don't you recognize me?"

"Not with your clothes on," he quipped.

Over dinner, I told him that I collected stories about him. He asked for a few. I told him that I heard he once went to see Louis B. Mayer and told the MGM studio boss that he wanted to make a film about Nijinsky. I recreated the story for him.

MAYER: Who's Nijinsky?

YOU: A famous Russian ballet dancer.

MAYER (*perplexed*): You want to make a film about a famous Russian ballet dancer?

YOU: Yes, and at the end of his life, Nijinsky went crazy.

MAYER (*growing agitated*): You want to make a film about a *crazy* Russian ballet dancer?

YOU (*deadpan*): Yes, and he had these delusions that he was a horse.

MAYER (*nearly irate*): You want to make a film about

a crazy Russian ballet dancer who thinks he's a horse?!
Get out of my office!
So you got up to leave. On the way out, you delivered a
parting salvo: Louis, you are missing out on one of the
great boffo endings of all time.
MAYER: What's that?
YOU: Nijinsky wins the Kentucky Derby.

Billy laughed and verified that the story was true. He told
me he loved to get under Mayer's skin to amuse himself.

Later, we got around to talking about the film he was
shooting, *Fedora*, the story of a great reclusive movie
star who kills herself in the opening scene. I asked him
about Marthe Keller. I was interested in what Billy might
say about her, as I was never a big fan of her acting.

"Ted," he said, "I shot a crucial scene with her today,
and her acting was absolutely brilliant. Take after take, she
gave a performance of tremendous depth."

"Really." I was a little surprised and wondered if he was
covering for her. "What was the scene?"

"She lay dead in a coffin all day."

I have to say that our dinner was one of the most
amusing and enjoyable I've ever had. And he was so generous to me, having seen several of my films and praising
them. My feet didn't touch the ground for days afterward.

99

Billy Wilder and I actually crossed cinematic paths, on paper
at least. We both made films based loosely on *The Front Page*,
Lewis Milestone's 1931 film that was based on a Broadway
play by Ben Hecht and Charles MacArthur. But my film,
Switching Channels, used the twist from Howard Hawks's *His*

Filming a scene with Kathleen Turner and Burt Reynolds for Switching Channels.

Girl Friday, which was also based on the original film but changed the main character from a man to a woman. Billy's remake, which starred Jack Lemmon, Walter Matthau, and Susan Sarandon, was based on the original.

In some ways, Billy and I were both facing the same problem, namely that any remake will suffer from comparison with the original, particularly when the original is a classic. Critics will always make invidious comparisons in these cases, though Billy Wilder would deservingly be given a longer leash than Ted Kotcheff. Perhaps as a defense mechanism, I did not have any of the three previous movies in mind when I made *Switching Channels*, nor did I watch them again to prepare. But perhaps I should have, because my film did not come together.

I have never been fond of remakes or sequels — indeed I've never directed a sequel to a film of mine — but I felt

I'm in deep discussion with Kathleen Turner on the set of Switching Channels.

that *The Front Page* could be updated to the world of television news. The Elizabethan dramatists continually borrowed plots and used them to their own ends, and that was what I wanted to do in this case. Or, to quote Ezra Pound on the subject of art, "Make it new."

Switching Channels was cast with Kathleen Turner as the newswoman, Michael Caine as her producer, and Christopher Reeve as the man she was giving up her career to marry. Kathleen was cast first. With her energy, feistiness, and quick tongue, I felt that she was in the tradition of the great comediennes of the 1930s and 1940s, like Carole Lombard.

However, the production hit a detour during rehearsals. Michael Caine, after a week of rehearsal, was forced to drop out due to a contractual hold that Universal had on him for *Jaws: The Revenge*. I had to replace him with Burt Reynolds.

Burt has a light touch as a comedic actor and always sees the ironic outlook of a scene, but from day one, Kathleen showed her displeasure with having to work with Burt, feeling him to be inferior to Michael Caine and making no bones about it. The situation was demoralizing and hurtful to Burt, and consequently, he became irritated with Kathleen. It didn't help matters that Kathleen failed to tell the producer, Marty Ransohoff, that she was pregnant. Consequently, I had to keep moving the camera higher and higher up her body as production moved along.

Burt had been the biggest star in the world in the 1970s. He was trying to find his footing as a movie star in the late '80s, having come off a series of tongue-and-cheek police comedies in the early '80s, like *Rent-a-Cop* and *Heat*, that had not reached the level of his '70s successes. Kathleen, by contrast, had just come off of a series of hits — *Peggy Sue Got Married*, *Prizzi's Honor*, and *The Jewel of the Nile*, the sequel to *Romancing the Stone*. For his part, Chris Reeve later wrote in his autobiography that he felt like a referee on set between his sparring co-stars. As a result of all the negative emotions, the film suffered terribly, and I think that was part of the reason it became apple juice rather than champagne.

Overall, the final product turned out to be uneven. It was an old-fashioned romantic comedy in the first half, but in the second half, the comedy went over the top and the film also went on too long, a cardinal sin for a comedy. It lost its zip. Looking back, cutting the film down in the second half may have helped. Commercially, the film did not do well at all — costing $19 million, it grossed $9 million. Critically, oddly, it was a mixed bag.

Roger Ebert gave it a few positive notes, writing: "Turner has perfect timing as the long-suffering anchor, and she and Reynolds work up a nice sweat and some good chemistry in their relationship, which seems to be based on a few good memories and a whole lot of one-liners. The Reeve character is unnecessary much of the time, but Reeve has fun with it anyway, with his floppy tailored suits, his newly blond hair and his willingness to accommodate the obviously derailed Turner."

However, Vincent Canby of the *New York Times* was less forgiving. He correctly pointed out that "the movie never finds the proper mixture of farce and melodrama that should be its style." Then he got snarky: "The saving grace is that you don't have to admire *The Front Page*, or even to have heard of it, to find the new movie an utter waste of time. It fails so successfully on its own that it makes the benign *Broadcast News* look like a work of seminal satire."

Comedies, I learned from making *Switching Channels* and *Fun with Dick and Jane*, are very fragile pieces of art. They are binary: they work, or they don't. There's no one moment that changes everything. They come together as whole, like *Fun with Dick and Jane*, or don't, like *Switching Channels*. I wondered then if Billy Wilder felt the same way. Given how sure-handed he was with comedy, I guessed that such an analytical thought never crossed his mind.

But then, listen, as this chapter title suggests, every film has its quotas of cinematic problems that are individually specific to the world that the film inhabits. To say comedy is the hardest is true, yes, but when you're in the middle of a difficult shoot, it all seems tough, and the difference between the genres is academic, and seems minuscule and hardly noticeable.

PETER SELLERS

I nearly worked with the incomparable Peter Sellers. The project was *Ghost in the Noonday Sun*, which came to me from MGM with Peter attached to play the lead. Along with a friend of his, the great funny man Spike Milligan, Peter and I worked on the script for two weeks. For a variety of reasons, the film never got made by me, but I loved the experience of working on the script with him.

Peter defined his characters by their accents. He would ask me, "Scottish or Irish?" I would say, "Irish might be interesting." He would then ask, "Which dialect? Galway? Dublin? Cork?" I opted for Cork, which I knew. On cue, he would do a pitch-perfect Cork accent. He was also the greatest mimic I have ever met. Minutes after meeting someone, Peter could flawlessly impersonate them, the way they spoke, their accent, everything right down to their mannerisms. Peter knew my American agent in Los

Angeles, and he captured him perfectly with an impeccable American accent.

I had heard one of the great acting stories about Peter fighting with Woody Allen. I told Peter the story I had heard and asked if it was true. It went like this:

In the mid-1960s, Peter did *Casino Royale*, a James Bond spoof, with Woody Allen. The two famously did not get along. They detested each other. It reached the point where in the scenes they had together, Woody would shoot his part, talking to a stand-in, and then leave. Peter would then come out of his dressing room and onto the set to do his part of the scene, also talking to a stand-in. Not surprisingly, due in part to the fact that it was taking twice as long to shoot their scenes, the picture was going way over schedule and way over budget.

Mike Frankovich, the executive at Columbia Pictures who was supervising the film, was irate. He called the producer, Charles Feldman, in London where the film was being shot and started screaming at him, telling him that he was totally incompetent.

"You're hopelessly over budget and you can't even control your actors," Frankovich railed. "Everybody's heard about the misbehavior of your two stars that's delaying shooting and costing us a fortune!"

He informed the producer that he was flying over from Los Angeles to straighten this movie out, once and for all. The next day, Frankovich landed in London and checked in to the Dorchester Hotel. He headed down to the bar for a late night snack and drink. Lo and behold, he spotted Woody Allen at the bar.

He tapped Woody on the shoulder. Woody turned around. "We've never met, but I'm Mike Frankovich, the head of production for Columbia Pictures, and I just flew over to straighten out the mess your picture is in," he told Allen. "I understand you've been having trouble with that prima donna English asshole, Peter Sellers."

"Yeah, he's difficult," Woody mumbled.

"Well, don't worry, Woody, tomorrow, I'm going to kick his limey ass so hard, he'll choke on my shoe," Frankovich said. "I'm on your side in this stupid mess, Woody. I promise you, I'm on your side."

Woody said that he was very appreciative, and the two shook hands, ending the brief exchange.

The next day, there was no filming scheduled, as the director, producers, and department heads had all been summoned to meet with Frankovich to figure out how to bring the budget under control. Frankovich entered the room and with the full bravado of a blowhard Hollywood executive declared, "I'm going to straighten out this movie!"

Feldman, the producer, laughed and said, "Well Mike, you're off to a very good start. Peter Sellers has quit the picture. He's on a plane to Rome."

"What's that got to do with me?" Frankovich asked.

"You know the guy you talked to in the bar at the Dorchester last night," the producer said. "That wasn't Woody Allen. That was Peter Sellers."

The master of disguise and accents, Peter was the same height as Woody, wore the same owlish glasses, and, most critically, could imitate Woody's accent and mannerisms perfectly.

A shaken Mike Frankovich walked out of the room and took the next plane back to Los Angeles.

After I related this to Peter Sellers, he smiled. "True story," he said.

CHAPTER EIGHTEEN
Frank & Dino

There are people in power in Hollywood who know what they are doing, and then there are people who don't. Sometimes the same ideas come out of those who do and those who don't. The difference is, those who have power can execute. Oftentimes, that is because they have people who can help them.

Like most filmmakers over the history of cinema, when I started out making films, I had no access to these types of movers and shakers in Hollywood. Yes, I realize some people get into the game through nepotism. But that clearly wasn't going to happen to me. Born a poor Canadian who was barred from the U.S., I cut my teeth in live television in England. Even with four films in England, it wasn't until I made a film that Hollywood wanted that anyone bothered to call.

For me, the *Apprenticeship of Duddy Kravitz* was my ticket. It became the gift that kept on giving. The film was picked up for distribution in the U.S. by Paramount Pictures, which was run by Frank Yablans. When Paramount bought the rights, I flew to New York to meet Yablans. I'll never forget the meeting.

We met at the top of the Gulf & Western building on Columbus Circle. Looking out over Central Park and beyond, I remember thinking that the view at the top of the movie business is pretty good. Yablans, who was dressed in a suit that cost more than I had earned directing the film, told me that the film was two hours and ten minutes long, which I knew. "I need you to cut out ten minutes," he said.

I asked why.

"I know this may be hard for you to do, and maybe not that artistic, but the theaters like to have showings that are at 2, 4, 6, and 8," he said. "What they don't want is 2, 4:10, 6:20, and so forth."

Though I wasn't pleased because the film was done exactly the way I wanted, I told him I understood. What choice did I have anyway? I was an inexperienced Canadian director hoping to use this film to get a job to make his first Hollywood feature, and he was the president of Paramount. From talking to him, it was clear that he also knew as much about filmmaking as anyone. He had been promoted to president of the studio because of his genius marketing campaign for *Love Story* and had just overseen a revolutionary wide release of *The Godfather*.

Curious, I asked why he bought *Duddy Kravitz*.

Yablans smiled. "Because it's the story of my life," he said, with a wink.

Now I knew why he was the head of a studio.

"

Several years later, my ICM agent, Guy McElwaine, called me. Frank Yablans had left Paramount and become a producer. He had a hot hand, having just produced the Gene Wilder/Richard Pryor hit *Silver Streak*. Guy told me that Yablans wanted me to direct a film for him about American football. I told Guy that I wasn't interested in football and to give Frank my best and tell him that I was passing.

Five minutes later, my phone rang. Frank Yablans was on the line; he wasn't going to take my rejection lying down. People in Hollywood rarely take no for an answer. "Ted, this film is not about football," he said. "It's about manipulation, alienation, people being treated like property."

"Sounds interesting, but I don't think . . ."

He kept talking, as all good producers do until they get over a no and get a yes. "It's about the players being used by owners of teams in a manipulative and harmful way. It's a story of corporate greed at its worst. There's a great line in the script when the chief character says to the owners, 'We're not the team. You're the team. We're just the equipment.' Most of all, it's authentic, because it was written by Peter Gent, who played tight end for the Dallas Cowboys. He knows this world inside and out. Peter Gent is an artist in the body of an athlete."

Frank's enthusiasm and Shakespeare-like description of the world of football had me intrigued. I read Peter Gent's book and loved it. Because I wasn't a football fan, I didn't view the sport with any reverence, a plus when it came to showing the unvarnished truth. I agreed to come on board.

We hired one screenwriter and then another, but the script wasn't coming together the way we had hoped. As

Frank and I were talking about which writer to bring on next, in a moment of frustration, I blurted out that I could write a better script in a weekend than the ones we had paid so much money to get. Frank called my bluff. "What are you doing this weekend?" he asked.

He rented a bungalow at the Beverly Hills Hotel, and the two us of went to work. It was intense, but it was the way I love to work. I would write scenes and then Frank would revise them. By Sunday night, we had a draft we were happy with. We then sent it to Peter Gent to punch up the dialogue and maintain its authenticity.

Frank turned out to be the best traveling companion on a film that a director could hope for, and one of the most entertaining as well.

Heading into preproduction, casting, and locations, we set up offices in one of those classic cottages on the Paramount backlot. Frank and I shared the main room, which was spacious but cozy, allowing for constant interaction. Our secretaries were in the kitchen.

One day, I was talking on the phone to my business manager, who, because I was earning quite a bit of money that year, was urging me to buy an expensive car like a Mercedes for tax purposes. I said to her, "I'm sorry, Teresa, I grew up during World War II. What the Germans did to the Jews, Gypsies, and homosexuals, I can never forgive them. So I don't buy anything German."

Frank overhead the exchange. Afterward, he said to me in his typically blunt delivery: "Kotcheff, what are you going on about? The war finished over thirty years ago! You won't buy anything German, that's ridiculous. You're not even Jewish — at least, you say you're not Jewish. My grandparents died in a concentration camp and I have three

Mercedes. They're the best cars, beautifully engineered. Forgive and forget, Kotcheff, forgive and forget."

Again, I succumbed to his rhetoric. Frank immediately phoned his Mercedes dealer. Master negotiator that he was, he hondled him down from $35,000 to $30,000.

A few days later, Frank walked into the office and told me that my car had been delivered. It was sitting outside. I charged out of the office. There it was, a long beautiful silver gleaming Mercedes 450SL — hanging in the rear window was a genuine Nazi SS flag. Only Frank . . .

"

The standard we wanted for the film was total authenticity — which turned around and hit us in the face.

The film was set in Texas. Frank secured the Rice University stadium to shoot our football scenes. He made a deal with the Houston Oilers NFL team to let us use all their facilities, exercise rooms, etc., and provide us access to their organization. Days after the Houston Oilers owner, Bud Adams, agreed to give us all access, he called us and told us that he had to back out of the deal. The issue was the Murchison family, who owned the Dallas Cowboys. They did not want the film to be made because of its unflattering portrait of the NFL and the Dallas Cowboys. And because a former Cowboy had written it.

"Boys," Adams said in his heavy Southern drawl, "after you finish the film, you get to go back to Hollywood, but I have to stay in Texas and they will make my life miserable."

The Murchisons were going to make our lives miserable too.

Rice University soon informed us that they would also have to back out for unspecified reasons. In an effort to mobilize opposition within the NFL, people in the Murchisons' circle began to spread ugly rumors about me. One was that in my film I was going to show the Murchisons getting blowjobs from the Dallas Cowgirls in the owner's box during a game. They threatened to blackball a former Cowboys receiver who now had his own sports radio show if he took a part in the movie.

Because of the Murchisons, Texas was now out of the question for our film. Our only option was to film in California. It turned out that as we were coming to this conclusion, the budget came in at $12 million, but Paramount insisted the film be made for $10.5 million. Therefore, shooting in L.A., which was far less expensive than going on location to Texas, would serve a dual purpose.

However, there was one problem. The actors' contracts, including Nick Nolte, Mac Davis, and a few others were all going "pay or play" in three weeks, meaning that the production would have to start paying them whether we were filming or not. It had taken me two months to find all the locations in Texas; I now had three weeks to find them all in California. To speed up the process, Frank provided me with a helicopter, and we went to work.

The most critical location was the football stadium and its facilities. We had three weeks of shooting scheduled at that location. At the time, the Rams played in Los Angeles. We toured the facilities. They were perfect for us, and we met with the team's general manager, Don Klosterman. Being sensitive to any controversy, we agreed to cover up the Rams logos when we were filming. We made an agreeable deal with Klosterman, who was very excited at the prospect of us shooting there.

Another important location was a sprawling mansion with a spacious outdoor pool area for a big party scene. At the time, both Mac Davis and I were bachelors, and we frequently visited the Playboy Mansion. I called Hugh Hefner. I explained to Heff that I was under the gun and asked if we could shoot at the mansion. He had never allowed a director to film there, but he might be open to us filming there.

"

Two days before filming began, Frank Yablans and I were in the production office making final preparations when the Rams GM Don Klosterman called. Frank put him on speakerphone. Klosterman told us that the NFL had called him and very strongly asked him not to let us film at the Rams facility.

"But we have a deal!" I protested to Klosterman. "This is totally unethical."

"You're right, it's unethical, sorry," Klosterman replied. And then he hung up.

I couldn't believe it. I began to rant to Frank that the NFL was going to sabotage our film. I cursed the rich owners for not standing up for themselves. Most of all I wondered what the hell were we going to do now.

Frank stopped me. "Bridget," he called out to his secretary, "get me Dino Conte on the line."

The name rang a bell. While trying to find cuts in the budget with my line producer, Jack Bernstein, I remembered seeing an item in the budget: "Dino Conte — $150,000." The strange part was not that I hadn't heard of him, as there were 200 people working on the film, but that a guy making that kind of money was listed with the electricians and the grips, rather than above the line with the producers, actors, and director. At the time, I had asked Jack who Dino Conte was. His response was a quick "don't ask." So I didn't. But I was about to learn who Dino Conte was.

Within a minute, a guy with a thick American-Italian accent was on speakerphone. Frank introduced me. Conte asked what the problem was. I filled him in on the Rams backing out of our deal in the eleventh hour.

Conte listened. He didn't say more than a few words, and the call ended. Frank seemed pleased, so I changed the subject to other impending production issues.

Fifteen minutes later, Don Klosterman called. "I've been thinking about what you said, Ted, and you are right, it is unethical for me to back out of our deal," he said. "You can film at our facility."

Wow. This Dino Conte was something else.

Back to work I went to secure the Playboy Mansion. I called Hugh Hefner and pressed him for a yes. He explained he was having a change of heart. He told me how fond he was of me personally, but the fact was that he had never allowed any of his other director friends to film at the mansion and simply could not set a precedent.

I told Frank what Hugh had said. Unfazed, he called out, "Bridget, get me Dino Conte on the line!"

Dino was back on the phone. I explained the situation with the Playboy Mansion. Again, Dino said very little, and the call ended.

Minutes later, Hugh Hefner called me. "Come on up to the mansion, Ted, maybe we can work something out," he said.

Any time there was a problem in preproduction, some roadblock, it was always "Get me Dino Conte on the line!" Now I had to know: "Frank, who the hell is Dino Conte?"

His response: "He's an old friend of mine and what does it matter, we got our locations." Indeed we did. Ever grateful that I had a producer who knew people who could get things done, I promptly dropped the matter.

Out of respect for my friendship with Hugh Hefner, I spared him the embarrassment with his other director friends and found another location.

"

The first week we shot every night until midnight. On Friday night, at the end of the week, Frank Yablans was so pleased with the results that he wanted to take me to dinner. When I asked him where we could possibly go at midnight, he told me that my driver (who took me to and from set every day) knew a place. I could hardly say no.

Tired but exhilarated, I climbed in the front seat of the car, where I always sat. As the driver pulled away, a voice came from the backseat. "Ted . . . I'm Dino Conte. Nice to meet you."

Startled, I turned around. This was our first personal encounter. There was a man lounging in the backseat, legs crossed. He had a heavy five o'clock shadow and was wearing a black suit and white shirt with an oversized shirt collar that cascaded over the lapels of his suit. His gold watch glowed. He looked like he had walked out of *The Godfather*. I shook his hand.

We went to Gatsby's, a well-known restaurant with a dance floor. The place was like a scene out of a mob movie. We walked in. All the waiters and waitresses were lined up from the entrance to the dance floor. The tuxedo-clad maître d' rushed over to us and ebulliently greeted Dino with so many Mr. Conte's that it seemed like he feared for his life. Either that, or he was angling for a huge tip. He ushered us to a table for four that had been set up right in the middle of the dance floor.

Soon after, Frank Yablans arrived with a beautiful girl on his arm, one of my film's background extras. As Frank was busy romancing the lady, I was left with the dubious task of talking to Dino, who frankly scared the shit out of me. I quickly ordered a double Glenlivet, gulped it down, and asked for another.

Dino could not have been more pleasant. He asked how production was going. I nervously launched into a story of how I was having trouble getting a work permit for my film editor who I always used, Thom Noble, a Brit. Owing to the fact that I was totally intimidated, and my brain fatigued by work was now fuddled by the Scotch, I garbled my way through the story. Dino misunderstood and thought that I was the one who needed the work permit.

Dino put his hand over mine and patted it, "Teddy, my boy, for a person of your eminence, there is no problem in getting a work permit," he said with a knowing twinkle in his eye.

For a split second, I imagined myself indebted to Dino Conte for life. "No, no, it's not for me," I said nervously and over-emphatically. I prattled on that I was certain that everything would be worked out, and he should not give it another thought. Dino smiled and told me that if I needed any help to let him know. I ordered another Scotch and never brought it up again.

Later, I asked Jack Bernstein, my line producer who had told me not to ask about Dino Conte, to explain to me what Dino had on people like Rams GM Don Klosterman and Hugh Hefner.

"Ted," Jack said, brushing me off, "I have no idea. And if I did, I would never tell you."

Point taken. In the end, it didn't matter. I had learned that every film should have a Dino Conte.

CHAPTER NINETEEN
Gridiron Characters

Films endure, no doubt. But if you ask filmmakers, actors, grips, or cameramen what they liked most about a film they worked on, my guess is they will not talk about a scene in the finished product, or about walking down the red carpet at the premiere, or about the box office numbers. They will talk about the process of making the film, of working in the trenches with like-minded creative people day after day, and of the tribe they formed during the long days of shooting.

North Dallas Forty was that kind of film for me, one that was about the people who worked on the film. We had an assortment of characters that I never really came across again. I had a producer more Hollywood than Hollywood itself in Frank Yablans, and the fixer of all fixers watching my back in Dino Conte. My cast was unique in that it was made up of one of the greatest actors of his generation, a singer with no acting experience, some terrific character actors as supporting players, and several former NFL players.

The film tells the story of wide receiver Phil Elliott and his quarterback, Seth Maxwell, who play for the North Dallas Bulls professional football team (standing in for the Dallas Cowboys). The two are very much into the sex, drugs, and rock 'n' roll scene that lured in many sports figures of the 1970s. They play for a coach who looks the other way to their consumption of painkillers and an owner who treats all of his players like commodities.

Nick Nolte was cast as the wide receiver. To date, most of Nick's credits had been in TV. He had shot to stardom in the miniseries *Rich Man, Poor Man*. His diversity showed through when he then starred in two very different movies back to back, the popcorn thriller *The Deep* and the gripping drama *Who'll Stop the Rain*. He had an old soul look that I wanted in the character.

For the quarterback, I went with Mac Davis. I knew Mac socially. He was a superstar country singer with a long list of chart-busting hits, but he had virtually no acting credits to his name. I wanted the character to have that rock star status with the "howdy man" drawl. I saw the quarterback as a good ole Texas bullshitter who is your friend — though if it comes down to it, to save himself he will throw you under the bus.

Nick was unconventional in every regard. He is easily one of the finest actors I have ever worked with, and he brought enormous depth to the character. But he also played hard every night.

To shoot one sequence, we went to a distant location in the country and both stayed in our motor homes so that we did not have to commute back and forth in heavy traffic.

We were parked in a field next to each other. All night long, I would hear him partying and carrying on doing God knows what in his motor home, female voices crying out. But the next morning, he would arrive on set totally prepared for the scene, his face virginal with no signs of debauchery.

Finally, I asked him how he was able to burn the candle so hard at both ends.

"I just get used to it," he said nonchalantly. "It's my form of relaxation."

”

For authenticity and also for information, I had my casting team look for real NFL players to use in front of the camera and behind the camera as coaches in *North Dallas Forty*. Fred Biletnikoff, a former standout receiver with the Oakland Raiders, worked with Nick Nolte. He showed Nick how to line up and coached him on which passing routes to run.

In the football scenes, I ended up using around 18 current and former NFL players, including Louie Kelcher and Harold Jackson. But none had a bigger impact on the movie and on me than John Matuszak, who, interestingly, got the part when the Dallas Cowboys' Harvey Martin backed out at the last minute likely due to pressure from the organization.

Nicknamed "Tooz," Matuszak was an original, and a misunderstood one at that. He entered the league full of promise, as the first pick of the 1973 NFL draft by the Oakland Raiders, and he fulfilled every bit of that promise in eight seasons with the team. He gained a reputation as one of the toughest defensive players — and hardest partiers — in the league. I met Matuszak because he was trying to make inroads into acting before he retired.

Matuszak became like a back-up assistant director to me. He would constantly feed me information that I needed for authenticity. I was preparing to shoot a scene in the locker room in which the players are getting ready to take the field. He came up to me and said, "Ted, just before a game, everyone is so nervous they have to shit. All the toilets are full. We are like actors going onstage. We have to go out on that field in front of all those people and the TV cameras, and we are all worried we will make asses out of ourselves. It's worse than opening night on Broadway." So I shot a lot of players having to crap before the game.

I once asked Tooz if he shot up with painkillers and steroids. "Ted, did you actually expect me to go out on that field and face those huge monsters who are shot up to the eyeballs without being shot up myself?" He told me there are certain physical effects to shooting up. The neck muscles tighten up and begin to twitch. I asked him to act this in the film, and players later told me how accurate it was.

I became something of a father figure to him. Between takes, he would actually sit on my knee and air out his problems. Mind you, he was 6-foot-9 and 270 pounds! He was so large that if I stood behind him, at 6 feet, no one would be able to see me. However, he was a big softie at heart. At the time, he lived with a mother and her adult daughter in an apparent ménage à trois relationship. His real persona was the complete opposite of the one he had cultivated on the field. His hard hitting and hard partying spilled over into the media and became the way people saw him. This created problems everywhere he went. "My image is so wrong," he told me once, sitting on my knee. "I'm not a big mean violent guy." But everywhere he went, people thought he was, and every tough guy tried to pick a fight with him.

Once we were in a bar together having a drink and a medium-sized burly redneck walked up to him. The redneck stood over the seated Tooz and challenged him. "You think you're so tough, don't you . . ."

Tooz told the guy he had no quarrel with him and wasn't looking for one. I piped in, "Hey, please leave us alone."

The redneck moved aggressively closer. "Oh yeah, you think you're one fucking tough hombre." Tooz stood up.

"Don't do it . . ." I said to the redneck, just as he took a swing at Tooz.

Tooz ducked under the punch and countered with an uppercut. Tooz popped the guy so hard that he went sailing through the front picture window of the restaurant and landed on the sidewalk. There was glass everywhere. The guy was so cut up, we had to call an ambulance.

I was happy that *North Dallas Forty* was the beginning of a new career for Tooz as an actor. He played in the NFL another two years after the film came out, helping the Raiders win the 1981 Super Bowl. He retired after spending the following season injured and began acting full time. He appeared in a number of movies, including *The Goonies*, *One Man Force*, and *Caveman*, as well as on many popular TV shows such as *Perfect Strangers*, *The Dukes of Hazzard*, and *Miami Vice*.

Matuszak lived hard and fast and died young. In 1989, at just 38, he was found dead as a result of an accidental overdose of the prescription drug Darvon, a potent narcotic pain reliever with such debilitating side effects that it is no longer on the market.

Tooz was revered by those who knew him. *Los Angeles Times* sports columnist Mike Downey wrote, "Death should have feared John Matuszak. The other way around makes no sense. When the Grim Reaper came by to touch the Tooz on the shoulder Saturday night, the big guy should have sprung from his bed, ripped open his hospital gown from the neck down, roared like a primal beast, and then poured the two of them a drink. He should have scared Death to death."

,,

The great thing about having the football players around was that when I needed authentic material, I could ask them. No slight against a screenwriter's imagination, but the players' stories not only rang true, they were true.

Case in point: I had been struggling with the climax of the film. I needed one scene that encapsulated how the players were used as pieces of meat, as animals there to win games for the management without regard for their health or well-being. One former NFL player working on the film told me the most amazing story.

The player, a veteran, said that the team's head coach stopped by his room the night before a playoff game. The player was injured and not scheduled to play. The coach said to him, "I know you are injured, but I need you to play. I'm not supposed to do this but I need you to shoot up so you can play tomorrow. The team is counting on you."

The player said, "Anything for you, coach."

The coach thanked him and told the player how much he needed him for the game and how much it meant to the team. The player shot up and suited up. But the coach never played him in the game.

"Ted," the player told me, "I finally realized that the reason he had me shoot up was so he could go to a young star player suffering injuries who did not wish to shoot up and say, 'See that old veteran shooting up, he's a real team player. He'll do anything for the team, so you need to shoot up, too. You want to succeed in this sport, you've got to play with injuries, and sometimes you have to shoot up.' So he did."

When I heard that, I thought, *Eureka*. There's my climax. To me, that was the ultimate manipulation.

"

The two most important shots in any film are the first and the last. The first shot is a taste of what the audience is in for, and the last shot is what remains of the experience.

In the opening shot of *North Dallas Forty*, I defined the physical brutality of the NFL experience. I had Nick Nolte lying in bed and waking up. There was dried blood on his nose and lip and on the pillow. It was such a strong image that the *New Yorker*'s Pauline Kael called to tell me what a brilliant opening shot it was.

But I couldn't find the last shot in my head. The novel ended with Phil Elliott (Nick's character) being dumped from the team and driving to the country to start a new life with his lady friend, only to find her dead. To me, that was too melodramatic. I kept thinking the ending would come to me during filming, but the night before we needed to film it, I still did not have the shot. I stayed up until 2 a.m., pacing and pondering.

I wanted the film to end after Nick's character is forced to testify at the team office about drug use. When he leaves the building, he bumps into Mac's character, the quarterback, who is waiting outside the hearing on the steps. Mac is playing with a football and stewing to find out what happened. When Nick, his favorite receiver, emerges, he asks Nick if he has squealed on him. Nick, whose character is being run out of the game on a trumped-up charge, says that he did not give him up. But that was all I had.

Finally, the morning of the shoot, I had a eureka moment. I would keep the scene going a bit longer.

As Nick walks away, Mac calls to him. Nick turns around. Mac throws him a pass, a perfect spiral. But Nick doesn't catch it, he opens his arms and lets the ball hit his chest and bounce off. He is going to start his new life with his lady friend, who is still alive. He shrugs his shoulders philosophically. Freeze frame. End of film.

Robert McKee, the top screenwriting guru for decades, flattered me by citing the ending as one of great archetypal endings in modern cinema in one of his courses.

"

Though my memories are of the people, *North Dallas Forty* undoubtedly had both an immediate and lasting impact. Leading up to its release, the NFL pushed back hard against the film, calling it a fictitious account of the league. There were even accusations that players who appeared in the film were blackballed. The San Francisco 49ers Tommy Reamon claimed that he was cut in training camp because he took part in the film. Tom Fears, a former player and now a scout, did a fabulous job helping me stage the football formations and actions. He claimed that his scouting service was dropped by three NFL teams.

There was no proof that these players were shunned because of the film, and the NFL called such claims ridiculous. Frank Yablans, however, played it up in the media as being possible. "Those are pretty strange coincidences," he said. "With a borderline player, this movie might be the catalyst for a team to get rid of him."

The reviews were positive. Janet Maslin of the *New York Times* wrote, "The central friendship in the movie, beautifully delineated, is the one between Mr. Nolte and Mac Davis, who expertly plays the team's quarterback, a man whose calculating nature and complacency make him all the more likable, somehow." *Time*'s Richard Schickel wrote: "*North Dallas Forty* retains enough of the original novel's authenticity to deliver strong, if brutish, entertainment." *Newsweek* critic David Ansen said that the film "isn't subtle or finely tuned, but like a crunching downfield tackle, it leaves its mark."

There was much talk about the verisimilitude of the football sequences and the realism of its violent, body-wrecking culture. Frank Deford, the highly regarded *Sports Illustrated* correspondent, wrote, "If *North Dallas Forty* is reasonably accurate, the pro game is a brutal human abattoir, worse even than previously imagined."

On Super Bowl Sunday in 2009, the *Los Angeles Times* chose *North Dallas Forty* as the best film ever made about football. ESPN ranked it the eleventh best sports movie of all time. Even the folks in Dallas later came around to recognize the merits of the film. In 2010, *Dallas* magazine named the release of *North Dallas Forty* one of the 35 biggest pop culture moments in Dallas history.

CLOSE UP

NICK NOLTE

Stanislavski might as well have been talking about Nick Nolte when he said, "Play well or play badly, but play truly."

Nick is deeply and commendably committed to the integrity of his characters. He never does anything in a performance that he thinks violates his conception of the character. It sounds strange, but this is at odds with becoming a movie star, as many stars are more concerned that they look good than they are about staying true to the film.

Here's what I mean. On *North Dallas Forty*, we were shooting a scene with Nick and Mac Davis. The two team-mates, who had been at a party carousing the night before, are in the team's training room, full of stainless steel equipment designed to soothe aching joints and muscles. Mac Davis, the quarterback, is going to soak his sore throwing elbow in swirling warm water. Nick is taking off all of his clothes to soak his whole bruised body in a whirlpool bath. We rehearsed the scene and got ready to shoot.

I called action. Nick took off his trousers and was stripped down to his underwear — I yelled cut. Nick asked me what was wrong. I told him that his underwear had visible skid marks.

"Yeah, I know," Nick said. "This guy would have skid marks on his underwear."

"I don't care what he would have," I shot back. "I'm not having shit-stained underwear on my leading man being thrust in the face of the audience!"

Nick pushed back. "You're a sell-out, Kotcheff!" he bellowed. "You don't want to follow the truth of this guy! This guy would have shitty underwear."

"You can call me all the insulting names you want, but I won't shoot the scene with skid marks on your underwear," I railed. "I'm going to my office, and I ain't coming out until you change your underwear!"

I stormed off the set. I sat in my office for 15 minutes and stewed over what Nick had called me. I shouted for the AD and asked him to have Nick come to my office.

A few minutes later, Nick walked in, wary of what I was going to say.

"Nick, I have an idea. Instead of the skid-marked underwear, we'll get another pair that is full of holes so we can see your ass through it."

A big smile came across Nick's face, and he banged his fist on the desk in excitement. "Kotcheff, you're a genius!" he said.

This depth of character was classic Nick Nolte. There probably wasn't a big star in Hollywood who would have let me put hole-filled underwear on him. I know if I had asked a star to wear underwear with skid marks on it, I would be fired that evening. But Nick was all about the character and cared not a lick about his image. I believe that these types of unselfish actions that were true to the movie were why he never became a classic leading man. But Nick also refuses to play the Hollywood game of showing up at every possible glitzy industry event. It goes against his grain; he just won't do it.

I remember in a party scene there was a close-up of him watching his girlfriend across the room laughing with another football player. I gave him the direction to be jealous. Now, some actors would blatantly send telegrams with *JEALOUSY* written in red letters across their foreheads, but Nick knew instinctively at what level of depth in his psyche jealousy would be found. You saw it, but it was subtle, fleeting, amazingly lifelike.

Nick is a great cinematic talent, and he has won and been nominated for many acting awards. Even so, I feel it doesn't reach the level of recognition he deserves. I put Nick up there with one of cinema's great performers, Gene Hackman.

CHAPTER TWENTY

Rambo

Rambo. The iconic character played by Sylvester Stallone conjures up images of American supremacy and the jingoistic Reagan administration foreign policy of the 1980s. When President Ronald Reagan was playing hardball with the Soviet Bloc, he was dubbed "Ronbo." Posters of a bulked-up Reagan brandishing a machine gun began appearing in the media. The "Ronbo" reference was coined by his detractors to show Reagan as a warmonger, but it was immediately adopted by his supporters, as it implied that Reagan could singlehandedly take on all of America's enemies. President Reagan himself embraced the image. He used Rambo as a paragon of his unified vision of America as the world's policeman against all evildoers. Notably, in a press conference at the end of the 1985 hostage crisis in Beirut, Reagan quipped, "Boy, after seeing *Rambo* [the sequel] last night, I know what to do next time this happens."

A related tangent. Bruce Springsteen's anti-war, anti-government anthem "Born in the USA" was appropriated by the right as a hawkish call to arms in the 1980s. The pulsating chorus was adopted by the right as an affirmation of Reagan's "Morning in America" mantra. However, the song conveyed the exact opposite. It was actually a gut-wrenching tale of a Vietnam veteran who is shunned by his government and his own community when he returns home from war. As Springsteen has ironically noted numerous times, "Apparently, the money is in the misinterpretation."

That also applied to the transition of John Rambo from the first film to the next three.

The character, as conceived in the novel *First Blood* by David Morrell and put on the big screen in the first Rambo movie which I directed, was the opposite of his depiction in the sequels. I saw him as a man who had seen too much senseless killing and wanted it to stop. But by the second movie, the one referenced by Reagan in his Beirut speech, Rambo had come to be regarded as a hyper-patriotic, one-man killing machine.

First Blood is, in fact, a film about the aftermath of the Vietnam War, a war which I had opposed on every level. All wars are stupid, but the Vietnam War was especially stupid. A war that could and should have been avoided. It was based on the dubious "Domino Theory," that if Vietnam went Communist, the rest of southeast Asia would fall like dominos and become Communist. Well, we all know the validity of that idiotic idea, as American tourists now sun themselves on Vietnam's beaches. The soldiers there knew it was a pointless and unwinnable war: 58,000 young Americans and a million Vietnamese died there for absolutely nothing. The veterans who survived felt they had dirtied their souls for no good end.

The war had disastrous effects on the psyche of the American people and was physically, mentally, and emotionally crippling to those who served. The statistics involving veterans were horrifying. In 1980, it was reported that 1,000 veterans a month were trying to commit suicide and one-third of those were successful. To state the obvious, war involves murdering people. It takes a long time with a lot of communal support for a mind to become reacclimatized to ordinary society. This, the Vietnam veterans never received.

When Vietnam veterans came home, they were not only rejected, they were vilified: the right wing of this country treating them as a bunch of losers; the left wing as "women killers" and "baby killers." I heard a story from one vet, who, after finishing his service in Vietnam came to McGuire Air Force Base and was greeted by protesters who threw garbage, feces, dead rabbits, and baby dolls covered in fake blood. They carried signs saying in large, lurid letters, "Baby Killers!"

When I was researching for *First Blood*, another vet told me how, on his last day of service in Vietnam, the Vietcong attacked their camp. He machine-gunned dozens of Vietcong at very close range, while many of his close friends died all around him. The next morning, his tour of service over, he was put on a plane that flew directly to San Francisco. Arriving at midnight, he was dumped out into the dark streets with no one to greet him, no one to assist him, his mind still full and haunted by all of the nightmarish ghosts of the previous day. He wandered through the dark streets, not knowing what to do with himself.

The contrast to previous wars was stark. In the past, when American veterans returned from war, they were celebrated as heroes in parades with marching bands, banners, and ice cream trucks welcoming them home. All of these things helped the vets return to normal, civilian society. The World War II veterans received generous government benefits and became part of the so-called Greatest Generation. The Vietnam veterans were humiliated and basically left out in the cold.

What's incredible is that the terrible treatment of Vietnam vets goes on to this day, with veterans waiting endlessly for medical treatment from the Department of Veteran Affairs. All vets wait many months, with some dying before they receive needed treatment. It fills me with heartbreak and anger to think that these men, who did not ask to go to Vietnam and risk their lives, came home to America to find that there was no place for them, so they turned their guns on themselves. That's why I conceived *First Blood* as Rambo's suicide mission.

In my film, Rambo's treatment by the redneck sheriff and his deputies was a microcosm of the way America had treated their returning veterans. I think the film touched a nerve of guilt and shame. Indeed, many veterans thanked me personally for what the film had to say.

"

For me, the subject of unjustified violence is personal. When I read David Morrell's novel *First Blood*, I thought of my heritage. My family was raised in a violent culture, and the more I learned about their history, the more I abhorred violence.

My mother grew up in Macedonia under the violent and oppressive rule of the Turkish Ottoman Empire. In 1903, a faction of Macedonians stood up and rebelled against Turkish rule to gain their freedom. This turned out to be a horrible mistake. In ten short days, the Turkish Army crushed the resistance and savagely punished all Macedonians. The Turkish authorities announced that, for this heinous rebellion, 50 Macedonian towns and villages would be totally obliterated and their inhabitants massacred.

My great-grandfather on my mother's side feared for his family's safety. With regret, he decided to abandon his very successful farm, and to save his family, they set out to flee Macedonia. Fifty members of my family who lived and worked on the farm, including my mother, attempted to escape to the free part of Bulgaria. This incredible odyssey, full of dangers, adventure, and murder — and all the time being pursued by the cruel Turkish cavalry — was so dramatic that I came within the drawing of a straw of never existing.

Even more harrowing was how that violent culture affected another one of my mother's cousins, Stavro Grozdanov (the fat one), my hero, who you recall was a commander of the Macedonian rebels who failed to commit suicide, and via Turkey, Syria, and Italy ended up in Canada. Something I learned about him many years later was that he suffered an excruciating tragedy, probably the most searing that any human being should have to endure in this world of pain. The Macedonian rebel commanders, including Stavro, laid down a strict law: no Macedonian woman should fraternize with any Turk on pain of death — with no exceptions! Consorting with the enemy was punishable by death. Stavro's mother, an attractive young widow, became romantically involved with a handsome Turkish officer. Stavro had to order his mother's execution! What he went through afterward was unimaginable. My mother, who told me about this horror, said it pained and haunted him for the rest of his life.

Many years later in the 1950s, when I was an adult, I

was involved with saving my mother's brother, my intellectual mentor, Uncle Andrew, from yet more oppression. The situation started while Andrew was living in Canada. He was invited by Marshal Tito, the Communist dictator of Yugoslavia, to return to his original homeland and be a part of the ruling government. Because my uncle was Macedonian, Tito made him the vice-president of the province of Macedonia. Andrew decided to return for the cause. He was so committed that, as he boarded the boat to Yugoslavia in Montreal, he ripped up his Canadian passport, the fool. He announced to the press, "Goodbye capitalist Canada! I'm going back to the paradise of the workers!"

However, once Uncle Andrew became involved in the inner workings of Tito's regime, he saw the Communists' true colors. The government was arresting artists, intellectuals, and lawyers and jailing them without just cause, even executing some of them. Totally disillusioned, he began to show his disdain for the Communists and fearlessly voiced his feelings of disapproval — actions that put him in mortal jeopardy.

My uncle Andrew, the lifelong unwavering advocate of social equality, was deeply disturbed that he had become what he had always despised. He and his family lived in the mansion of an executed aristocrat. He had a limo and a chauffeur, Ivan, who always clicked his heels when Andrew approached, no matter how much my uncle told him not to. And whether it be agriculture, the position of women, or the arts, Ivan always spouted the correct Communist line. Even my Communist uncle got impatient with him and said, "Ivan, don't you have any opinions of your own?" Ivan replied, "I do, sir, I do, but I don't agree with them."

Finally, my uncle had a nervous breakdown, which manifested itself in him endlessly playing the violin all day long. He wanted to return to Canada and freedom, but the problem was he had no passport. And would Tito let him go?

Before he could figure a way out of Macedonia, government enforcers took him. In what was like a scene out of a Solzhenitsyn novel, two guys knocked on his door at midnight and hauled him away. They brought him in front of the head of the secret police. There was a large, menacing Luger on his desk pointed straight at my uncle. Uncle Andrew stared back at him. "If you think that gun is going to frighten me, it isn't. You know why? You have already killed my soul. You have killed my mind. You have killed my idealism. There is nothing left of me to kill!" The chief put the gun away, but Andrew was not out of danger.

Andrew's wife, my aunt Luba, suspected that her husband was going to be killed. She was a wily, cunning woman. It turned out that she was friends with Tito's mistress, who was an opera singer. She rushed over to her friend's house and told her that the secret police had taken Andrew away. She begged her friend to appeal to Tito for her husband's life. The woman said that Luba was in luck; Tito had sent word that he wanted his mistress that night.

The opera singer went to the palace and had sex with Tito. Over pillow talk, she told him that he could not kill Andrew Palmeroff, because he was a well-known intellectual and journalist in Slavic circles in Canada. If he ordered Palmeroff's execution, she told Tito, then many Canadians would hate him. Reluctantly — and we can only guess not entirely focused — Tito called off the execution.

Now came the problem of getting Uncle Andrew back into Canada before Tito changed his mind. My parents came to me for help, as I was the most articulate member of the family. They asked me to go to the RCMP and convince them to let Uncle Andrew back in the country.

In 1958, when I was still banned from entering the United States, I met with the colonel in charge in his office — he had the comic-book name of Colonel Fast. On his totally clean desktop there was only an inch-thick file with my name boldly emblazoned on it. So they had been watching me, but I was not intimidated. I pleaded my uncle's case forcefully. Colonel Fast asked why Canada should allow a troublemaker who gave speeches and wrote articles in the *New Times* espousing Communism back into the country.

"Because he has seen the light, and he can help others see the light," I replied.

The argument went back and forth for some time, with me continually making the point that my uncle was a totally changed man. The colonel was skeptical to the point of mocking me as a Communist. "I never could win an argument with a Communist," he said ironically, but he relented. Uncle Andrew was allowed to return to Canada.

The Colonel never opened my file.

My father's side of the family was not to be outdone on the question of suffering police and government violence. My father's brother, Gyorgi, my favorite uncle, who lived with us in Canada during the Depression, was deported back to Bulgaria, the fate of all immigrants who committed an illegality. Gyorgi didn't really mind. He never cared for Canada; remember what he said: "The weather in Canada is cold. So are the people." He loved the mañana way of life in Bulgaria — why do anything today if you can put it off till tomorrow? He enjoyed sitting around cafés laughing, joking, drinking endless cups of Turkish coffee. But don't get me wrong, he was very enterprising.

He started a small shoe-manufacturing factory that proved very successful. It was upended when World War II hit, and at war's end, Bulgaria, having been on the

German side, was awarded by Churchill to Stalin as victory booty. Stalin executed all Bulgarian politicians who were not "reds" and instituted a Communist government. One of the first things this government did was to nationalize Gyorgi's shoe factory. So he went back to making shoes by hand, which were very prized, especially by the Communist nomenklatura.

But Gyorgi was never one to hold his tongue. He openly commented that the Communist government officials were totally incompetent, not anywhere as efficient as the capitalist government in Canada. He made quips like, "Under capitalism, it's dog eat dog, but under communism it's the other way around." Someone betrayed him to the Commies. So one morning, two cops showed up at his shoe shop and declared that Gyorgi had to come with them to police headquarters. He went to get his jacket, but they said he wouldn't need it; he'd be right back at his business after lunch. A blatant lie. He was taken to police headquarters and incarcerated.

Gyorgi was put on trial, accused of being a Turkish spy. At his trial, he spoke in his defense to the judge: "Your honor, you're obviously a very intelligent man; now, if you were going to be a spy, who would you work for? Obviously, you'd spy for the United States. They're rich and would pay you handsomely. What do the Turks have? Lice!"

The whole court burst out laughing, including the judge. The Bulgars hate the Turks, as they had ruled Bulgaria cruelly and tyrannically for 500 years, with Bulgaria only becoming a free country very recently. However, as amused as they were by his wit, they nevertheless found Gyorgi guilty and sentenced him to seven years in a gulag. The trial obviously had been a total, pre-ordained sham.

The gulag was a sadistic experience. He slept on a cold

cement floor, lightly covered with straw and nothing else in a very long, narrow shack alongside 50 other prisoners. They were fed fish broth with only fish bones in it. Early every morning, the prisoners were forced to run to a work site a mile away, smash rocks all day, and then run back to the gulag.

It took his wife six months to find out which gulag he was imprisoned in. When she finally ascertained his location she sent him food packages, which were not given to him. Instead they were placed in full sight but out of reach, so that Gyorgi could watch the food rot. He was a man of my size, six feet and weighing about 200 pounds. In six years, he was reduced to 100 pounds, and on the edge of death. Gyorgi understood that these gulags were not places of incarceration but places of execution, charnel houses where a slow, relentless death was administered. But Gyorgi was a fiercely determined man. He was not going to let these "fucking Commie bastards" kill him.

Gyorgi had the good fortune that he slept on the freezing cement floor next to an Oxford-educated Bulgarian Orthodox prelate, who for some reason was allowed to keep his priestly robes. He would wrap himself and Gyorgi in them, saving Gyorgi's life in a last act of Christian compassion. At the six-year mark, of the original 500 prisoners who were there when Gyorgi first arrived, he was the only one left. Four hundred and ninety-nine had died, including his saintly savior, to be replaced of course by fresh prisoners.

Gyorgi, now the longest-serving prisoner, was be-friended by one of the nicer guards who felt sorry for him. The guard told him that with the coming freezing winter and continued deprivation of nourishing food, Gyorgi was not going to make it. The guard furtively suggested to Gyorgi a plan: "Get some prisoners together and say that you want to organize an escape. There are insufficient guards here and an escape could be entirely possible. One of your chosen prison colleagues, I'm sure, will immediately go to the commandant and betray you for a slice of bread. You'll be moved to a proper prison in Sofia: warm, your own cell, and with a proper bed." Gyorgi took his advice and sure enough, my beloved uncle was moved to a high-security prison in Sofia where he managed to survive the last year of his sentence. When he was finally released, his wife, who was waiting for him outside the prison, did not recognize the 100-pound boy coming toward her. She kept looking beyond the approaching figure for her husband.

And those goddamned Yanks accused me of being sympathetic to Communism. Ha!

These stories of my family facing violence informed the way I saw the world. The recurring violence in their lives caused me to personally detest any kind of violence and also to be ever mindful of any violence that I put on the big screen as a filmmaker.

And so, even though I am not an American and the Vietnam War was not personal to me, I held on to this conviction when I approached *First Blood*.

"

First Blood came to me from Robert Shapiro, my former William Morris agent and a very dear friend who had become president of Warner Bros. He called me into his office one day and told me about this novel by David Morrell, who happened to be Canadian. A number of filmmakers had tried to adapt the novel into a film, but no one could seem to get the script right. I told him I would read the book.

First Blood is the story of John Rambo, a Vietnam

veteran and a Congressional Medal of Honor winner, who is picked up hitchhiking by a small town Kentucky sheriff. Rambo is not looking for trouble, but rather searching for himself and for a home, wandering through America after being discharged from the Army. The surly sheriff makes a brash judgment of Rambo's appearance as he looks like a derelict hippy. He will not let Rambo even stop in the town to buy a hamburger: he drives him to the edge of town and orders him not to return. This is too much for Rambo: he's been treated like this repeatedly, so he turns around and walks back into the town, knowing what's going to happen. When Rambo does return, he is jailed and treated like an animal, which triggers flashbacks of him being tortured in Vietnam. He escapes jail and becomes the target of a massive manhunt.

After finishing the book, I immediately agreed to take on the project. The story had a strong metaphor: an engine of violence like Rambo, once created, goes on existing and can wreak damage on the people who created it, despite the fact that he is trying to return to a normal state.

I took an office on the Warner Bros. backlot and went to work on the screenplay with Mike Kozoll. Three months later, we had a solid draft, which I was very happy with. I turned it in to Robert Shapiro.

For several weeks on pins and needles, I heard nothing. Robert finally called me into his office. He informed me he had bad news. "Ted, the Warner board feels that the American public wants to forget about Vietnam," he explained. "It represents the most colossal failure in American military history, and many people associate it with the massacring of women and children. With Ronald Reagan being our president and creating a strong aura of patriotism, the audience is hungering for patriotic films, according to the board. You can hardly describe *First Blood* as a patriotic film. Ted, they just don't see a market for this movie."

Of course, I was pissed off. I asked him why he hadn't considered all of that before I spent several months working my ass off on the script, but it was no use. I disagreed strongly with their reasoning, but Warner Bros., obviously, was out.

Months passed, and I moved on to other projects. Then one evening, I was having dinner at the house of a producer named Andy Vajna, who was a social acquaintance of mine. Andy loved to cook Hungarian food, which is similar to Bulgarian food, so we hit it off. Andy mentioned that he and his partner, Mario Kassar, who also loved to eat, were ramping up their production company, Carolco, and asked if I had anything I wanted to direct.

I told him about *First Blood* and what had happened at Warner Bros., but I had to say that I doubted that Warner would let the script go. Never mind that the studio was never going to make the film. The issue in these situations is always the same: if Warner let the script go, and the film became a hit, then the executive who made the decision *not* to make the film and gave it to another company would look like an idiot — which, of course, is exactly what happened. I have seen other examples of this where the guilty executive was even fired. So I was not optimistic that they would give it up.

Andy and Mario both loved the script. They went to work trying to maneuver the project away from Warner Bros. It took nearly a year of tortuous negotiations, but they finally convinced Warner to sell it to them.

Carolco was one of the first to pre-sell foreign rights country by country based on the overseas appeal of a film's cast, and then borrow the money to finance production against those pre-sale contracts. Their strategy was to wait to sell the U.S. rights until the film was finished, hoping to bring a larger advance.

So, the first order of business was to cast the part of John Rambo. My first choice was Sylvester Stallone. At that time, Stallone's career was stalled. The first two Rocky movies had been huge hits. But he had followed them with *F.I.S.T.*, *Nighthawks*, *Paradise Alley*, and *Victory*. None of those films were very successful at the box office in the U.S. and the received wisdom in Hollywood was that Stallone only sold tickets as Rocky.

That kind of dogmatic thinking did not bother me. I thought Stallone had both the toughness that the role demanded but, more importantly, the poignancy. And, watching all of his performances, I thought that with the right material and me as the director, he could give as outstanding a performance as Robert De Niro or Al Pacino. With Andy's blessing, I sent the script to Stallone's agent on a Thursday night. For the first time, and only time in my long life of working as a film director, I received a reply the very next day, instead of the usual three months.

Stallone called me personally the next morning and told me he wanted the part. But he had one condition to coming aboard: he wanted to work with me on the rewrite I was planning. Of course, I immediately agreed.

"

Sylvester Stallone and I went to work on the script. By the way, I never called him "Sly," as everybody else did. I didn't like it; I always called him Sylvester. For *First Blood*, we both wanted something unique and unpredictable that was also true to the spirit of the novel. I discovered right away that our sensibilities for the movie and the character were completely aligned.

In one scene, Rambo manages to get his hands on a rifle. He is being chased by the National Guard, a ragtag bunch of weekend warriors. Rambo begins to pop them one after the other, dropping them like figures in a video game. Sylvester rejected the scene. "This guy is a Green Beret and a Congressional Medal of Honor winner," he said. "These National Guard guys work in drugstores and put on uniforms on the weekend to try to keep their community safe. The audience will hate Rambo for killing them." Sylvester possessed a keen populist sense, knowing what audiences like to see and what they don't like to see.

I didn't have to think about omitting the National Guard scene for very long. I wholeheartedly agreed. We stopped writing and opened up a dialogue about the Rambo character. We talked about how he had killed soldiers and innocents alike in Vietnam and had seen a horrendous amount of killing and death. I said, "The last thing Rambo would want to do is return to America and start killing." At the end of our conversation, Sylvester said, "He shouldn't kill anyone in the movie." I wholeheartedly agreed. It was absolutely true to the character.

We decided that we would draw a parallel to the Vietnam War itself. The Vietnamese did not wish to kill American soldiers. They wanted to incapacitate them, cripple them, put them in wheelchairs so they would be seen in every American city and town when they returned, a permanent living reproach to America's interfering actions in Vietnam. So we had Rambo do exactly the same thing with his pursuing attackers: immobilize them, not kill them.

A few days later, Sylvester came into the office and said that he had a crazy idea: Rambo never says a word in the whole movie. Of course, I loved the idea. I always favor extreme ideas, and this felt like something that had not been done before in an action movie.

Without telling the producers, for obvious reasons, we went through the script and took out all of Rambo's dialogue. We played around with the scenes and talked about how they could be staged wordlessly. But after a couple days, we came to the conclusion that it looked forced and unnatural to have Rambo say nothing at all. Still, it had a very salutary effect both on the character and the script. Rambo became a man of very few words and everything he said had power and substance to it. For example, "They drew first blood, not me," six words, but how powerful, resonant, and charged. And the script itself became very laconic. As Michelangelo Antonioni had shown me, films are a sequence of connected images, and so, in my opinion, the fewer words, the better.

The biggest change we made in *First Blood* occurred during shooting, in British Columbia. The entire picture had been conceived as a suicide mission. Rambo feels there's no place for him anymore in American society. People dislike him intensely, sharing the country's irrational feelings about all Vietnam vets. When Rambo turns around and crosses the bridge back into town, he knows that he is not going to survive. This is the end of the line for him.

The day came to shoot the ending. In the final scene, Rambo, who has been tracked down and arrested, lays siege to the police station and ends up inside by himself. He's surrounded by the police and the National Guard. His former commanding colonel enters. A distraught Rambo tells the colonel: "You created me and now you should just kill me. I know you've got a gun underneath that jacket."

The colonel pulls out his gun and aims it at him. He

has come to put Rambo out of his misery, but he can't go through with it. Rambo then leans in, presses the trigger, and blows himself away. The film was conceived as Rambo's tragedy that mirrored the tragedy of so many of those veterans who killed themselves, and how they came to this sad conclusion.

We shot the scene the way it was written, and it was very moving. Sylvester played it perfectly with tremendously deep feeling. It was some of his best acting in the film. But after I had gotten the various angles I needed, Sylvester pulled me aside and asked if he could talk to me privately.

"Ted, we've put this character through so much," Sylvester said, "The police abused him. He has been endlessly pursued. He has been hunted by dogs. He has jumped off cliffs into the boughs of trees to break his fall. He has run through freezing water. He's been shot and had to sew up his own wound. We put him through all this, and now we're gonna kill him?"

I nodded, following his train of thought. "Well, Sylvester, you have a point."

"The audience is really going to hate this," he said.

There was Sylvester's populist sense in action again.

Sylvester's wise words addressed something that had been simmering in my mind for some time. The quintessential American town that Rambo finds himself in was emblematic of the United States. America had not dealt with Rambo like the Congressional Medal of Honor hero that he is, but had treated him like an enemy. So he will return the favor. He attacks this American town like he has been trained to take apart an enemy town. This symbolic action is what makes the conclusion to the film so satisfying. To then have him kill himself means the enemy would have won. The audience had got the message, it didn't need excessive piling on; it was just too much.

I agreed with Sylvester. I knew the character so well that a great idea immediately popped in my head. I explained it to Sylvester:

> I will cut out of that scene we just shot before the colonel pulls out the gun, then in one long tracking shot, it will start with you and the colonel and a state trooper coming out of the police station. Rambo stops and looks, the camera pans over and down to show that the sheriff, who has pursued Rambo throughout the film and been shot, is being loaded into an ambulance and is still alive. A relieved Rambo and his escorts come down the stairs and walk down the main street past all of the townspeople lined up to see the man who practically destroyed their town. He climbs into a jeep with the colonel, and they drive away. All this in one incredible long effective tracking shot.

Sylvester loved it.

As I began instructing the crew how to set up the shot, the two producers came running over to me, demanding to know what I was doing. We were supposed to be wrapping for the day. Why was I setting up another shot?

I told them I was shooting an alternate ending and explained what it was.

Predictably, they went nuts. "We agreed that this film was Rambo's suicide mission, and now you are altering it,

PROD.
'A' CAMERA
SCENE 115A TAKE 3
FIRST BLOOD 17·3·82
DIR: T. KOTCHEFF
CAM: A. LASZLO DAY

A compilation of four First Blood *moments. Clockwise from top left: Stallone and I discuss the big jump into the trees. Bad cop Jack Starrett gets his death makeup. My wife, Laifun, handles the clapper board. Rambo is poised to leap from the cliff face.*

plus you're over budget and over schedule." In short, they told me no, I was done for the day.

I told them, whether they liked it or not, I was shooting the scene. I've never taken any shit from producers. It would only take two hours. "And then when the American distributor wants a happy ending, which I'm sure they will, then you won't have to spend all that money to bring the whole cast and crew back here three months from now. You'll be kissing my ass in gratitude," I said.

In spite of their protestations, I proceeded to shoot what proved to be the closing shot of the picture.

99

As I finished shooting the film, every major foreign distributor was present in Los Angeles for the American Film Market. Thom Noble, my brilliant editor, had assembled forty minutes of some of the best scenes of the film and screened it in a major movie house in Westwood for all of the foreign distributors. The distributors went totally crazy for the film. Three competing Japanese distributors pushed Andy Vajna against the wall in the lobby waving big checks in his face. Through the American Film Market screening, Vajna was able to secure distribution for the film to practically half the world! I was still busy shooting when all this occurred, but obviously the film seemed set to make a lot of money.

After I finished editing the picture, the next big hurdle for the producers was to find a U.S. distributor. Orion Pictures, a brand new distributor, was very interested. However, Mike Medavoy, the head of Orion, disliked the original ending in which Rambo kills himself and wanted it reshot — oh, my prophetic soul! Andy Vajna pushed back, reiterating that the film was always thought of as a suicide mission. It was structured that way. The argument got very heated. With both sides at such fierce loggerheads, they agreed to hold a test screening in Las Vegas with the original hari-kari ending to see how an audience would respond.

The producers and Orion executives were there with their PR people. The audience reaction was amazing. They were screaming out loud. "Look out, Rambo! He's right behind you!" They were cheering for Rambo and constantly trying to warn him where the bad guys were. And then the final scene played out, with Rambo killing himself.

The theater went dead silent for a full minute. The credits began to roll. Then a voice in the crowd yelled, "If the director of this film is in the theater, let's string him up from the nearest lamp post!" People began seconding his motion. I felt like the evil sheriff in the movie. I turned to my wife, Laifun, who was sitting beside me, and I said, "Let's get the hell out of here before these crazy people do what they are threatening." We rushed out of the theater.

After the screening, the audience test cards were all collected. Andy, Mario, and I read one after the other. And with minor variations, the cards all expressed similar reactions to the film: "This is the best action picture I've ever seen! But the *ending*!! *Horrible*!!!," another card: "*How could you kill Rambo?!?!*"

I saw the gathering consternation on the face of my two producers. "Well, boys," I said, "not to worry! I just happen to have this other ending in my back pocket."

In the face of this universal disapproval, reluctantly they agreed to change the ending. The film was retested, and the results were across the board wildly positive. If you ever want to see the original ending, some DVDs of *First Blood* include it as part of the package.

Orion purchased the domestic rights, and the film

Stallone and I work on the original ending of First Blood.

LAIFUN CHUNG

Stallone, stunt coordinator Conrad Palmisano, and I discuss the jail escape scene.

ended up grossing $47 million in the U.S. and an even more impressive $78 million overseas, making it a huge hit. Of course, by not killing Rambo, the door was also open for sequels.

As the saying goes, unhappy endings are intellectual endings, and happy endings are popular endings — to which I might add for Andy Vajna and Mario Kassar, who produced three Rambo sequels, profitable endings too.

"

Sequels are not my thing, because I do not like to repeat myself. I prefer to live in the world of a film and then move on to another world. The producers and Sylvester wanted me to direct the sequel. Out of curiosity, I read the script for *Rambo: First Blood Part II*. It had Rambo agreeing to rescue a small group of American POWs, but it was incredibly violent, which was disheartening to me.

The Rambo character was being taken in a different direction, a direction that later defined the iconic image of a jingoistic American soldier out for violent retribution. In *First Blood*, he was a man who, because of his experience, abhorred violence; wrestled with the moral dilemma of violence in Vietnam; and did not kill anyone. In the sequel, John Rambo was turned into a gratuitous killing machine, running up a body count of 74, as he tried to singlehandedly leave a stamp of American might on what had happened in Vietnam. My film was against the Vietnam War; this film seemed to be enthusiastically for it. So I passed.

Personally, I felt it was an opportunity lost to create a pacifist military hero. But there's no disputing the numbers. *Rambo: First Blood Part II* was released in 1985 and did $300 million worldwide. *Rambo III* came out three years later and grossed $189 million worldwide. But by 2008, audience fatigue had set in with the franchise. Sylvester Stallone wrote, directed, and starred in the third sequel, which earned $113 million worldwide, which was less than the $125 million earned by *First Blood* some 26 years earlier. My stupid principles . . . I could have been a very rich man today.

There is also no dispute that Rambo is cemented in popular culture as a unique American hero. No matter what part of the world I travel to, there are two films of mine that seemingly everyone has seen: *First Blood* and *Weekend at Bernie's*, and further, everyone always says the same thing: "We've seen all the Rambo films; yours is by far the best."

SYLVESTER STALLONE
AND KIRK DOUGLAS

What a pairing! Sylvester and Kirk. What opposites. Maybe so, but not how you would think . . .

Sylvester Stallone and I worked closely together on the *First Blood* script with an almost identical view of it. When filming commenced, on the very first day of shooting, Sylvester came up to me and said, "Ted, I just want to say, it's been so rewarding working with you on the script. But now, I don't want you to be concerned that because I'm a director as well, I'm going to try to muscle in and interfere with your work. This is your film; I'm just the actor from now on." I was very touched by this sensitive display of consideration, and he was true to his word. He went on, "In any case, I'm going to have my hands full with the portrayal of Rambo, and getting to the truth of him."

Early on in the shooting, I filmed a scene where the nasty deputy falls out of a pursuing chopper and dies, landing on

Rambo escaping from jail on the stolen motorbike.

a huge rock. I had Rambo, seeing this, rush toward his dead body, hoping to get his jacket for some protection against the freezing cold. Rambo stops close to the dead body. As I was lining up a close-up of him, I said to Sylvester, "When you look at the dead deputy, I want to see in your eyes all the death you witnessed in Vietnam, all the dead bodies of enemies and friends that you saw all around you in your time in that war." Sylvester nodded thoughtfully, said nothing. Well, he did it brilliantly and movingly.

The next night at dailies, we all saw that close-up. The lights came up. Sylvester, who had been watching, sitting alone, came over to me and said, "Ted, that close-up is one of the finest bits of acting I have ever done, and I owe it all to you."

The director-actor relationship was now perfectly cemented. From that moment on, whatever hesitations he might have had about me evaporated. We were as one, total trust had been achieved between us. As I said in writing about Ingrid Bergman, every important actor, no matter how exalted, must have some trepidation in placing his or her performance, and whole career indeed, in the hands of a director of unknown capabilities. After all, *First Blood* was my very first action film.

Sylvester is an actor capable of deep emotion, and a moving sensitivity. The last long speech he gives about his painful experiences in the war at the end of the film, where his bottled-up feelings erupt in a volcanic outburst of words, so poignant and intensely affecting, is one of the finest single bits of acting that I have ever received in one of my films. No one could have done it better.

And Sylvester always gave me 100 percent. In the film, Rambo makes an incredible leap from a high cliff face into the boughs of some evergreen trees to break his fall, finally hitting a thick branch lower in the tree, and then falling to the ground. Of course, I used one of the great stunt men, Buddy Joe Hooker, to do this life-threatening leap, falling almost 100 feet. I wanted to cut to Sylvester when Rambo falls to the ground. Sylvester insisted on doing the last slamming fall onto the thick branch himself. I tried to dissuade him. "It's too dangerous," I said. But he would not be deterred. Of course, it would add tremendous realism to have Sylvester do it and not a concealed double. Very rarely do I allow my star actors to do their own dangerous stunts for obvious reasons. Finally, I agreed against my better judgment.

Stallone falls on the thick branch, cracking four ribs.

With the cameras rolling, Sylvester leapt from eight feet above onto the unyielding bottom branch of this tree; he let out an incredible cry of pain and slipped off the branch to the ground. Only one thing, that cry of pain wasn't acting; it was real. Hitting that thick branch that had no give whatsoever, he cracked four ribs. For many days after, Sylvester played with those cracked ribs. Any action I gave him was extremely painful, but he did it all, never complaining or revealing his agony. That's Sylvester: deeply committed and unsparingly, always giving his all.

"

Kirk Douglas was cast as the colonel in *First Blood*. I'm always asked which actors were a pain in the ass to work with. There have been very few times where the experience I had with an actor did not go smoothly. But this was one of them.

When I offered Kirk the role, he was doing a play in San Francisco with Burt Lancaster about Huck Finn and Tom Sawyer in their later life. I flew up from Los Angeles to meet with him. He told me he liked the part. He was very receptive and professed to be excited about working with Sylvester Stallone and me. Sylvester was looking forward to meeting him because he told me that Kirk Douglas's film about boxing, *Champion*, inspired his film on the subject, *Rocky*. So I expected nothing but smooth sailing, one younger actor playing alongside his inspiration.

However, by the time Kirk arrived on location in Hope, British Columbia, something had gone seriously awry. We had already been shooting for three weeks, as his character enters later in the film. He started quarreling about the content of his scenes. For starters, he had a disconcerting habit of talking about himself in the third person. He would say things like, "The sheriff shouldn't say this line, Kirk Douglas should say this line." I would disagree, explaining to him that the line in question was not appropriate for the Green Beret commander but it was for the redneck sheriff. He would then say, "It's a funny and original line, so Kirk Douglas should say it."

A producer friend of mine I spoke to afterward said, "Ted, why didn't you call me? I've produced three films with Kirk Douglas. He's always trying to steal other actor's good lines."

Content wise, he wanted his character to be like a military commander from a 1940s B war film. He suggested trite lines that the commander would say to Rambo like, "Boy, spit shine your shoes! Polish those brass buttons! Your hair is too long!"

"That's how Kirk Douglas would play this part," Kirk said.

Sylvester and I tried to accommodate his ideas. After shooting all day in the freezing cold and rain, he and I would work late into the night, rewriting the script, hoping to please Kirk. After all, he was a major star, and a great distribution asset to the film. Then I would meet with Kirk and discuss the changes and hear his thoughts, but we could never satisfy him. I can't tell you how many rewrites we did.

Finally, exhausted, I went to the executive producers, Andy Vajna and Mario Kassar, and told them that Kirk Douglas was more trouble than he was worth and that if we started shooting scenes with him, the whole production would grind to a halt. They agreed. Buzz Feitshans, the producer, and I went back to Kirk in the charming lakeside cottage we had obtained for him and his wife. We told him he had to do the role as it was originally written in the script and which he had contractually signed on to play or he would have to leave the production. He packed up and went home.

After Kirk's oh-so-welcome departure, I got on the phone to my great casting director, Lynn Stalmaster, who has done most of my films, told him what had happened, and we discussed possible replacements. We finally agreed on Richard Crenna. "Tell him to get on the next plane; we start shooting that character the day after tomorrow!"

Richard arrived post-haste. He said to me, "Ted, I haven't got a clue as to what I should be doing. You're going to have to feed me spoonful after spoonful of performance."

I did. It was gratifying that Richard made a big name for himself in this part, and in all the sequels.

Kirk wrote about the experience in one of his memoirs — only he got it all wrong. There is not a single word of truth in what he has written. Ted Kotcheff is here to tell you it is total bologna, that or another b-word.

CHAPTER TWENTY-ONE
Partying with Bernie Lomax

"Ted, I can't get this image out of my mind: two guys are dragging around a dead guy pretending he's alive . . ."

"Well, how did this come about, Bobby?"

"I don't know."

"What happens to them?"

"I don't know, but I want to work with you to find out."

Normally if I'd heard that idea for a movie, I would've rolled my eyes. But this idea was coming from Bob Klane, who had written the cult novel and script for the iconic, jet black, outrageously funny comedy *Where's Poppa?* This film, adapted by Bob Klane from his own novel, was directed by Carl Reiner in 1970 and starred George Segal and Ruth Gordon. If you haven't seen it, get a DVD of it. It is original and brilliantly funny.

I asked Bobby if he had written anything on the new idea. "There's a script, but it's not good, more like a treatment. The hard parts are left out. But it has a salvage-able idea: the two guys have shown up at a beach house for a weekend of partying and find their host dead, but they're determined the party will go on regardless."

Well, I loved the idea. I loved it because it was so extreme. I thought it was not only hilarious, but also dark and full of comedic and satirical possibilities.

At that time, the successful high-concept comedies had been much more mainstream. *Three Men and a Baby* had been the top-grossing movie of 1987, and *Crocodile Dundee* had been the second-highest grossing movie in 1986. Hollywood is always looking for the next big comedy, so I was sure we could get the film made if we could nail the script.

Bob had come up with the idea in the '70s when he had worked in New York in advertising. On weekends in the summer, all the machers of the agency would decamp to their houses in the Hamptons and Fire Island. Occasionally, they would invite their underlings. But he always won-dered what would happen if the underlings got a house all to themselves — inmates taking over the asylum.

The plot of the script was that two guys working for an insurance company discover that someone is stealing great sums of money from the company. They report the larceny to their boss, Bernie Lomax. But the boss is actu-ally the thief. He invites them to his beach house for the weekend, where he plans to have them bumped off. Bernie then assures the mob guys behind the scam that he will take care of things. The mob guys decide to cut their losses and have Bernie killed instead. When the two guys arrive for the weekend at Bernie's beach house, Bernie turns up dead. But the party isn't.

Bob had written a script for 20th Century Fox, but it lay

dormant. Victor Drai, the producer and a good friend of mine, convinced a company called Gladden Entertainment to buy the script from Fox and to back the movie.

Gladden, interestingly, was the business reincarnation of David Begelman. He had become infamous when he was fired from Columbia Pictures for forging Cliff Robertson's name on a check and for other financial misdeeds. The story was laid bare in the runaway bestseller *Indecent Exposure*. In any other business, Begelman would have been at best finished and at worst prosecuted. But in Hollywood, that den of thieves, he merely waited things out until someone would make a deal with him again.

Begelman liked me; thought I was his lucky charm because the film I made for him, *Fun with Dick and Jane*, had made him so much money, some of it belonging to George Segal, Jane Fonda, and myself — our share of the profits for which we had to threaten to sue him. But that's another story. My threatening him didn't seem to tarnish our relationship. He liked *Weekend at Bernie's* and still liked me, as I said, so we were launched.

Both Bob and I agreed that the script needed a tremendous amount of work. So we vamoosed to the Biltmore Hotel in Santa Barbara to escape the daily distractions in our lives — agents, managers, producers, writers with scripts, wives, children. I told my secretary, "Don't tell anyone where we are. Just take messages. And don't phone me. I'll phone you at the end of each day."

The two best things about working in a hotel, which I had previously done with producer Frank Yablans rewriting the script of *North Dallas Forty*, are that nobody bothers you and there's room service.

We took a suite on the second floor with two bedrooms on either end of a spacious living room, so we had plenty of room for us to pace up and down. We had a large balcony off the living room that overlooked the pool, which was teeming with tourists. Some of the time, we would pace out onto the balcony, intensely batting around ideas, and arguing what was funny and what wasn't. Back and forth we would go, as the tourists sunning themselves kept looking up at these two grown men squabbling. From the looks on their faces, it was clear that they thought we were a couple of gay guys having a spat.

I must say that the most pleasurable part of filmmaking for me is dreaming about it, imagining it in my head day and night, and not having to deal with the difficulties of turning it into a reality. Over the course of a few days, and many club sandwiches, we did a lot of dreaming. Bob and I had broken the back of the script.

We returned to Los Angeles, triumphantly, and Gladden gave us the green light. While Bob tidied up the script, I began casting the film. I cast Andrew McCarthy and Jonathan Silverman as the two young guys, Catherine Marie Stuart as the wide-eyed love interest, and a TV actor named Terry Kiser as Bernie Lomax.

Jonathan Silverman was best known for the sitcom *Gimme a Break!*, and Andrew had been lumped in with the group of young actors dubbed the Brat Pack. He was well known by young audiences and had been in several successful films, including *Pretty in Pink* and *St. Elmo's Fire*. He had also played the sought-after role of the protagonist in *Less Than Zero*, though the movie did not perform as expected.

I found Andrew to be the opposite of a spoiled actor. In addition to having great comedic timing, he was very humble and a pleasure to work with. He was also endlessly fascinated by what I was doing as the director. In fact, when

I was pressed into service in front of the camera, I let him direct the scene.

Now I don't fancy myself as Alfred Hitchcock in any regard. Hitchcock put himself in his films, usually in the background doing something benign. In my case, I ended up putting myself in *Weekend at Bernie's* because of a mistake I had made.

Admittedly, there was an odd parallel. One of the few comedies that centers on a dead body is Hitchcock's *The Trouble with Harry*, the story of a small town that finds a corpse on the side of a hill and can't figure out what to do with it. The difference is that Hitchcock's dead guy is left in one place and mine does everything from hot tubbing to water skiing.

In *Bernie's*, there is a scene in which Jonathan Silverman's character, Richard, comes home with a girl. In an attempt to gain her sympathy while romancing her, he tells her that his parents died in a plane crash. But then his father walks into the living room. Thinking fast, Richard pretends that his dad is his butler.

Addressing his dad, he says, "Henry, will you lay out my suit for tomorrow?"

His dad shoots back, "How 'bout if I lay you out!"

The girl turns to Richard and says, "You let your butler talk to you like that?" And she leaves.

I had cast a New York stage actor in the part, but I misdirected the scene. I wrongly played it for farce, and the poor actor couldn't land the line. After I saw the scene in dailies, I asked the producer, Victor Drai, to let me reshoot the scene with a different actor. He gave me the go-ahead.

Hoping for a favor, I called Alan Arkin and tried to convince him to fly down from New York to North Carolina to do the scene. He would have been perfect. Graciously,

Alan told me that he simply didn't have the time to do a two-day turnaround trip for a one-line part.

Victor Drai convinced me to do the part, telling me I looked like Jonathan Silverman's father. With my options limited, I reluctantly agreed and cast myself. I feel safe behind the camera and have never sought to change that, but here I was, about to lose my virginity.

I lined up the shot for Andrew and asked him to watch the performances. He became the director for the scene, and I became the nervous actor. I'll never forget the momentary stage fright that hit me. I stood in the hallway waiting to enter the living room and nearly froze. I thought to myself, "Kotcheff, how do you walk? Oh yeah, you put — one foot — in front of — the other. How do you talk? Uh . . . you open your mouth — and the words come out."

Andrew shouted action. I took a deep breath, pulled myself together, and walked into the living room in my underwear. My respect for actors increased exponentially that day.

I did the scene, and it got a laugh when we played it back. I give Andrew McCarthy all the credit. When the film first came out, I used to tease my two young stars: "I got the first big laugh." Oh, by the way, Andrew McCarthy subsequently became a director working very successfully in episodic television.

But I'm ahead of myself.

"

In the preproduction of a film, the two most important activities are casting and finding the locations. One of the most important locations, in which most of the film takes place, is Bernie Lomax's summer mansion. We shot the

I'm setting up the night shot where Bernie is washed up by the tide.

film in the Outer Banks of North Carolina. We originally found an appropriate house for Bernie on Bald Head Island. The homes on the island were preponderantly owned by affluent doctors and dentists. They strenuously objected to a film company coming into their peaceful community and campaigned to block us. One of them said, "We don't want these AIDS-ridden people in our community, druggies partying all night, playing loud, heavy metal music."

Understandably, I was furious. I'm not known to keep my cool, even at the best of times, but in the face of such inanities, I started speaking very emphatically. "Do you know how hard it is to make a film? We work twelve hours a day, six days a week. Stay up all night?! I go to bed at

10 p.m. because I have to be up at 5:30 in the morning to be on set with my entire one-hundred-man crew to start shooting precisely at 7 a.m.! And I mean precisely, because it costs $100 per minute to shoot a film; so if you're five minutes late, that's $500 that doesn't get on to the screen. And drugs?! I have a film in my head that has to be turned into a reality. I can't befuddle my clear vision of it smoking Mary Jane!"

Calming down, I took a breath. "Oh, by the way, I prefer classical music. All the actors and directors I know, and I know many, are almost all bourgeois family folk who want a quiet life for their wives and kids, just like you. I have a two-year-old daughter, and another child on the way very soon. Where do you get these scurrilous fantasies about us? The *National Inquirer*?"

I became forceful again. "It would be tantamount to me saying, 'All you doctors are corrupt abortionists who are paid huge bribes by Big Pharma to prescribe expensive, unneeded, body-damaging pills to indigent patients, when simple, low cost, naturopathic approaches would do the job.'"

All the cajoling and arguing was to no avail: they refused to let us shoot there.

So I decided to build Bernie's summer home. Luckily, the municipality of Wilmington was eager for us to shoot there. They knew we would be spending millions in their community on hotels, car rentals, taxis, lumber, hardware, and restaurants. They gave us a beautiful ocean-side spot on their unspoiled state park.

Bernie's indulgent, over-the-top, two-story, modern millionaire's weekend mansion, complete with terrace and swimming pool, and its huge, lavishly furnished interior was beautifully created by our production designer, Peter

Jamison, and built by our crew. The state park officials allowed us to do so, with the proviso that, on the completion of shooting, the mansion would be torn down and every inch of it removed. So it no longer exists. One would be hard pressed to even find the location where it once stood.

There were two benefits to our constructing it. One, there were no other summer homes around it; it was in splendid isolation. And secondly, the house was artfully designed to accommodate all the action and staging required by the film. It made my mis-en-scène effortless.

"

When we went on location to Wilmington, North Carolina, Laifun was nine months pregnant. She did not want to remain in Los Angeles and have the baby by herself. And I didn't want to miss my son's birth. So she came to North Carolina with me. Well, you guessed it: we were shooting in Bernie's summer home when word came up that Laifun had gone into labor. I was staging the climactic moment of the movie where the hitman is wrapped round and round with a telephone wire by Andrew McCarthy and completely immobilized. It was an elaborate shot, the last of the day. Laifun later told me that the baby was stirring early in the morning but, like a good film baby, he waited to come out until the last shot of the day.

I instructed the director of photography where to put the camera, and as I was backing out of the door, I yelled out further directions, leaving the crew to finish the shot. Yes, one might say that I'm totally obsessed when I'm making a film. I charged down to my car and driver, jumped in, and told him to burn rubber. Laifun was groaning in pain in the backseat as we set out for the hospital.

The production had a terrific relationship with the police in Wilmington. They loved us shooting in their town, and we appreciated them for all that they did for us, controlling traffic and onlookers, helping us gain access to locations. Officers were stationed at every intersection, holding up the traffic and waving us through the red lights. Then, halfway to the hospital, a police car joined us and gave us a siren-blaring escort all the way there. The hospital sent a fully equipped ambulance to follow us, in case Laifun gave birth en route.

At the hospital, Laifun was taken straight to the birthing room. The obstetrician rushed in from dinner. "Oh my god, the baby's head is halfway out!" Everybody sprang into action. The baby came out with incredible speed. After all, he'd been waiting all day to make his entrance.

The birthing room was furnished like the parlor of a southern plantation house, based on the theory that the baby should not be greeted by stainless steel and cold, white tile. I sat in the corner in a granny rocking chair as my son entered this world. At one point during the proceedings, the obstetrician turned to me, rocking in my chair, and said, "Who are you?" implying that I was totally unnecessary to the procedure.

Everything turned out fine, but we did cut it very close. And no, we didn't name him Bernie. We named him Thomas.

"

My producer, Victor Drai, did a very clever thing during the shoot. Being French, he shared with his countryman,

TING CHUNG

Our children, Alexandra (along with Don Ameche) and Thomas, on set with us.

LAIFUN CHUNG

Napoleon, the philosophy that a film crew marched on its stomach. Victor hired a top-class Italian chef to prepare dinner for us every evening. The four main actors — Jonathan, Andrew, Catherine, and Terry Kiser — Victor, and I were housed in the same delightful apartment complex, right on Wrightsville Beach. After looking at dailies, we would retire to Victor's apartment, where we would be greeted by

Last directorial words to Jonathan Silverman, Terry Kiser, and Andrew McCarthy in a red golf car about to be towed away by the vehicle loaded with camera and sound.

the genial chef with a tray of bruschetta or some other delicious antipasto, and a comforting glass of chianti red, followed by a wonderful Italian repast.

For hours, we would sit gossiping and laughing at some of the antics of the day's shooting. Aside from saving us precious time in not having to go to restaurants every night, the dinners' friendly atmosphere created a warm, easy camaraderie between us. This carried over to our work together, with an uninhibited flow of ideas and feelings so important to any joint artistic endeavor, but especially vital to a comedy. It made our work together so much easier.

Replete with fine food and wine, and cosseted by being so richly looked after, we would retire to our adjoining apartments to sleep well and get physically and mentally prepared for the fray of the following day. Victor was always a warm and outgoing host. He was a terrific creative producer and production facilitator, and this was a really inspired thing that he did. I must add that Victor went on to become a famous restaurateur in Los Angeles and Las Vegas.

"

20th Century Fox distributed *Bernie's*. Bobby's original title for the film was *Sitting Ducks*, which no one liked. The marketing executives proposed calling it *Hot and Cold*, and they were very enthusiastic about this title. Victor and I resisted.

From my point of view, I didn't want to read in every review variations of the line, "Sometimes this movie is hot, other times it's cold." Never give a film critic easy ammunition. But I was not sure I was going to win this battle, remembering Julius Epstein's observation that in a fight

Jonathan Silverman, Terry Kiser, Andrew McCarthy, and I discuss Bernie's dead man walk.

with distributors, there are two areas you'll never win: titles and endings.

The good news was that we knew the film worked from the test screenings. You can tell a drama is working if there isn't too much coughing during the previews. For a comedy, it's much easier. Is the audience laughing? Our test audiences were rolling in the aisles with deep, belly laughter.

After the screening, one of the Fox PR people said to me, "Okay, smart guy, you come up with some titles." I always thought Bernie was a funny name, so I came up with *Weekend at Bernie's*. Lo and behold, everyone agreed. I won on this occasion, but most of the time Julius Epstein is right.

As a result of our audience testing, and the cards containing their reactions, we thought our film was set to be a big hit. Nevertheless, in the release of a film, timing is often everything. I don't profess to know much about the finer points of marketing and distribution. However over my career, there is one thing I have learned about the release of a film: it helps if the picture comes out at the right moment and it must have a generous publicity budget.

Who's Killing the Great Chefs of Europe? did not fare well when it was released in 1978, as there wasn't much interest in chefs, aside from maybe Julia Child. Had it been released in the last few years, in our era of *Iron Chef*, *Top Chef*, cooking competitions, and celebrity chefs all over television, the film would have done much better.

I had another somewhat disappointing experience with the 1983 release of *Uncommon Valor*, which starred Gene Hackman. The film was initially dogged by comparisons to the real-life story of Bo Gritz, a former Army operative who led a failed POW rescue mission into Laos. Though we assiduously avoided the real-life parallels, Paramount's original marketing campaign centered on the plight of POWs, rather than the father-son drama that is at the heart of the film. The studio changed the campaign at the last minute. *Uncommon Valor* was released inappropriately with limited publicity over Christmas. In February, the *New York Times* called the film "the year's biggest movie surprise," but it was too late. Barry Diller, who was running Paramount at the time, later apologized to me for the studio not spending enough money on marketing. "I didn't realize the picture would have such a broad appeal," he said.

Weekend at Bernie's was released July 5, 1989. The film did very well at the box office, grossing $30 million on a $15 million budget. I think the film could have done even better if Fox had followed the original plan to release it in late summer with the fading of all the other spring and early summer releases. But Fox hurried its release because their big tentpole picture wasn't ready, so we came out with curtailed pre-publicity, competing with all the big-budget blockbusters from all the other studios.

The film broke box-office records in Italy, beating out *E.T.*, the biggest sci-fi hit of the time. Wherever I went, people had seen it and were thrilled to meet the director of *Weekend at Bernie's.* They would tip their heads as if they were dead, smirk, and do the Bernie wave.

The ensuing DVD sales of the film were absolutely astronomical. Even now, so many years later, it's still a big DVD seller, especially during Christmas. The film's satirical edge about human behavior connected with audiences. These two guys want something so bad, something that they've never had and may never have again — a weekend of extravagant partying at the beach — that they don't care if their host is alive or dead. The people around them are so selfishly involved in their own needs that they don't notice Bernie is dead. I especially like the moment we created where a young woman at the party reaches into Bernie's inside pocket to pull out a bag of cocaine that she knows is there.

The film's success was enough for a sequel to be put in motion (co-financed by an Italian company, naturally). As per Directors Guild of America guidelines, I was given first right of refusal to direct it. Victor Drai tried to cajole me with the promise of bringing his wonderful Italian chef back to the set, but in the end I passed. The sequel to *Weekend at Bernie's* was written and directed by Bob Klane and, of course, starred our original trio of Andrew McCarthy, Jonathan Silverman, and Terry Kiser.

But it was what happened after the release of the original film that continues to surprise. The film got into the zeitgeist in a way that you cannot manufacture and has remained there to this day. In 2010, a rap group in Miami started a song and dance craze called "Movin' Like Bernie" that got 12 million views online. In 2015, in the Oakland Raiders' first game of the season, the players all came out onto the football field doing the hysterical dead-man Bernie dance. Not surprisingly, there are dozens of political references: *MAD* magazine did a parody "Weekend at Bin Laden's" with President Obama and Vice President Biden holding up the deceased al-Qaeda leader. On a lighter note, in 2015, Rep. Bernie Sanders showed his self-deprecating side in a CNBC interview by donning sunglasses, flopping his head, and doing his best Bernie Lomax. The image of two guys holding up a dead Bernie was used all over Venezuela during the 2012 presidential election.

On a more somber note, in 2012, two guys in Denver drove around with a dead guy in their car and used his credit card to fund their night at a strip club. Every single headline had some play on *Weekend at Bernie's*. In 2008, in the New York area, two guys tried to cash the Social Security check belonging to their recently deceased friend. They pushed his corpse, seated in an office chair, along the sidewalk to a check-cashing store. They claimed their friend was in a deep sleep. An article recounts, "They did not go about it the easy way, the police said, choosing a ruse that resembled the plot of *Weekend at Bernie's*."

I demonstrate to the off-camera actor how she will take things from Bernie, oblivious of him being dead.

There's even a six-bedroom, five-bathroom beach house named "Weekend at Bernie's" for rent in North Carolina. Of course, it's not actually Bernie's house. As I mentioned earlier, the day after we wrapped, the house was taken down.

In an entry in the Urban Dictionary, a "Weekend at Bernie's" is defined as "the friend everyone has who can't control their drug/booze intake. After they have passed out you have to carry their body from one party to the next. 'Look at Riley, she's about two beers away from *Weekend at Bernie's.*'"

Bernie's even entered academia. Dr. Mikel Koven, a

film studies professor at the University of Worcester in England, wrote a paper entitled "Traditional Narrative, Popular Aesthetics, *Weekend at Bernie's*, and Vernacular Cinema" that was published in the book *Of Corpse: Death and Humor in Folklore and Popular Culture*. His theory was that the movie satirized the solipsistic richies of the late '80s "whose self-indulgences and self-obsessions make them oblivious to Bernie's dilemma."

Even with the initial success and continued cult following, I never reaped any financial reward. Remember the $2 million fraud that the characters Larry and Richard reported to Bernie that resulted in Bernie getting rubbed out? Bob Klane and I found what we believed was our own fraud in the accounting for *Weekend at Bernie's*. We each had 10 percent of the film's profits, but despite its enormous success at the box office everywhere, and later on video and DVD, we have never been paid any profits from the film. To our dismay, we learned that it was too late to sue. There is a statute of limitations on lawsuits dealing with company profits after the ten-year mark; so all the money the film made in the first ten years is beyond our legal reach. MGM has agreed to give us our share of the profits that have been made in the time afterward.

To this day, 26 years later, people want more of Bernie Lomax. *Rolling Stone* just released a video "super cut" of The Weeknd's "Can't Feel My Face" with scenes from the film. The magazine drew parallels between The Weeknd's inability to feel his face and Bernie's inability to feel *anything*.

There is a Facebook page entitled "Campaign to Make *Weekend at Bernie's 3*." Bob Klane and his son, Jon, actually wrote a script for a remake of the first one, but it never got off the ground. The farcical *Bernie's* had taken on apocryphal overtones. The Facebook page falsely quotes Bob as saying that the Rolling Stones' Keith Richards would be the perfect choice for the new Bernie.

I wouldn't put it past someone in today's Hollywood to try to sell *that* idea to a studio.

CHAPTER TWENTY-TWO

Pretending to Be Someone Else

I have heard fools say, scornfully, "Actors are people who pretend for a living." I respond, "Okay, smartass, try it. And you'll find how hard it is to do — even badly." I found out in my own one-line cameo in *Weekend at Bernie's*.

Paul Bocuse, one of the world's great chefs, was my technical advisor on *Who Is Killing the Great Chefs of Europe?* One day I questioned him about the preparations of his fabulous dishes. "Well, first of all Ted, I say to all my supplying farmers, 'I want your best fruit, best vegetables harvested at that moment when they reach the peak of perfection! You give me the best; you'll find me easy to please.' You see, Ted, second-class ingredients lead to second-class cooking."

I said to him, "Well, Paul, that's exactly like making a film: second-class acting leads to second-class films."

When I first came to Hollywood, a Warner Bros.

executive said to me, "Kotcheff, are you an actor's director or a shooter?"

I was a bit taken aback, "Well, I think I'm both. Don't you need to be both if you want to be a successful film director?"

"No, there are certain well-known directors who are camera-obsessed and have never said one word to an actor."

I found this hard to believe. This wasn't going to be me.

There's no question in my mind that casting the right actors for the part and eliciting great performances from them is 90 percent of a film, for they are its most important element. Aside from the fact that actors are often the reason people buy a ticket to the movies, they engage the audience's interest, command their attention, and grab their emotions.

Some films try to disguise the acting with fancy wardrobe and special effects. An actor can wear all the costumes in the world, but I want to see the way they behave. I not only want to see them pretend to be someone else and duplicate real life with accuracy and verisimilitude, but also to reveal something about the human condition. This is what the audience is watching for too.

I always knew that to get my stripes as a director, I would need to be able to gain the trust of actors so that they would deliver compelling performances. To me, that is on par with the visual aspect of film directing. Inherently, I knew that the more I understood about acting, and the more aware I was of what's involved in creating a character, the easier it would be to direct actors and assist them to achieve their objectives.

So in 1957, when I was still cutting my teeth as a young television director, I enrolled in an acting class in Toronto taught by Basya Hunter to learn more. I was the only non-actor in her class; all the rest were top professionals. Basya's credentials were impressive: she had studied acting in New York with the iconic Mikhail Chekhov, nephew of playwright Anton Chekhov, my cultural hero.

Mikhail Chekhov had been taught by the legendary acting teacher and director Stanislavski, who called him one of his greatest students. Mikhail wrote a book entitled *To the Actor: On the Technique of Acting* that laid out his detailed observations on the craft. It became my bible. One of his compelling ideas is his theory that if you watch human beings, everybody's body is centered in different places, which results in psychological gestures that can define a character. His techniques, which cover the full spectrum of acting, were later adapted by Hollywood stars from Marilyn Monroe to Clint Eastwood.

Gregory Peck, as you'll recollect, was also a student of Mikhail Chekhov. When we worked together communication between the director and the actor was very easy. We shared a common lingo. Gregory Peck starred in a Hitchcock film entitled *Spellbound* in which Mikhail Chekhov played a psychiatrist. Mikhail's performance is beautifully shaped, embodying all of the acting tenets to be found in his famous book.

During a summer break in the *Law & Order: Special Victims Unit* series that I executive produced, Chris Meloni, my great leading man, was hired to play the lead in Arthur Miller's *View from the Bridge* in Dublin. Chris had not worked in the theater for some time. I gave him my copy of Chekhov's book with Gregory's introduction. The central character in the play is a longshoreman. Since the character worked with his hands all day, Chris chose to make his hands the center of his character's body. It was amazing: his hands seemed to be the size of huge plates; the way he picked up things, the way he embraced people, his hands were omnipresent. They got in his way; they defined him. The "center" worked wonderfully well. Afterward, I hugged Chris and whispered in his ear, "Mikhail Chekhov would be incredibly proud of you." He never returned my copy of the book.

Studying Chekhov's acting techniques from a directorial point of view provided me with the criteria with which to judge an actor's performance. I learned that every scene must contribute to the protagonist's objective, for example. He or she may have a larger, super objective, like becoming a somebody in life. In a smaller scene, his or her objective might be to obtain something seemingly minute, but that short-term goal must contribute to achieving the character's long-term goal. I also learned about playing your relationship. This means that the way a person talks to a guy changing a tire is different from the way he would talk to the president of a corporation, or to his parents.

After I had studied with Basya for about a year, she had to move to England. Her husband was a specialist in food co-operatives, then a nascent business in America but very common in England. Basya suggested to me that I take over her two acting classes. She said to me, "Teaching acting will be invaluable for your directorial aspirations."

I took over teaching both her professional and her amateur classes, the latter being held at the Holy Blossom Synagogue. The amateur class was composed of middle-class Jewish professionals, like accountants and lawyers and their wives, who used acting as an emotional and creative outlet. I directed a group of them in Arthur Miller's *All My Sons* (my very first stage production), which actually garnered very favorable reviews considering the troupe was totally inexperienced. In the professional class, one of my pupils was William Shatner. I ended up using him in one of the TV plays I directed for Sydney Newman's drama series at the CBC, which Shatner wrote. I cast him opposite a lovely actress, Gloria Rand — whom he ended up marrying. We became friends and remained so.

Between taking and teaching acting classes, I felt that I had a strong grasp of the actor's craft and what went into a performance. To paraphrase Stanislavski: good actors do this naturally but sometimes they need to be reminded. Great actors do this spontaneously. I have spent my entire career seeing these words validated.

There was one other thing I did for my directorial education when I was in my 20s and starting out. Because I felt I had lived a sheltered existence, I took summer jobs where I could see life in the raw, and meet real, ordinary people. So I worked in restaurants, a slaughterhouse, Goodyear Tire and Rubber, I took sustenance at night to the homeless and the derelict. I became an intense student in the school of life.

I am often asked by film students which film school I went to. In my time, there was no such thing as a film school. My film school was the slaughterhouse.

"

When it comes to acting, I have found that actresses go about the process differently than actors. Their surprising, unanticipated reactions to the directions I give them are a constant treat. When I give a man a direction, I almost always know how it will manifest itself in his face, his manner, his voice. When I give the same direction to a woman, I cannot predict how it will come out. It is unforeseeable.

The minds, emotions, and psyches of the two sexes are structured completely differently.

Men are like bulls: they see the red cape, they charge frontally, directly. Women see the red cape, they never go directly at it, they circle it and charge sideways. Women are oblique. I always love seeing this.

The first major actress that I directed was Jean Simmons in my second film, *Life at the Top*. I remember being mesmerized by her eyes as she performed my directions. Eyes full of ambivalences, contradictory thoughts, conflicting emotions, all swirling this way and that. I have seen the same quality in the eyes of many wonderful actresses I have worked with: Micheline Lanctôt, Jane Fonda, Jacqueline Bisset, Mariska Hargitay, Judy Geeson, Catherine Mary Stewart, Sylvia Kay, and many others.

An interesting postscript: When I worked with Jean Simmons in 1964, I remember trying to analyze what she was thinking as she played various scenes, and over 50 years later I am reading a medical publication and what do I see: men and women have different brains! All this as a result of 46,000 brain scans. Women's brains are more active than men's, especially in the prefrontal cortex that controls judgment and impulse control. Men's brains have less impulse control, so men are more likely to be impetuous. Remember the bulls charging the red cape? So what I intuited so long ago, the difference between the sexes, was now scientifically validated.

"

Filmmaking is an expensive business. The meter is always running, and the pressure is always on to get a scene right and move on. The director only hopes that his actors are prepared, can digest what he is saying, and know how to manifest it in the scene so that he does not have to give the producer a heart attack by doing countless takes. I love actors who know their characters, so that I can help shape their performances and seamlessly integrate them into the movie.

On *Who's Killing the Great Chefs of Europe?*, Robert Morley paid me a great compliment. "You know what I love about being directed by you, Ted," he said. "You think we're better than we are." The truth is that most of the actors I've worked with are just plain great.

GENE HACKMAN

One thing I discovered over the years working with actors is that you must find a way to reach them: figure out what language to use to bring out the performance you want. There's no set formula for this. Some actors like the Freudian psychiatric approach, whereas others just like to hear the emotion named — "get angry" — and they will find a way. And still other actors don't like any direction at all.

Gene Hackman was one of the latter. He found that direction got in his way. At our very first meeting for *Uncommon Valor*, Gene said to me, rather brusquely, "Kotcheff, I only want three directions from you."

"Oh yes, and what are those?"

Gene replied, "More, less — faster, slower — louder, softer."

I repeated them thoughtfully. "Okay," I said, "that's pretty clear."

"Anything else, Kotcheff, screws up my brain."

Of course I had no intention of restricting myself. I just had to find the right language so I could communicate to him the shadings I wanted without upsetting his artistic equilibrium. Different actors require different lingo; there is no one size to fit all.

What Gene did on *Uncommon Valor* was not acting; it was being. He plays a colonel who sets out to rescue his son, a Vietnam POW. He wasn't acting the colonel; he was the colonel. He had prepared for two months beforehand. Becoming the colonel took total possession of him. The benefit to me, of course, was that I could ask him to do anything or say anything. He never objected; he would do what I asked exactly as the colonel would.

His ability to switch in and out of character was mesmerizing. One day, he and I were standing right next to the camera, waiting for the cinematographer to finish setting up the shot. Gene and I often dined together after work at nice restaurants in Bangkok, where we were filming.

Gene said, "I hear the rooftop restaurant at the Oriental Hotel is just great."

The AD yelled, "Roll camera."

I said, "Yeah, and I heard they have a phenomenal wine list."

The AD yelled, "Speed!"

Gene [twinkling], "Well, you know how much I love my wine."

I said, "Action, Gene."

Snap: the bantering Gene turned from me and in a second transformed himself into the colonel, not just superficially, but seven levels deep. It was jaw-droppingly

Gene Hackman in Uncommon Valor.

incredible. For he had so digested the character, he was able to call upon this at a moment's notice. It made directing him a breeze.

Gene was also very intuitive about the filmmaking process and what made a scene work.

I was staging a scene in which he tells the other Vietnam veterans about what they are going to be doing on the rescue mission. Just before we rolled, Gene said to me, "Ted, you're not gonna have me stand here speechifying, are you?"

"Why, what would you like to do?"

"I want some business," he said. "I hate speechifying. Actors act better if you give them business, then they don't have to think about the words."

"All right, I'll tell you what," I said, "why don't you put on camouflage makeup while giving the speech?"

"Oh, that's wonderful, Ted," he said. "That's just wonderful." We rolled the cameras, and he applied the makeup to his cheeks and forehead while delivering the speech. The result was brilliant.

Gene was certainly right about giving actors something to do in addition to reciting their lines. This became one of the things that I follow and recommend to other directors: provide actors with business to make their performances become immediately more real. Because they will be preoccupied with the business and not the words, the lines will come out naturally as they do in life.

Gene had been a U.S. Marine in World War II, stationed in Asia for a couple of years after the war was over. In 1948, he decided he wanted to be an actor and went to New York to a reputedly good acting school. One actor that he befriended was Dustin Hoffman. Both being impecunious, the two of them worked together as furniture movers during the day. Then at night, acting school. After a short time, the head teacher of the school asked Gene and Dustin to come into his office. He told them they didn't have any acting ability, and there was no future for either of them in show business. And his advice to them was to stick to moving furniture. Boy, whoever that fool was, he sure had a perceptive eye for talent. The two finest American film actors of the 20th century, and he tells them they are only fit to be in the moving business. I'm glad, and the film industry is also glad, that Gene and Dustin ignored this idiot. I hate to think of other talented performers whose belief in themselves was totally destroyed and their futures wrecked by that teacher's purblindness.

An actor has to believe in himself, totally and unequivocally, if he is going to succeed as Gene and Dustin did. Doubts are destructive, and the first whiff of them must be suppressed and ignored.

One other thing: Gene is a very fine painter who has been exhibited successfully. If he had pursued it, I think he could have been a major American artist. When Laifun was painting, she and Gene would hire a model together. So I often saw him working in my wife's studio. We have several of his paintings in our house.

I conclude by saying Gene Hackman is the finest actor that I had the good fortune to work with — with Nick Nolte a close second.

CHAPTER TWENTY-THREE
Special Victims Unit:
No One Can Take the Children

Dick Wolf, the creator and executive producer of the hit TV series *Law & Order*, was a big fan of two of my films: *North Dallas Forty* and *The Apprenticeship of Duddy Kravitz*. When he was putting together his new one-hour drama, *Sex Crimes*, he called and asked me if I wanted to come onboard and help him get the series up and running.

Dick explained that the new series stemmed from an episode of *Law & Order* that he had written based on the "Preppie Murder" in New York's Central Park in 1986. A teenager from a wealthy family named Robert Chambers strangled his former girlfriend, Jennifer Levin, and claimed that it had happened during rough sex. Chambers ended up pleading guilty to manslaughter. Dick kept in the back of his mind that he wanted to do a series about sex crimes and the psychology behind them.

What connection Dick found between the existential problems of a pro football player or a Jewish hustler trying to become someone, and sex crimes in New York City, I didn't have the foggiest idea. But I wasn't about to complain. I accepted his offer: it provided me with a new challenge and the chance to work a muscle that I hadn't used in a long time.

I was the first person hired on *Sex Crimes*. I signed on for three months as a producer to help cast the series and shoot and launch the pilot, working alongside Dick's able head of production, Peter Jankowski. After I accepted the job, I had a call from a director friend of mine, Mark Rydell, who said, "Hey, Ted, I understand you've gone over to the other side." I was about to find that the transition from director to producer was a bit tricky.

"

The first order of business was to cast the two lead characters, detectives Olivia Benson and Elliot Stabler. A long list of names was narrowed down to three women — Samantha Mathis, Reiko Aylesworth, and Mariska Hargitay — and four men — Tim Matheson, John Slattery, Nick Chinlund, and Christopher Meloni. The final casting session was held in the spring of 1999 on the 67th floor of NBC's Rockefeller Center. It was a large space where all the secretaries had their desks. These were pushed out of the way. Rows of chairs were set up in the back half of the room, and the front half was left clear for the auditioning actors.

The seating chart was a classic study in Hollywood hierarchy. In the front row sat the three bosses, Dick Wolf, head of Wolf Films; Garth Ancier, NBC programming chief; and David Kissinger, head of Studios USA. Just behind these three emperors were their satraps armed with legal pads and folders containing the résumés, headshots, and credits of the auditioning actors. In the rows behind them were the people who would be working on the series, such as me, Peter Jankowski, and the casting director — the maids, butlers, and servants, as it were.

Ordinarily in these auditions, each actor reads with the casting director. However, Dick Wolf waved me over and suggested that I pair the actors so that they could read with each other. I went into the greenroom and paired them off randomly. Serendipitously, I paired Chris Meloni and Mariska Hargitay. The readings commenced.

After the final pair departed, silence fell over the room. Garth Ancier, as head of the NBC network airing the show, was the top emperor so, as I later found out, everyone was waiting for him to speak first. However, not knowing television casting protocol, and being used to life as a director where I was top dog, I blurted out, "I don't know what you are all waiting for! That last pair, Chris Meloni and Mariska Hargitay, were the best by far. We should cast them."

Simultaneously, all 16 people looked back at me like I was the drunken court jester. Again, there was dead silence. Then Garth spoke. "Ted is absolutely right. I agree one hundred percent. The last couple were the best, and that's who we are going to cast."

Everyone started nodding and mumbling in agreement. The biggest shock was not which actors had been cast, but the fact that the NBC honcho, Garth Ancier, was treating me, the television novice, this nobody, like I knew what I was talking about and had some power to participate in that decision. What no one in the room was privy to was that Garth was a wine connoisseur who had attended one of my monthly wine dinners, and we were social friends.

Me with my wonderful SVU *cast: Stephanie March, BD Wong, Tamara Tunie,*
Chris Meloni, Mariska Hargitay, Dann Florek, Richard Belzer, and Ice-T.

But that was that. Mariska Hargitay and Chris Meloni,
whom I had randomly paired, were cast as Detectives
Benson and Stabler.

NBC felt that *Sex Crimes* was too lurid a title, so it was
changed to *Special Victims Unit*, after the name of the New
York Police Department unit that deals with those crimes.
To brand the series, its full title became *Law & Order:
Special Victims Unit*, which became *SVU* for short.

As we were putting together the pilot script, I spent a
week in situ with the Special Victims Unit in New York,
located on 105th Street directly under a set of elevated
subway tracks. The time that I spent up there informed
my approach to the show. One of the interesting elements
of this police department was that there were more female

detectives than in any other New York police unit. It made sense, because a preponderance of these special crimes are committed against women and children, where women were again involved as mothers.

During the time I spent observing the detectives and case officers, two women came in sobbing with a five-year-old girl. The girl's hand was wrapped in a thick bandage. As they took a seat in the waiting area, they were all crying. I watched them closely. Later, I asked the sergeant, who was letting me tag along with him, what had happened.

"You won't believe this," he said. "The little girl was coming down for breakfast and her father was frying bacon on the stove. She was happily dancing around. Her father told her to shut up, but she kept singing and dancing. Again he told her to shut up. But being a five-year-old girl, she continued to sing and dance. He flew into a rage, grabbed her left hand, and plunged it on to the red-hot frying pan, burning her fingers off."

I couldn't believe what he was saying. One thing I cannot stand is child abuse, perhaps because of my own experiences. I sat down very slowly. "How do you stand it?" I asked. He shook his head.

"No one can take the children," he said. "That's why the average career for an SVU detective is only two to three years. And this is the only serious crime that has live victims. In homicide, the victims are dead. Ours are alive and often the age of our own kids."

During the filming of the first episode, ably directed by Jean de Segonzac, there was an artistic problem. It was a night shoot on a busy street in New York City, something that is never easy. At one point, I leapt from my chair to enter the fray. Dick Wolf, seated next to me, laid a restraining hand on my arm. "Ted, you're a producer now," he said with the calm of a veteran.

I sat down. Except for the few times I took the directorial reins, I had to continually hold myself back. This led me to coin the expression: "Watching someone else direct is akin to watching someone else drink champagne." Eventually, I became comfortable in my new role, so comfortable in fact that my three-month start-up gig turned into 12 years. Many series don't make it past those first three months because of low ratings. That was not the case with us.

The season began shooting in September and continued until June. At the end of each season, I would swear I was leaving the show to return to filmmaking. But then each September, I couldn't help myself. I would jump back on the plane to New York, where I lived during the shooting season, with a renewed energy to create great television. On top of all that, I loved living in New York; what a city.

"

Law & Order: SVU returned me to my roots of live television. Though *SVU* wasn't broadcast live, there was always a rush to filming on a tight schedule every week. The creative team I worked with was first rate, and we became like an extended family over the years.

First among equals was my fellow executive producer and showrunner, Emmy Award–winning Neal Baer, who was also our head writer. After *SVU*'s first year on the air, Neal was hired away from *ER*, where he had worked since the beginning of that series and risen to executive producer. He had a unique background. After starting out as a screenwriter, he left Hollywood for Harvard Medical School. Before he graduated, he was recruited to write for

ER, so he commuted from Boston. After finishing Harvard, he completed his residency in Los Angeles while working on *ER*.

Neal and I clicked immediately. He is a cinephile, and he constantly peppered me with questions about the star actors I had worked with over the years. He wanted to bring great actors on to the show and write guest parts for them.

Neal came aboard when we were working on episode entitled "Taken." Most of it had been shot, but the result was a mess, which sometimes happens. I took over the directing chores, and Neal spent his first weekend on *SVU* rewriting the script. We shot around the clock and pulled it off — the beginning of a productive 11-year partnership.

I ran the show in New York, supervising the casting, hiring the directors, and overseeing the physical production, while Neal ran the writers in Los Angeles. Neal and I worked well together and were always on the same wavelength. We spoke on the phone at least ten times a day. Each week, Neal and his writers would work out the script. On his office wall, Neal had a large whiteboard, and he would break down the episode scene by scene. He and the writers would put together the structure, and then one of the writers would go off and write the dialogue. The script would then come back to Neal for revisions.

The writers were several weeks ahead of production. When a new script was finished, Neal would send it to me. In the early years of the show, during the filming of each episode, I would have the actors do a table read of the script for the next episode at lunchtime so they could provide their input. I would combine their notes with mine and send it back to Neal and his team for a polish.

One of the best of the 239 shows that Neal and I worked on together was "911" in 2006. Neal was inspired to do a similar episode to one he had done on *ER*, in which George Clooney, dressed in a tuxedo, saved a child from drowning in a sewer pipe. In "911," Detective Benson was headed out for the evening in a cocktail dress when she takes a phone call from a girl who has been kidnapped, molested, and locked in the basement. A cell phone accidentally left behind allows the girl to phone the police. Detective Benson has to keep the girl engaged on the phone until the officers can triangulate her location to find and rescue her.

Because Neal was such a film junkie, he knew my entire résumé, right down to *The Human Voice*, the one-woman TV movie I did in 1966 with Ingrid Bergman talking on the phone the entire time. He came to me and said, "Ted, we should do our full hour with Mariska on the phone trying to save a little girl, and you should direct it."

We both wanted a tour de force episode for Mariska so that she could win the Emmy for best actress, which she so richly deserved. Mariska had been nominated twice, but had not won. Well, the script that Neal provided was a tour de force, and she got a good director — me. Mariska rose to the occasion magnificently. Her acting in *SVU* was always commendable, but her performance on "911" was extraordinary — deeply emotional. Her capacity for compassionate empathy for the molested and imprisoned young girl was heartrending. That year she took home the Emmy for "911." Yes! It was her only Emmy win on the series, despite the fact that she was nominated eight consecutive years from 2004 to 2011.

Oddly, Chris Meloni never received the recognition he deserved, which I consider one of the great injustices in the annals of the Emmys. He was nominated only once for an Emmy in 2006. The knock on him was that he wasn't empathetic enough, which is a crock of shit. He made every scene that he was in better, and Mariska often looked to him for guidance. I put the acting that Chris did on *SVU* up there with two of the greats I worked with, Nick Nolte and Gene Hackman.

From the very beginning, because sex crimes predominantly involve women, I wanted to hire women to the team. We had two talented female writers working for us, Dawn DeNoon and Judy McCreary. I also wanted women directors, but this proved to be more difficult than I imagined. I phoned the head of the Directors Guild in New York, Jack Shea, and asked for a full list of their women directors. He told me that only eight percent of the members were women. I was shocked and outraged. Jack was in sympathetic agreement: eight percent was unacceptable. When I asked why, he told me that, supposedly, it was because many of the male crew members working on shows did not like to be told what to do by women, which we both agreed was 100% nickel-plated bullshit.

"Women just don't get a chance to develop their talent and establish themselves," he told me. "Men do one show after another and build up a résumé. Women directors typically are lucky to get one show a year." Well, I was going to change that.

At first, I was lucky: I found Lesli Linka Glatter, and she did a fabulous job for me. I wanted to use her regularly, but I discovered that she was never available, working show after show for *Gilmore Girls*, *West Wing*, and *ER*. Then I imported two women directors from Canada, Helen Shaver, an actor turned director, and Holly Dale. Helen Shaver directed nine episodes for me, brilliantly. Then I hired Michelle MacLaren to direct one of her first TV episodes; she went on to direct and executive produce that great series *Breaking Bad*. And Amy Redford, a noted documentary filmmaker and daughter of Robert Redford, made her TV directorial debut on *SVU* in 2010. The episode was called "Shadow." During my 12 years as the executive producer of *SVU*, my desire to use women directors was always a problem for me. For the few women directors, like the aforementioned Lesli Glatter, were almost always unavailable.

Many years later I was talking to the distinguished filmmaker Mimi Leder, and I told her the eight percent story. I had been informed that the situation with women directors in the DGA had improved significantly. "Yeah," said Mimi dryly, "it's nine percent now." I was a bit taken aback, but she was right. In television, women directors accounted for only fourteen percent of production, and feature films was 4.7 percent. I don't know what it's going to take but the present situation needs to be rectified.

Interestingly, during my 12 years on *SVU*, one of the women who desperately wanted to direct an episode was not allowed to — Mariska. Dick Wolf maintained a strict policy against actors in the series directing, because he feared that once he let one do it, the floodgates would open. Eventually, in 2014, Dick wisely relented. Mariska has since directed five episodes and shown a tremendous talent and affinity for it.

We also featured big-name guest stars because of the love that Neal and I have for great actors, and these grisly stories lent themselves to emotional performances and a chance for actresses to explore the psychology of abuse. The list of guest actresses reads like a who's who. In no particular order and with absolute admiration for each one, we had Leslie Caron, Jacqueline Bisset, Ann-Margret, Dianne Wiest, Pam Greer, Margot Kidder, Amy Irving, Piper Laurie, Mary Steenburgen, Marlee Matlin, Patricia

Arquette, Jaclyn Smith, Chloë Sevigny, Angela Lansbury, Rebecca DeMornay, Ellen Burstyn, Cynthia Nixon, Mare Winningham, Amanda Plummer, Martha Plimpton, Kathy Griffin, and the budding actress and famous tennis player Serena Williams.

Neal and I saw an off-Broadway play with Viola Davis and gave her one of her first showy roles. Our sharp-eyed casting director, Jonathan Strauss, cast a young actress named Patricia Mara for an episode — she's now the award-winning movie star who goes by Rooney Mara.

The guest actresses who appeared on the show were frequently nominated for Emmys because they had a chance to shine in our wonderful scripts. Neal knew how to create situations where people were falling apart emotionally. Five of the actresses listed above — Amanda Plummer, Cynthia Nixon, Leslie Caron, Ellen Burstyn, and Ann-Margret — won Emmys for their intense emotional performances.

The list of actors who guest-starred was equally impressive: Robin Williams, Jeremy Irons, Richard Thomas, Ludacris, John Heard, Judd Hirsch, Eric Roberts, Eric Stoltz, Chad Lowe, Bob Saget, John Ritter, Lou Diamond Phillips, Ty Burrell, and an up-and-comer named Bradley Cooper. I reunited with many of the actors I had worked with on films, including George Segal, Andrew McCarthy, and Jonathan Silverman. Part of the fun was casting against type. Henry Winkler, the Fonz from *Happy Days*, and comedian Martin Short played dangerous psychotics.

We filmed the exteriors on location in New York City. The interiors, such as the police station and courtroom, were shot at NBC's Central Archives building in New Jersey. The space was a massive 53,000 square feet and was adaptable to any interior location we needed. New Jersey gave tax credits to film and television productions shot there until 2010. However, when Governor Chris Christie removed those tax credits from the state's 2011 budget, we upped stakes and moved to the Chelsea Piers studio in New York City where *Law & Order* had been filmed, for New York State still continued its tax breaks.

Dick Wolf was always urging me to show as much of New York City as possible, to make it almost a character in our series. He felt that the rest of America was really intrigued by NYC and loved seeing it: the skyscrapers, the Empire State Building, the financial capital of the United States, Wall Street, the bridges over the Hudson, the tunnels, the garbage piled up on the sidewalk, the energy, the hustle and bustle, the yellow taxis, those amazing New York and Brooklyn accents. I directed the small-part actors to always do that New York accent and act with that exterior of brusqueness and the snappy, no-nonsense manner of the typical New Yorker, exemplified in the joke: the out-of-town tourist approaches a New Yorker, "Excuse me, can you tell me the way to Carnegie Hall, or should I go fuck myself?"

For the 100th episode of *SVU*, which I directed, I decided to depict the essential New York, from top to bottom, starting in the bowels of the metropolis. In the episode, castrated genitals are found there in an abandoned subway station, deep underground. The station had 50 years of accumulated detritus, filth, and junk in it. I shot there with Chris Meloni for six hours. At midnight, we went up to have lunch. The crew and actors who were above roared with laughter at these two bedraggled human beings covered head to toe in oily dirt, soot, filth, and refuse, looking like two Neanderthal cavemen who had been digging for coal with their bare hands. We were practically unrecognizable. It took me almost a week to get clean.

Then we went to the very top, via a pit stop at an elegant

Madison Avenue antique store, continuing up to a lush and lavish apartment with a great view on the top floor of Trump Tower, belonging to the Jackie Bisset character. How our location manager, Trish Adlesic, got us into that place I'll never know. But she was always a bit of a miracle worker. So there it was: New York City, top to bottom. I'm sure Dick Wolf was very happy.

I worked as executive producer of the series for 12 years. In all that time, I never had one moment of bad behavior from any one of my performers. The detectives — Mariska, Chris, Richard Belzer, and Ice T — the Captain, Dann Florek; the psychiatrist, BD Wong; the medical officer, Tamara Tunie; and the prosecutor, Stephanie March, are all incredibly talented, but there was never any display of ego. They all worked congenially and respected each other. In my long directorial life, I've worked with some bad casts, actors who rubbed each other the wrong way, venomously spitting. "Are you going to touch me like that when I say that line?" No, there was none of that pettiness or silly jealousies. So, as the boss, it made my life easy, never having to put my foot down as I have in the past.

The stories on *SVU* were never easy. As an actor, you had to dig deep. A lot of the scenes were very emotional, dealing in difficult areas of human behavior: rape, child molestation, parental abuse, perverted behavior. What every member of the cast was focused on was making our shows real, lifelike, and moving week after week — committed artists giving their all. I loved every one of them. Mariska and Chris carried this show, and I think they were mainly responsible for its great success and longevity.

As it was with my actors, so it was with my production team: a great casting director, Jonathan Strauss, who assembled fabulous casts. Great writers: Dawn DeNoon,

Mariska makes fun of my habit of nervously hiking up my trousers.

Judy McCreary, Jonathan Greene, Daniel Truly. Great directors: Peter Leto, David Platt. Great producers: Arthur Forney, David DeClerque, Gail Barringer, Mike Ciliento.

Law and Order: SVU was truly a marvelous experience for me.

"

You never know who's watching your show! A memorable phone call came for me in the morning after one of my *SVU*s. The show, entitled "Limitations," was early in the series, episode 14, airing February 11, 2000. The show was a ticking-clock thriller. Someone had committed three rapes — and then he stopped. The SVU had his DNA but had not managed to find the perpetrator. There was a statute of limitations in the state of New York of five years for sexual crimes. The five years in our episode are almost up — only two and a half weeks to go. They have incontrovertible DNA evidence, but if the SVU detectives don't apprehend the suspect by the end of the two and a half weeks, he gets off scot free. He can't be tried for the three rapes he has committed. Ridiculous, I know, but true.

Under the leadership of Detective Olivia Benson and Detective Elliot Stabler, the whole SVU department makes an all-out effort to get this guy while they still can. The clock is ticking. The first rape case passes the five-year limit: the rapist cannot be tried for this rape. The detectives work night and day. The second case passes the five-year limit: the rapist can't be tried for this rape either. There are only four days of the statute of limitations left on the third rape case. The detectives bear down. This guy is on the edge of escaping any punishment for his three rapes. With only 24 hours to go, they finally catch him. He's charged with that third rape and convicted. That's the story of the *SVU* episode. And now, the phone call.

"This is Mr. So-and-so. I'm the personal assistant to the governor of the state of New York, Mr. George Pataki. Mr. Pataki is very angry with you, Mr. Kotcheff."

"What about?"

"Last night, in your show, you made an egregious error. In the state of New York, the statute of limitations for sexual crimes is not five years, it is ten years."

"My dear sir, do you think we're a bunch of doltish amateurs? We don't make errors like that. Every script is scrutinized for things that could possibly be incorrect: a New York Police captain examines the script for police procedures; a psychiatrist for the emotional effect of sexual attacks on women and children; and an eminent litigation lawyer examines it for its legal proceedings. All in the name of accuracy. Do you think that the main element at the heart of our story, the crucial statute of limitations of five years could have slipped by all that scrutiny? The whole point of the episode was to reveal to the audience the brainless imbecility of that five-year limit. Would we make such a mistake?"

"Mr. Pataki is convinced that you are in error. And who knows more about the subject than him?"

"May I suggest that the Governor open up his book of legislation and read the laws pertaining to sex crimes. If he doesn't have a copy, I'll happily lend him mine. Cheerio!"

I hung up.

I should have told him that many lawyers, both prosecuting and defending, watch our shows to see how these sexual crimes are dealt with by the law; that's how real and authentic we are. We are a textbook for the legal profession.

An hour later, the assistant to Mr. Pataki is on the line again, "Mr. Kotcheff, Mr. Pataki wants to extend his profound apologies to you. You are absolutely right. The cause of his mistake was he just could not believe that any group of legislators would pass a law of such ludicrous stupidity. He was incredulous and horrified. He wants to thank you for bringing it all into the open. He's now preparing a bill making the statute of limitations for sexual crimes ten years."

"I'm very glad to hear it, sir, but tell the Governor to make it twenty years!"

"I will, and thanks again."

I must say, it feels so good to have had a positive effect on such an important facet of our society. I was reminded of my film, *Wake in Fright*, and its role in saving kangaroos; of *Uncommon Valor* and *First Blood* that dealt with the mistreatment of the Vietnam veterans, earning me their

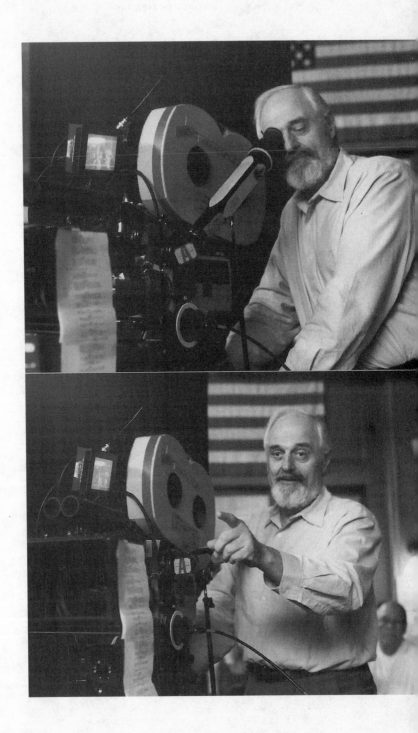

Me directing from the camera.

heartfelt gratitude; and of *Edna, the Inebriate Woman* and its effect on improving the hostels for the homeless and derelict. These are the best awards my work can receive.

Law and Order: SVU had another important beneficial result: rape, marital abuse, and child molestation were subjects that were all hushed up in the past. Our show brought them all into the mainstream so they could be dealt with. An amazing phenomenon was that Mariska, as Detective Benson, received thousands of personal letters and emails, and I mean *thousands*, from women disclosing their abuse experiences. She realized the desperation these scarred women must be feeling to open themselves up to a TV character, and the need to be heard and healed. So in 2004, she started Joyful Heart in Hawaii with the intention of helping these abused and violated women heal and reclaim a sense of joy in life. Mariska financed every aspect of the therapeutic experience, including flying the women to and from Hawaii. The organization has now spread to L.A. and New York, carrying on innovative ways to treat the trauma of rape and child molestation. Mariska is also working to abolish all statutes of limitations pertaining to sex crimes. These statutes still have some validity in other kinds of crimes, where human witnesses are essential; so for a crime committed 15 years ago, a witness's memories may have faded, faces of the guilty may have changed with age. This is not the case with rape, for we now have DNA, the witness that is eternally ready to point out the guilty. A statute of limitations has no place in the prosecution of sexual crimes. So Mariska and Joyful Heart are campaigning to have it abolished.

The other area in which Joyful Heart is campaigning is for rape kits to be processed. After a sexual assault, the authorities, with the consent of the victims, prepare a rape kit. It's not a pleasant experience for a woman. A woman who went through the process told me that it's almost like being raped again. But having gone through that, the victim expects that the DNA will be extracted, but many authorities don't spend the money required to extract the incriminating DNA. It's rendered a useless, sham operation. There are not just a few unprocessed rape kits, but a backlog of over 175,000. Most rapists are serial rapists, and they often escalate their crimes, ending up murderers. That is why Joyful Heart has an "End the Backlog" program. Processing the kits is so important: rapists may be apprehended, lives may be saved.

It is with much pride that I say that *Law and Order: SVU* was the instigating spark that lead Mariska into this mammoth, vital undertaking.

But what I can I say about Mariska herself. She is truly a Wonder Woman, a brilliant actress with not a single nasty bone in her body, good humored, beautiful, warm hearted, idealistic, generous in every way. I cannot say enough about this extraordinary woman.

"

Law & Order: SVU became an evergreen show for NBC, despite the fact that we were bounced around the prime-time schedule. Many new series were launched by airing in our wake. But even more amazing is that the show has been so widely syndicated that everywhere I go in the world, it seems to be on TV every day.

Mariska Hargitay and Chris Meloni, who were on for 11 consecutive seasons together, ended up becoming the longest running duo in the history of dramatic television. (Only comedy duo Ozzie and Harriet were on the air longer, at 14 years.) Mariska, who remains on the series to this day in its 18th season in 2016, plays the longest-running female character in dramatic television.

Both Neal and Chris departed in 2011. Neal signed a production deal with CBS and executive produced *Under the Dome*, and Chris successfully moved into feature films. I left following the 2012 season, having worked on 289 episodes. I never would have or could have spent 12 years on a television series if it was not for a wonderful crew and a talented cast, so free of destructive ego, so free of internecine friction, and so deeply committed to getting it right. It was one of the richest — and certainly the longest contiguous — experiences of my career.

I had started working in television in 1952 in Canada when the medium was in its infancy. I had cut my teeth as a director in the heyday of live television in England. Amazingly, 59 years later, I put a button on my television career. That is, of course, until another alluring opportunity comes along.

CHAPTER TWENTY-FOUR
Make Room for the Music

For me, life without music would be utter hell. There is a song by Schubert, one of my favorite composers, in which he voices a similar sentiment. "An Die Musik" (To Music) expresses how music takes him out of life's madness and transports him to a better world where the warmth of love is kindled in his heart. It's a very beautiful piece that always results in a flow of tears. All the great composers write music where they reveal that it does rain every day for them too, giving me solace and the consolation of communion.

One of the bedazzling mysteries of music is that all the great classical masterpieces, from Bach to Bartok, all the Mozart, Verdi, and Puccini operas that I love, all that jazz, and the beguiling songs of the Beatles and the Rolling Stones, all of it comes from a meager 12 tones — 12! Seven tones from A to G, and five semi-tones in between. Twelve tones endlessly drawn on, but never repeated in all this vast music. It's incomprehensible!

From the outset, I was surrounded by music. My mother and her sister, my aunt Sophie, would sing Bulgarian folk songs together all day long as they did the household chores. My mother played the mandolin, accompanying herself as she sang. My father would join in; he was an extraordinary harmonizer. And our whole extended family sang and danced together every Sunday.

My father loved country and western music. His favorite was Wilf Carter, the Yodeling Cowboy, a.k.a. Montana Slim. Dad had all his records, as well as those of Hank Williams and the Sons of the Pioneers.

At the age of five, my parents started me on the violin. I seemed to have a natural propensity for it. I had the best teacher, Frank Geleff, known as Koteh, which means "cat," as in Cat Stevens. He was the sweetest, kindest, most gentle of men, passionate about the violin. He was not a great believer in scales and academic studies. His approach was: "If you want to practice the key of E minor, why, we'll study the Mendelssohn violin concerto; G minor, a Mozart sonata; D major, a Beethoven opus."

He was always exhorting me to "play with fire." His English was shaky, but his meaning was clear. Fire meant intensity, passion, spontaneity, all blocks and inhibitions cast aside. Fling yourself heart and soul into the music. "Fire, Billy, more fire."

He took me to see all the great violinists. "If you aspire to be the best, you must see and hear the best." During the Great Depression, when I was six, seven, eight, he took me to Toronto's Massey Hall and Eaton Auditorium, and I saw the best: Fritz Kreisler with his seraphic bowing of the violin, Yehudi Menuhin playing the sublime Elgar violin

Proud violinist.

concerto, Tossy Spivakovsky, Nathan Milstein, Isaac Stern, and, of course, he whom I called the Zeus of the Pantheon of violinistic gods, the greatest of great, Jascha Heifetz. Koteh was right. Seeing those great violinists did inspire me. I saw myself playing at Massey Hall, performing in London, Paris, and at the ultimate — Carnegie Hall in New York.

And that dream was encouraged when, at the age of eight, I won a gold medal at the violin competition at the Canadian National Exhibition. Or, should I say, Koteh and I won it.

At nine, I started to compose: my first opus was "Bulgarian Dance." When I performed it for Koteh, he looked at my parents pointedly and said in Bulgarian, "I think we have someone special here." He had in mind Fritz Kreisler and Pablo de Sarasate, great violinists who performed the music they composed. My parents wanted me to be a concert violinist. So my dreams about my future became even more vivid, even more omnipresent.

Then came World War II.

I lost Koteh; he was drafted into the Canadian Army. My new teacher was an aging lady who was well meaning but dryly academic, with an emphasis on scales, arpeggios, studies. She was thorough, but fireless. I was stalled for three years.

I missed Koteh desperately.

Then Koteh was sent home, having been wounded. I was so happy to see him. He appeared to be whole and unhurt. Then he raised his arm, and I saw a sickening sight. His left hand was mangled, fingers smashed beyond repair. A German bullet had struck and destroyed his fingering left hand. He was never to play the violin again, and as he taught by demonstration, he could not teach.

I cursed God! Such calculated cruelty! Was He some cosmic prankster? What happened to Koteh's hand almost made me a Bogomil — a Bulgarian heretical Christian sect, described to me by my grandmother. They believed that this Earth did not belong to God, but to Satan and his demons. And we did not have guardian angels here, but guardian demons who ensured that we had evil thoughts and provoked us to commit evil deeds. In a word, this Earth is Hell!

I could not accept Koteh's calamity with equanimity. But this sweet, gentle man accepted it with an utter lack of bitterness.

Considered alongside the horrendous atrocities committed during that dark time, our loss might seem slight. Still, for Koteh and me, it was a pain without end, an irrevocable loss; a man, his fingers, a boy, his dreams. But I never surrendered. Fire, Ted, more fire! Yes, Koteh, yes — always! For all my creative work, it has become my mantra.

For me, it was not a total loss. My musical training helped me tremendously later in that most important aspect of filmmaking: the creation of background music. When I directed my second film, *Life at the Top*, I was 34, and as far as filmmaking was concerned, still wet behind the ears. Wet?! Hell, I was soaking! But it turned out to be a great learning experience.

My director of photography was the brilliant Oswald Morris, who later was nominated for an Academy Award for his work on *Oliver!* and won for his cinematography in *Fiddler on the Roof*. But Ozzie was a bit of a sourpuss, and he regarded me as a film-ignorant upstart TV director. But he taught me a lot.

I recall there was quite a long scene between my two stars, Laurence Harvey and Jean Simmons, playing husband and wife, which I staged very statically in a TV style. When I turned it over to him to light, Ozzie said sarcastically, "Kotcheff, it's called 'motion pictures,' not 'standing around talking pictures.'" I immediately restaged it with a lot of movement.

On another occasion, we were just about to shoot the hallway of their house. Ozzie said, "Kotcheff, do these people have children?"

"Yes, two."

"Well, you'd never know it from the bare look of this hall."

"Props!" I shouted. "Bring me a lot of toys, an electric train, a rocking horse, some dolls." All through the film, he gave me useful directorial lessons.

When I finished shooting *Life at the Top*, I began its editing. The lessons continued. I had a very genial, experienced editor, name of Derek York. There was a tense, emotional scene between the husband and Laurence Harvey, who had an adulterous affair with the man's wife, who had died in a car crash. At the end of the scene, the husband rose and crossed away from the camera down a long hallway in his home, a broken man, always to be tormented by his grievous loss. Coming from TV, as soon as the last word of their scene was uttered, I said to Derek, "Cut to the next scene."

"No, Ted. First of all, it's a great shot of this broken man stumbling down the hall with the guilty lover in the foreground. But more importantly, you have to leave room for the music. It's an opportunity for a great music cue, the pathos of the husband, the self-reproach of Laurence Harvey." That became our maxim during the editing: "Make room for the music."

Not only after the film is shot, but when I am scripting it, I give a lot of thought about the music. I say to myself, "We'll need music here, so I need to make room for the music when I shoot this scene."

After the editing is completed, the chosen music composer, my editor, and I run the film, and together we do music spotting; that is, we choose where to have music, where it should start, and where it should finish. Then we discuss what the function of the music should be for every cue.

I cannot exaggerate the importance of music in a film. It shapes the audience's sensibilities, affects the way they look at what's occurring on the screen; it creates mood, telegraphs what is about to happen. It expresses what's going on under the dialogue, in a sense, telling the audience what they should be feeling. Music can fulfill so many purposes. It's a great artistic tool for the director.

Many years ago, when I was shooting *The Apprenticeship of Duddy Kravitz*, its editor and I conducted an interesting experiment. I think it was Thom Noble's idea, the brilliant, Oscar-winning editor who has cut most of my films since the early '70s. Thom took a shot from *Duddy* and put three totally different kinds of music over it to see what the effect would be. It was a wide shot that showed Duddy and his girlfriend happily running down a sloping rural field. The first piece of music was a sweeping, joyful, bucolic melody reflecting the euphoric bliss of being young, those salad days that are the happiest times of one's life. It worked marvelously. The second was a very tender piece of romantic music. Love was in the air and was about to come to an amorous climax. The last piece of music was ominous, which seemed to presage that, unbeknownst to them, something untoward was about to happen to the two lovers.

The same shot, but one derived totally different thoughts and feelings from it because of the music. It proved to me pretty conclusively what a strong role music played in a film. Not that it needed proving.

"

There are two elements in creating a film that are of great importance: structure and pacing.

Getting the structure of my film right is my preeminent and paramount concern. For it is of the essence, the very crux of the matter. A misshapen narrative will never work. One of the things I use to guide me is the sonata form. What is it? It is the artistic structure of most symphonic works and instrumental sonatas.

It starts with a very short, slow introduction, then it becomes allegro (lively and brisk) for quite a while, laying down the basic motifs, then it goes into largo, a slow period of exposition, probing and exploring. In the third movement, scherzo is very light and quick. And then, finally, the last movement is allegro con fuoco (fiery), appassionata (passionate). It builds to a climax and finishes in a blaze of emotion — a satisfying denouement. I use that as a model in my overview of the whole structuring of my film.

Pacing, the dynamic and continual flowing forward of the narrative, is also crucial. Pacing is not achieved by playing every scene fast. That becomes tiresome and soon feels slow. No, you get pace by contrast, the juxtaposition of opposite tempi. When I'm preparing to decide the pacing of a scene, I use musical tempi notation, which I put on the top of every scene in my script, so I don't forget its pacing in the hurly burly of shooting. Allegro, adagio, presto, andante, vivace, con fuoco. I suppose because of my musical upbringing, the Italian speaks more clearly to me than its English translation.

"

I have worked with some really fine composers over the years, who provided my films with memorable scores.

The charming Henry Mancini did the music for *Who's Killing the Great Chefs of Europe?*, a brisk, playful, melodious score, perfect for my comedy. As the first title came up at the beginning, his jaunty tuneful music created a stylish, droll atmosphere. The audience knew they were going to be in for a jolly time.

Jerry Goldsmith did the music for *First Blood*. I had worked with Jerry before when he did the music for one of my TV films, but *First Blood* was our first feature film collaboration. The music that Jerry wrote for this film was flawless, capturing the dark, impassioned urgency of the action. And it was sonorous with plangent empathy for Rambo's existential dilemma. For the end of the film, Jerry wrote a superb, poignant song, "It's a Long Road," that movingly encapsulated all that has gone before. It always makes me cry.

The composer who wrote four great scores for me — and I mean great — was British, John Scott. He did *North Dallas Forty*, *Wake in Fright*, *Billy Two Hats*, and *Winter People*. *North Dallas Forty* was set in the world of professional American football. The music had two aspects: one was full of the sport's energy and the pizazz and hoopla of the game; the other a haunting intimate music that underscored the physical and emotional damage suffered by its players, a mixture of the glory and the pain of the gridiron.

What impressed me tremendously was how John Scott got into the head of Nick Nolte's character musically. You understood his deep dilemma between his love of the game and his sense of being unfeelingly and ruthlessly exploited. The main theme, a bluesy melody, was tender for the emotional moments and haunting as it underscored the heartbreak of the sport.

John Scott did me proud again in his score for *Wake in Fright*, set in the very centre of the Australian continent. From the very first shot, a 360° look at the vast, baking nothingness of the Outback, John's music speaks so powerfully of the physical and emotional isolation of this place, the imprisoning emptiness of this inhospitable, inimical land, so far away from civilization. The eerie, disquieting, foreboding music sets the mood for the film and sustains this atmosphere throughout the whole film. John Scott's music is masterful — truly great.

"

There was one other unexpected benefit from my early musical training. I was invited to direct one of the most acclaimed sopranos in the history of opera, Joan Sutherland, in abbreviated versions of famous operas.

Nathan Kroll, a New York producer, called me in England. He was going to produce eight shows for PBS entitled *Who's Afraid of Opera*, all starring Joan Sutherland, designed to introduce young people to the beauties of opera. I readily agreed. In the first opera that I did with Joan, Donizetti's *Daughter of the Regiment*, she played Marie, the orphaned tomboy raised by an army regiment, with an engaging, awkward girlishness. She displayed an extraordinary acting capability.

I did three more operas with Joan, playing Marguerite in *Faust*, Rosina in *The Marriage of Figaro*, and Violetta in *La Traviata*. She loved the way I directed her as Violetta, so she asked me to direct her in a production of *La Traviata* at the Metropolitan Opera House in New York! I was thrilled! I thought we would go straight to New York after the completion of the TV production. When I inquired as to the date, she said it was two years away! Of course, this is typical of opera stars who are booked years in advance. Regretfully, I had to decline for it might have come right in the middle of a film.

Oh goodness! A might have been!

CHAPTER TWENTY-FIVE
It Might Have Been

As the poet, John Greenleaf Whittier wrote,

> Of all sad words of tongue or pen,
> The saddest are these:
> "It might have been!"

This applies so often in the film business, that one almost becomes inured to it — or at least, to maintain your sanity, you *should* become inured to it. You complete a script, you dream about it incessantly, and, for one reason or another, the film doesn't get made. More often than not, for monetary reasons. As I said, you shrug your shoulders, shake off the frustration and disappointment, and move on to another dream. But sometimes, the pain of its loss did not go away, either because I came so close to realizing it, or because it meant so much to me.

The first case of this was a film entitled *Mozart in Prague*. I had played his great violin concertos and all of his many violin sonatas, so I can attest to what the conductor George Szell said: "Mozart's huge, fantastic output is astounding in that it includes hardly one work less than a masterpiece." And to what Georg Solti said: "Mozart makes you believe in God because it cannot be by chance that such a phenomenon arrives into the world and leaves such an unbounded number of unparalleled masterpieces." And I have to agree with Tchaikovsky: "I not only love Mozart, I worship him." That was why I wanted to make a film about him.

My good friend Clive Exton wrote a superb script with a very interesting structure. Prague was where Mozart was appreciated most; so he went there to produce his new opera, *Don Giovanni*, which I consider one of the best operas ever written. The script follows its rehearsal and, within the opera, there are moments that trigger flashbacks to his earlier life, his relationship with his father, his early musical experiences in Vienna, and so on. The script was a masterly piece of work by Clive. I couldn't wait to work on it.

I had a very good producer, John Heyman, who told me that if I could obtain a piece of important casting for Mozart, he could raise the money. I came up with Joel Grey: he had just won the Oscar for Best Actor in a Supporting Role for his wonderful performance in *Cabaret*, in which he played the Master of Ceremonies. I had always known him to be a fine actor, but now the Academy Award launched him into prominence. And physically he looked like Mozart, short and slim, finely featured, and he obviously was very musical.

Full of hope, I contacted his I.C.M. agent in New York who sent him the script. His agent was a bit of a fan of mine, having seen *Wake in Fright* and admired it, so he let me meet Joel without an offer. Usually, most agents won't let their clients read your script without a Pay or Play offer, meaning they get their money whether the film is made or not. This approach leads to the old conundrum: you can't get the money without the actor, and you can't get the actor without the money.

I flew from London to New York, hired a car, and drove up to New Haven, Connecticut, where Yale University is located and Joel lived. Joel was a real charmer, he had a good understanding of the material, and we talked the afternoon away. I congratulated him on his recent Oscar. I thought the meeting was a great success, and I was full of optimism that we were off and running. I flew back to London, where I gave my producer, John Heyman, the good news.

Two days later, I got a phone call from Joel's I.C.M. agent. "Ted, I'm afraid that Joel is passing on your Mozart project." What?! "He loves you, loves your script, but he's looking to follow up his Oscar with a big Hollywood blockbuster to consolidate his stardom. Rather than your European art film, which, good as it is, will only have limited exposure in art houses. I'm sorry. Joel sends you his best wishes for your project."

I never did succeed in getting the film cast with the required star, and it drifted into the netherworld of the unmade. Having lived with it so intensely for such a length of time, I saw the film *Mozart in Prague* in my head, every frame of it. I gotta tell you, it was one terrific film. Too bad you didn't get a chance to see it.

"

The next "it might have been" was even worse: it was based on Anthony Burgess's novel *A Clockwork Orange*. I had a great script by Terry Southern. I had my star, Mick Jagger of the Rolling Stones. I had the money from British Paramount Films, which loved the script and the package. I was cock-a-hoop! Let's start shooting!

And then, out of nowhere, a major stumbling block in the form of the British Board of Film Censors. I was told by its head, whose name I'm glad to have forgotten, that my film would never be screened in Great Britain. Whereas the MPAA (Motion Picture Association of America), which functioned in a somewhat similar fashion classifying films, was lenient in matters of violence but tough on sexual display, the British censors were the reverse: lenient on sexual matters but very tough on violence. They had banned Marlon Brando's film *The Wild One* for 14 years in England because of it. They were especially hard on my film because it was full of "youthful violence against people and property." A total no-no as far as they were concerned.

My film, if made, would be banned forever in Great Britain. I argued with the head of the censors' board, told him I would do the violence in an impressionistic way and not graphically, but it was to no avail. I then tried to persuade the British Paramount executives to make the film in England for distribution in America. "Ted, we can't give you British money for a film that will never be seen here." I came so close to making the film, but now I was so far away.

Many years later, the British Board of Film Censors mitigated the severity of their prohibition on the depiction of violence and allowed *The Wild One* to be screened. And Stanley Kubrick would make a great film of *A Clockwork Orange* in 1971.

"

In the early '90s, I was approached to make a film about Muhammad Ali. I got Evan Jones involved as the writer. You will recall that Evan and I had collaborated on *Two Gentlemen Sharing*, a film dealing with the racial situation in London in the '60s, and on *Wake in Fright*. We had become good friends in the process. Another strong reason to use Evan on this particular film was he is an African-Jamaican. As Evan was in London, I arranged to spend a few hours with Muhammad and get all the pertinent biographical information from him for our film.

I went to see Muhammad in his apartment in south Los Angeles. It was swarming with boxing managers, agents, TV people, personal assistants, and black Muslims, the latter all bearing large handguns and warily watchful of me.

Muhammad and I immediately liked each other, and he trustingly opened himself up to me. He was a sensitive man, very intelligent and articulate. A prolonged intimate connection between us was impossible, what with the noise of the crowd and his assistants rushing up to him every two minutes and whispering in his ear requests for interviews and public appearances. Muhammad got up and said, "Ted, follow me."

We went into the bathroom. He locked the door; he lay down comfortably in the empty bathtub, and I sat on the toilet with my notebook poised. And for the next four hours, he delineated the salient experiences of his life. They were so vivid, so dramatic: I immediately saw the theme and structure of the film — a story of incredible moral courage, of a man with a deep commitment to his beliefs, in a ceaseless battle with the white racist establishment.

The black people in his birthplace, Louisville, Kentucky, were treated like dogs. He remembered, as a boy, being denied a drink of water in a store because of the color of his skin. At age 18, he won the light heavyweight boxing gold medal in the 1960 Summer Olympics in Rome — bringing great honor to his country. But was he treated any differently upon his return? No. There follows what I called the black Hamlet scene.

He is on a bridge over the Ohio River. It is midnight as he gazes down at the rushing waters, pondering his role in this world, as he suffers the slings and arrows of mindless white racism. A sudden vision: he realizes what is to be his mission in life — to be the voice of black people and to struggle with America to live up to its founders' principles. He rips the gold medal from his neck and hurls it into the Ohio River.

There have been some who say this never happened — that the missing medal was actually stolen. Sorry, boys! I heard it from his lips.

He converted to Islam shortly afterward, rejecting the fake Christianity of his oppressors.

Muhammad described another strikingly eloquent scene which exemplified his moral bravery, and Evan and I put it into the script verbatim. Here it is.

He had made his views on the Vietnam War very clear: he was not going to kill one Vietnamese person. "No Vietcong never called me 'nigger.'" "My enemy is the white devils, not the Vietcong."

Still he appeared for his scheduled induction before the draft board in April 1967. At the time, he was the world heavyweight champion, having defeated Sonny Liston. When his name was called, he refused to step forward. He was called three times but still did not step forward, citing his religious beliefs and opposition to the Vietnam War. A military officer approached him. He warned Muhammad that he was committing a serious felony: draft evasion, punishable by five years in jail and a $10,000 fine. Despite knowing what would happen to him, when his name was called for the last time, Muhammad Ali courageously refused to budge. He was immediately arrested, tried, and found guilty of draft evasion and sentenced to five years in prison, plus the fine. He appealed the sentence to the Supreme Court, so he didn't have to go to jail until they decided his fate. It took four years — four years of no fights. The New York State Athletic Commission stripped him of his title and suspended his boxing license. Other state commissions followed suit. He was also stripped of his passport. The World Boxing Association had already stripped him of his title when he joined the Nation of Islam in 1961. This is what I mean by his moral courage. He put his championship on the line, his celebrity, all the money, all the endorsements, everything sacrificed for what he believed in. He was also deeply involved in the Civil Rights movement. Four years of no fighting in his prime. What guts! He reminded me of some of my uncles who displayed the same kind of courage. He became an icon for me and my generation. What he was willing to do inspired people of all races.

The U.S. Supreme Court overturned his conviction in 1971 since the lower court gave no reason for the denial of a conscientious objector exemption to Ali. His license to box was reinstated.

Muhammad Ali and I talked for two whole days. On the third day, he asked me to accompany him to a predominantly black high school in south L.A. where he delivered his Black Is Best speech, which he gave to many colleges as well. He was a very popular speaker. He spoke in favor of the Black Muslim movement. He gave a very funny diatribe against eating pork entitled "The Evils of Bacon" — the reason bacon sizzled when fried was that all the vile, repulsive maggots and grubs in the meat were dancing around. The students gagged at the disgusting picture, heightened by Muhammad's hand beating out the rhythm of the maggots' dance on his lectern.

One story Ali told me intrigued and puzzled me. I wasn't sure what to do with it in the film. Ali got himself invited to a Ku Klux Klan cross burning. I can only conjecture that he wanted to see the worst and oldest American racists and white supremacists in action, who now murderously opposed the Civil Rights movement and desegregation. The robed and masked klansmen welcomed him and treated the heavyweight champion of the world with due deference. But at one point, they brought out a coil of thick rope with a noose at one end and hurled it over a branch. The white hooded men turned to look at Ali. He was frozen. Then they all burst out laughing. "Only joking," said the head klansman. Some joke.

There is one other moment of interest in our time together. I don't know what possessed me but I said to Muhammad, "I'm going to stand dead still. I want you to jab at me as close to my head as possible." I wanted to personally experience his hand speed, the deft jabs he threw from all angles, the rapid fire of five jabs in succession. Well, I never saw them. I only heard them: the whistling sound as they came within millimeters of my ears. It was an extraordinary experience. Had one of them hit me, it would have put me in the middle of next week.

Why the movie didn't get made, I never discovered. The English producer, whose name I've forgotten, didn't come up with the money to pay Evan Jones to start writing our script. Then suddenly, he became incommunicado and didn't have the good grace to tell us why he withdrew from the project.

My suspicion is that when he went to the money people

for financing, they did not want to get involved with this film, feeling that white audiences would be angry to be depicted as the racists that most of them were and they would reject the film. But this is pure conjecture.

But what a great three days I had with the Heavyweight Champion of the World!

"

My final "it might have been" had an unforeseen happy outcome. I always wanted to make a film about a Canadian hero who had an epic life, a doctor named Norman Bethune. He fought in China with Mao Tse-tung and helped him defeat Chiang Kai-shek and Japan.

Up to that time in China, the battle wounded were taken by horse-drawn wagons on non-existent roads to military hospitals 25 miles back of the lines. The mortality rate was 97 percent — most of the wounded bled to death on the way. Bethune stopped that. He had tent hospitals moved half a mile back of the battle front, becoming mobile army surgical hospitals. The mortality rate dropped close to zero. The Chinese army made Bethune into a great hero.

There were not enough surgeons. Bethune ingeniously took farm boys who had worked with farm animals and knew their innards and taught them how to operate on humans, how to remove bullets. After all, we're not that different from pigs, who are genetically very close to us. The new surgeons helped save many soldiers' lives. Mao put Bethune's face on their stamps, the only white person ever to receive this honor.

A Canadian playwright, Ted Allan, who lived in London, a good friend of Mordecai and mine, had written a book about Bethune, and he adapted it for my film. I persuaded

John Kemeny, my old colleague who produced *The Apprenticeship of Duddy Kravitz* so successfully, to partner up with me again. An added plus was that John had produced a documentary on Bethune. Bob Shapiro, my good friend who was then head of Warner Bros., wanted to fund the project. The three of us went to China together to look at possible locations and to negotiate the cost of shooting there, hoping it would be reasonable. The script had huge battle scenes with thousands of extras. When we arrived in Beijing, Bob opened negotiations, while John Kemeny and I scouted locations and met with Chinese military officers.

The Chinese proved to be totally unrealistic, hoping to bilk these capitalists for all they were worth. For example, they wanted to charge us Hollywood union prices for the thousands of extras. Ridiculous! We had hoped to make it for less in China; otherwise the price would be prohibitive. Bob, an excellent negotiator, gamely struggled on, bargaining with the obdurate Chinese. Finally, he lost his patience and told John Kemeny and me, as he left for Hollywood, to think about shooting the film in Taiwan or the Philippines. John and I went into northern China, near Manchuria, to visit where Bethune had built a hospital, stopping all along the way for other possible locations.

It was late November, freezing cold. The hostelries where we stayed had no heating, as the government wanted to save money and didn't turn on the heat till mid-December. John and I froze. I slept in an army great coat given to me by a Chinese military officer we had talked to, but still never got warm. And one morning, honest to God, I woke up with an icicle hanging from my nose. Also, there were no toilets; it was always squat jobs.

We returned to Beijing to the special hotel for foreigners. "Look, John — toilets! Radiators!"

The next day, exhausted, we sat having lunch in the hotel when two very attractive Chinese ladies came in and went to a table and talked to a man sitting there. They were definitely not Chinese, as they were not allowed into the hotel dining room. And anyway, they were wearing American clothing, and not wearing Mao suits. They had to be North American Chinese. I said, "Look, John, let's ask those two women to dinner tonight."

"What? Importuning women in a public place? No, no, Ted! Please!"

"We're not going to rape them, John; just invite them to dinner."

"Please, Ted, so unseemly, so embarrassing!"

While we were having this Pinteresque discussion, the two women, who I thought were going to have lunch, turned around and left. "John, the only two women we've seen who are not members of the henna rinse brigade, and we lose them because of your silly inhibitions. You're a great companion, but if I don't talk to someone soft soon, I'm going to lose my mind." I had broken up with Micheline Lanctôt recently and was getting very antsy. "I'm tired. I'm going for a nap."

"Oh please, Ted. I want to visit the Temple of Heavenly Peace. Come with me."

"John, the last two weeks we've seen twenty Temples of Heavenly Peace. Red tile roofs, curly cue corners, and columns in the middle."

"Please, Ted, awfully boring to go by oneself."

"Okay, John."

So we went to the Temple of Heavenly Peace, and there it was as I predicted: red tile roof, curly cue corners, and columns in its middle. "Okay, John, back to the hotel for a nap."

"One more thing."

"One more thing? What?"

"I have a hot tip for an antique store, way off the beaten tourist track."

"Antiques? John, you've spent twenty grand already on Chinoiserie. You're gonna buy more?!"

"Way off the beaten tourist track. Please, Ted."

"Okay, but promise, right after, back to the hotel."

"On my mother's grave."

When we arrived at the antique store, I couldn't believe my eyes. Inside were the two women that I had admired in the hotel dining room! I thought *Thank you, God! I understand that woman is meant for me. I had to be forcefully dragged to my destiny, but I will not fail you this time!* I immediately crossed to one of the women and said, "Excuse me, you don't know me, but we're having dinner tonight."

"Are you crazy?"

"I may be crazy, but there's no way we're not dining together tonight!"

She looked around for help from her friend. I looked over and saw John, laying down sand with the other woman, who was older than my intended, who had to be in her 20s. They came over. "Mr. Kotcheff, I know you," said the other woman. "I am the cultural attaché at the Canadian Embassy. Why didn't you contact us? I could have helped you in your negotiations with the Chinese." She turned to her friend and said, "Ted Kotcheff is a well-known film director."

"Film director! I'm not having dinner with some druggie Hollywood director." I loved her Bette Davis spunk.

The cultural attaché said, "You don't have to take us out; come to my place. The Chinese government has given me a lovely apartment with a full staff, cook and all. We'll have dinner there."

Well, that's how Laifun and I met. I overcame her reluctances and ultimately we married. Laifun has provided me with 37 years of marital happiness and two amazing children: Thomas, a composer and concert pianist, and Alexandra, an auteur filmmaker. By the way, in Mandarin, Laifun means the "fragrance of a beautiful flower."

I returned to Los Angeles, where Ted Allan, the writer, and I waited for Bob Shapiro and Warner Bros. to decide whether they would finance the expensive *Bethune*.

Ted Allan had a heart attack, and I had an attack of kidney stones. Both of us were in Cedars-Sinai Hospital at the same time. I put on a dressing gown and pushed an I.V. stand with two bottles attached to my arm down the corridor — tinkle, tinkle, tinkle — and entered Ted's room where he lay prostrate with numerous wires attached to his body and an oxygen mask on his mouth. A muffled sound came from under the mask. "Have you heard from Shapiro yet?"

I hadn't.

But ultimately Warners passed, and the film became moribund. It was made later at a much-reduced price by two Canadian producers whom I didn't care to spend a year of my life with.

I lost a dear film, but I gained something infinitely better: Laifun.

CHAPTER TWENTY-SIX
Escape to Freedom

Filmmakers, writers, and artists of all stripes draw on their family's history as they produce their work and grapple to find their identity. Over the years, I have often drawn on the inspiring resilience and tragedy of my family's history.

In 2008, my daughter, Alexandra, who has traveled the world and had a unique perspective for a 24-year-old, came to Laifun and said that she had been listening to my family's tale of survival all her life. She was tired of hearing me constantly say that it had all the dramatic elements of a great film. She told Laifun that she was going to take on the project with her boyfriend at the time, Zak Cheney-Rice, a writer.

That summer, when I was on hiatus from *Law & Order: SVU*, Alexandra and Zak sat me down with a tape recorder, and I went through the story in detail. They then took the real-life recollections and wrote a treatment that Zak converted into a screenplay entitled *Flight of the Andreyevs.*

OVER BLACK, TITLE CARD.

The Balkans, 1903.

On Saint Ilinden's Day, 300 guerrillas from the Internal Macedonian Revolutionary Organization (VMRO) captured the town of Krusevo, Macedonia. They drove out the occupying Ottoman troops and set up a new revolutionary government.

Two weeks later, 5,000 Ottoman soldiers returned and gutted the town, killing, raping, and pillaging for four days. Some of the Macedonian guerrillas were killed. Many willfully withdrew or managed to escape.

With the town of Krusevo back under its control, the Ottoman Empire swore revenge on the Macedonian people.

My mother was raised on a beautiful farm owned by her grandfather. She was actually born in the farm's vineyard. My grandmother went into labor while picking grapes, and the other women pulled her off to the edge of the field where she delivered my mother. Nothing could interrupt the harvest! My grandmother left my swaddled mother in the hands of one of her older siblings and went back to picking grapes!

My great-grandfather, Dedo, had five sons. When they were all married and had children, the families continued to live together under his roof. The men worked the wheat fields and fruit orchards and tended the sheep, while the women cooked meals and watched after the children. Fifty people sat down every night to a dinner prepared by five women. Though they were Macedonian peasants, they were self-sufficient, hard workers, and had purpose to their lives.

The farm, however, turned out to be so productive that it caught the attention of the local Turkish commissar. The man would visit the farm unannounced and marvel at its productivity. He would ask my grandfather how he kept 500 acres so actively planted and the livestock so healthy. This was disconcerting for Dedo, because the Turks ruled Macedonia and often took what they wanted. The Turkish Ottoman Empire had controlled Macedonia, as well as Albania and parts of Bulgaria, Serbia, and Greece, for some 500 years. Every Macedonian lived in fear that his property may one day be taken over by a local commissar. There was nothing they could do about it.

The threat to my great-grandfather's farm reached the danger point in 1903. As related earlier, that August, a faction of Macedonians rebelled against the ruthless Turks. The uprising lasted only ten days, and the Turkish Army crushed the resistance and savagely punished all Macedonians. Dedo's son, Fat Stavro, participated in the revolution, which put the family at further risk. The Turks were even more punitive than the Nazis. By one historical estimate, as retribution for the Macedonian uprising, more than 200 villages were burned and destroyed, and more than 4,500 people were killed. Some 30,000 refugees fled to the free part of Bulgaria.

After the uprising was crushed, Dedo feared for his family's safety. He knew that the local commissar was eyeing the farm and would likely take it over. Though it broke his heart, my great-grandfather told his sons that everyone had to leave or risk being killed. The women packed up everything that could be carried, and the men burned the farm to the ground, killed all their animals, and poisoned the wells with dead animal carcasses. Then they all set out for Bulgaria.

EXT. ANDREYEV HOUSE — NIGHT

The family loads their belongings onto a pair of horse-drawn carts.

In the pastures, COTE and TIME grab a few sheep and scare the rest off. The animals bleat and run aimlessly into the countryside.

DEDO watches as his house is cleared of everything he and his family own.

> STAVRO
> We're about ready to go, Papa.

> DEDO
> Burn it.

> STAVRO
> What?

> DEDO
> Burn the house. I don't want anything left the
> Turks can use, no food, no supplies, nothing.

STAVRO

But the soldiers will see the smoke.

DEDO

They're coming anyway, smoke or no
smoke. Burn the house down.

STAVRO nods and runs out back with LUDMIL
and DONO. They return with barrels of wine.
Together, they douse the inside and outside
of the house, then clear out and light it on fire.

DEDO watches, pained but without tears.
Wine soaks the earth like blood as the house
is engulfed in flames.

The ANDREYEV family caravan, tearful and
quiet, rides into the countryside toward the
mountains. GYORGI, aged seven, looks back
and watches his home, consumed by fire, as
it disappears in the distance.

Their journey was treacherous, as they hiked over rough
terrain with few supplies. They had several children with
them, including seven-year-old Gyorgi, my mother's
cousin. They had to eat what they scraped up along the
way. At a certain point, the group received word that the
Turkish cavalry was in pursuit of them. In the already cruel
world of the Turkish army, the cavalry was considered to
be the cruelest. They had a reputation for the most heinous acts. Every Macedonian knew the stories about how
15,000 Bulgarian prisoners were taken by the Turks who
ripped out both eyes of all but 100. The somewhat lucky

100 were left with one eye so they could lead the blinded others back to Bulgaria, thereby allowing the people to see what the Turks were capable of.

When my family was just ten miles from the border to the free part of Bulgaria, they spotted the Turkish cavalry in the distance gaining on them. My great-grandfather decided that the group had no choice but to split up: so they could move faster, and more importantly, he wanted the family to survive, and splitting into two groups gave a better chance of this happening. One group would take the river valley, considered the more dangerous route. The other group would go through the mountains on the safer route. The group drew straws for who would take which route. My mother, who was three at the time, was with the people who went along the river valley, the route to near certain death, as were her brother Andrew and sister Sophie. My great-grandfather was on the mountainous route, as was little Gyorgi and his parents.

In an unexpected twist, the Turkish cavalry chased the group headed into the mountains, instead of those traveling through the valley. The cavalry fired at the group and wounded one of the men. The cavalry dismounted their horses and chased the group on foot. As the cavalry closed in, the group hid in a cave. Though there was a maze of caves, the Turks were able to track the group because the man who was wounded left a trail of blood.

INT. CAVE — DAY

> COTE lies on the cave floor, bleeding from his
> chest. Blood pours from his mouth. His eyes
> roll back and close forever.

Then, a wave of gunshots. NADESZDA instinctively covers GYORGI with her body as the Andreyevs begin falling to bullets all around her. They scream as their bodies are filled with lead.

GYORGI hides under his mother's bullet-filled body, crying but unharmed. He watches as all his family in the cave are killed, his sisters, his cousins, his uncles, his aunts.

The gunfire stops. NADESZDA rolls over and looks into GYORGI'S eyes, barely breathing. She lifts a forefinger to her mouth.

> NADESZDA
> Shh —

Her eyes close as she falls to the floor, dead. GYORGI'S eyes widen, filled with tears.

EXT. CAVE – DAY

The SOLDIERS lower their rifles. They listen for any noise inside the cave, but hear none.

> SOLDIER #1
> I think they're gone.

> SOLDIER #2
> There's no way anyone survived that.

                         YAVUZ
            Go make sure. Cut an ear off each body
               and bring it to me. And make sure
               Stavro Andreyev is among the dead.

SOLDIERS #1 and #2 nod and step into the cave, knives drawn.

INT. CAVE — DAY

GYORGI lies beneath his mother's dead body, completely still. He hears the SOLDIERS enter the cave. They begin hacking at the ears of his dead relatives.

Soon, they reach his mother's body. He lies still as SOLDIER #1 cuts her right ear off with a knife. Then they reach him. GYORGI remains still, as though dead. The SOLDIER grabs his ear and, in one swift motion, slices it right off. GYORGI is silent and motionless through the whole ordeal. The SOLDIER walks off, carrying GYORGI'S ear, while GYORGI is left alive.

Gyorgi lived to tell the horrifying story. Everyone else was killed. After his ear was hacked off, Gyorgi somehow waited for the cavalry to leave. Summoning an incredible inner fortitude, he pulled his way out of the pile of dead bodies and walked ten miles to the Bulgarian border. Amazingly, he was reunited with the other half of family that had taken the river route.

My mother's group had made it safely to Varna, a Bulgarian town on the Black Sea. There, her father (my grandfather) got a job building houses. Her mother died when she was eight years old. Consequently, my mother was yanked out of school to take care of her father, her older brother Andrew, and her younger sister Sophie, so she never properly learned to read or write. She lived there until age 18, at which point she and several family members immigrated to Canada to start new lives.

As an adult, Gyorgi ended up in Chicago. I met him a couple times. He was, of course, immediately identifiable because he had no right ear.

"

My family's stories and experiences defined me, from my mother's escape to freedom, to the grisly story of her cunning seven-year-old cousin living to tell the tale of 24 family members being massacred around him, to the adventures and tragedies of my mother's cousin Stavro. Though I had trouble processing these harrowing tales in my childhood, as I grew up they created a prism through which I viewed the world.

Albert Camus once said of writers, "The nobility of our calling will always be rooted in two commitments difficult to observe: refusal to lie about what we know and resistance to oppression."

The stories of my family became my calling. They imbued me with an ideal — that it is incumbent upon all of us to leave this earth better than when we entered it. They made me wary of any ruling government that wielded unnecessary power over its citizens. They made me believe that violence is not the answer to anything. The recurring violence in my family's lives caused me to abhor violence and be ever mindful of any violence I put onscreen as a filmmaker. They showed me that perilous situations can be survived with stern self-preservation, and that a strong will is the cornerstone of heroism. And they taught me to hold on to freedom and independence at any cost.

Collectively, these stories became the foundation of my creativity, as well as a trigger for themes I have explored as a filmmaker. Perhaps, if I can round up financing for *Flight of the Andreyevs*, those two worlds will join.

99

Every director I know has a film within them that they have always wanted to make. I have two: *Flight of the Andreyevs*, and the story of King Boris the Third of Bulgaria and how this wily fox managed to save all 50,000 Bulgarian Jews during World War II. Not one was killed and, in fact, the Bulgarian Jewish community was the only one in Europe that grew in numbers during that period. With Laifun as the lead producer, we are trying to get our film about King Boris financed. If we're successful, there will be another chapter to add to my memoirs in the future. If not, it will be added to the chapter — It Might Have Been — regretfully.

ACKNOWLEDGMENTS

I'd like to extend my ardent gratefulness to these friends who shared their lives and their prodigious talents so generously with me and so, enriched mine, incalculably.

Josh Young, who co-authored this book so inestimably.

Joel Gross, for introducing me to Josh Young. Boy, you hit a home run there, Joel.

Andrew Stuart, my literary agent, introduced to me by my co-author. Andrew found the ideal publisher for our book. You also hit a home run, Josh.

Neal Baer, in whose imagination and artistry I basked so often.

Robert Lantos, to whom I'm so grateful for being such an inspiring producer on the film we made together, *Joshua Then and Now*.

Bob and Sandy Shapiro, oh, those London card games, those times in China and Africa, and the best agenting ever.

Tim and Susan, my supportive brother and sister in every way.

Thom Noble, my congenial companion as he shaped my films so consummately.

Timothy O'Brien, you turned our shared visions into unforgettable realities.

Evan and Joanna Jones, Evan, for his magical writing, Joanna, for being Joanna.

Peter and Phyllis Bart, what wit, what perspicacious discernment, the man who brought me to Hollywood!

Victor Drai, you filled every part of me, my tum, my mind, my pocket.

Ted Pakozdi and Judy Haines, affectionate, convivial, outgoing, sympathetic.

James Orr, my protégé, sapient, articulate, a masterful screenwriter.

Helga Stephenson, boundless affection, constant sagacity.

Buck Snyder, my godson, and Linda Snyder, his vivacious mother.

The Leder sisters, Mimi and Geraldine, so sparkling, so astute, and their smart men,

Gary Werntz and George Beckerman, who have given me so much pleasure both fleshly and intellectually.

Scott and Lorna Granger, for their enhancement of the sunset years of my life.

Alan Mandel, for his fecund mind and entertaining sense of humor.

My World Organization of Wine camaraderie, those bon vivants:

George Caloyannidis,

Joe Smith,

Ralph Shapiro,

Mike Miller,

Si Litvinoff,

Bob Uhl, for 35 years of fabulous wines, gourmet repasts and endless sophisticated drolleries and yucks.

And my gratitude to the following, who edited and enhanced my memoirs:

Crissy Calhoun, my chief editor. Every page of my memoirs is peppered with her Illuminations and refinements.

Emily Schultz, my assistant editor, who held my hand as I took my initial faltering steps with the formidable task of creating this book of my life.

Mike Ciliento, my *SVU* producer, whose encyclopedic memory of all my 289 *SVU* episodes and all the times between made it possible for me to conjure up many important details and occurrences.

Jack David, my publisher, my heartfelt thanks for his belief in me and these memoirs.

Mariska Hargitay, the unreserved, rhapsodic, warm-hearted praise of me in the foreword you wrote to my memoirs moved me very deeply. Your golden words will be with me always.